W9-CHY-739

The Political Meaning of Christianity

The Political Meaning of Christianity

The Prophetic Stance

An Interpretation

Glenn
Tinder

HarperSanFrancisco
A Division of HarperCollins*Publishers*

The author gratefully acknowledges permission to quote from the following works: Karl Barth, *The Epistle to the Romans*, trans. E. C. Hoskyns (London: Oxford University Press, 1933); Dietrich Bonhoeffer: *Letters and Papers from Prison*, Rev., Enlarged Edn. (Copyright © 1953, 1967, 1971 by SCM Press, Ltd.) and *Ethics* (© Macmillan Publishing Company 1955. © SCM Press, Ltd. 1955); Albert Camus, *The Rebel*, trans. Anthony Bower (New York: Alfred A. Knopf, Inc., 1954); Andre Dumas: *Dietrich Bonhoeffer: Theologian of Reality* (Copyright © 1971 by Macmillan Publishing Company); *Murder in the Cathedral* by T. S. Eliot, copyright 1935 by Harcourt Brace Jovanovich, Inc., renewed 1963 by T. S. Eliot, reprinted by permission of the publisher and by permission of Faber and Faber Limited; and Simone Petrement, *Simone Weil: A Life*, trans. Raymond Rosenthal (New York: Pantheon Books, a Division of Random House, Inc., 1976).

FIRST HARPERCOLLINS PAPERBACK EDITION PUBLISHED IN 1991.
REPRINTED BY ARRANGEMENT WITH LOUISIANA STATE UNIVERSITY PRESS.

This edition is printed on acid-free paper that meets the American National Standards Institute Z39.48 Standard.

Library of Congress Cataloging-in-Publication Data

Tinder, Glenn E.
    The political meaning of Christianity : the prophetic stance : an interpretation / Glenn Tinder.—1st HarperCollins ed.
        p.   cm.
    Includes bibliographical references and index.
    ISBN 0–06–250893–8 (pbk. : alk. paper)
    1. Christianity and politics.   I. Title.
BR115.P7T42   1991
261.7—dc20   90–66795
                                                                      CIP

91 92 93 94 95 MCN 10 9 8 7 6 5 4 3 2 1

To the memory of my parents

Mary Frame Tinder
1893–1959
Glenn Erin Tinder
1890–1952

They who wait for the Lord
shall renew their strength.

Isaiah 40:31

Contents

Acknowledgments

I wish to thank several people for reading and commenting on my manuscript: my wife, Gloria, who is my most loyal reader; my older son Galen, a Lutheran pastor, who gave cheerfully of his limited time and abundant theological understanding; my friend Wally Mead, of Illinois State University, who is trained both in theology and in political theory and provided an extensive and extremely valuable set of comments; Richard Stivers, a sociologist from Illinois State University, who read the manuscript from pure intellectual generosity (since we have encountered one another personally only once and briefly) and strengthened my morale and deepened my understanding with a letter of praise, encouragement, and constructive criticism; and finally, my good friend Neil Riemer, of Drew University, who from the standpoint of Jewish faith has for some years been examining the themes I deal with in this essay from the standpoint of Christian faith and who, with his usual sensitivity and generosity, enabled me to understand better the ideas I was trying to develop.

I wish also to thank Professor Martin Marty, of the University of Chicago, who has read and responded generously and discerningly to a number of my writings in recent years and has done much to hearten me when the burdens of thought and composition seemed heavy.

The Political Meaning of Christianity

Preface

This book, as the subtitle suggests, is a personal statement. It is an interpretation and is not intended as a complete and definitive exposition of the political meaning of Christianity. It is a product of much solitary reflection and is shaped by my own temperament and interests. My reflections have been guided, it is true, by the Bible and by Christian traditions; and I believe that my temperament and interests are like those of many Christians in all ages. My views are presumably not altogether subjective. But I do not believe it is given to any of us, and certainly not to me, to grasp once and for all any aspect of the mystery of Christ. It would be presumptuous were I to discuss the political meaning of Christianity in a manner suggesting that no serious and well-informed person could disagree with me.

I say this mainly because I would like readers to feel that they are engaged, along with the author, in a process of inquiry and not that they are being informed of something to which it is hoped they will simply assent. I will try to be brief and thus shall not always be able to point out diverging lines of thought. I hope, nevertheless, that readers will feel that they are being invited to think and not just pressed to agree.

I stress the personal character of this book also because a principle is involved, and that principle is important in my interpretation of Christianity. We do not possess God, as God is envisioned in Christian faith, but God us. Hence, the truth given in Christ both illuminates our lives and evades our comprehension. Revelation and mystery are inseparable. Christian faith is consequently degraded when it becomes merely the acceptance of dogmas—verbal formulas set forth as final and inflexible embodiments of the truth. The spirit of Christianity, I believe, is inquiring rather than dogmatic and is accurately expressed in the biblical injunction, "Come now, let us reason together."[1]

Readers would be misled, then, were they to attribute to the author any dogmatic intentions. They would be misled also, however, were they to infer from these disclaimers that what follows is eccentric or extreme. I am not conscious of having departed in any way from the basic doctrines of traditional Christianity. I have said some things not to be found among these doctrines but nothing, at least knowingly, that contradicts them. In sum, my approach is at once undogmatic and orthodox. This reflects my own experience as a Christian. I have always believed that Christianity is a preeminently personal and liberating creed, for it rests on the faith that all truth was incarnate in a person, in Jesus of Nazareth. It has seemed to me essential that this truth be approached in an inquiring and uncoerced fashion. Yet I have found that the progress of my thinking has been marked by a spontaneous and steadily deepening respect for established doctrine.

Claims to orthodoxy must always, of course, be qualified, for devout Christians are not wholly in agreement. My own viewpoint is broadly that of the Reformation; hence, Catholics will at times disagree. My attitudes are more Lutheran than Calvinist; hence, some Protestants will take issue with certain of my interpretations. But I have been influenced by the writings of both Roman Catholic and Calvinist thinkers; further, I feel a deep affinity with Eastern Orthodoxy; and finally, I stand on ground, such as the doctrine of the Trinity, that is common to all who can claim unqualifiedly to be Christian. My interpretations of the political meaning of Christianity thus are not markedly denominational, although I think they are broadly orthodox.

Still, it would be misleading were I to create the impression that serious and orthodox Christians will disagree with me only on minor and unconnected matters. As an expression of Reformation attitudes, my position involves an emphasis on human fallenness that many Christians are apt to consider excessive. This emphasis is not merely personal; it represents a tradition often associated with Paul, Augustine, and Luther. However, there is another Christian tradition, closely connected in its own way with Paul and Augustine but reflected with particular clarity in Thomas Aquinas; this, of course, is the tradition embodied in Roman Catholicism and reflected, in limited ways, in Calvinism and Liberal Protestantism. For the sake of convenience, I shall call the tradition represented in these pages the "Reformation" tradition and the other the "Catholic" tradition, although both terms indicate very inadequately the breadth and richness of the respective traditions. (I shall use quotation marks to remind readers of the inadequacy of the terms.) The "Reformation" tradition, emphasizing human fallenness, is politically and historically pessimistic; the "Catholic" tradition, far less so. Hence, the two traditions divide on several key issues: for example, on the nature of Christian love, particularly on the extent to which it differs from and contradicts ordinary worldly love; on the character of society and the degree to which it reflects our fallen condition; on power, political action, and the state and whether these are in fundamental and inevitable conflict with Christian love.

My aim in this essay is not to refute, or in any way to suggest disdain for, the "Catholic" tradition. Either aim would be presumptuous in view of the rich and ancient character of that tradition and of the manifest wisdom of many of its representatives. Even to try at every turn to show why I do not follow the "Catholic" lead would make my essay far too long. What I hope to do is give clear expression to a version of the other tradition. This is a version shaped by my own efforts to think through afresh the political meaning of Christianity and shaped in some ways, too, by "Catholic" attitudes. It is therefore, I believe, distinctive, not simply a restatement of Reinhold Niebuhr or a political elaboration of Karl Barth. It does, however, rest primarily on "Reformation" principles; moreover, I have tried to define sharply the conclusions I have reached. It may strike some Christians as a rather uncompromising statement. I wish to stress, therefore, that throughout the essay my purpose has been to further the process of inquiry but not to obscure the breadth and diversity of the Christian mind or the fact that my conclusions are, as I say in the subtitle, an *interpretation*, not more.

If I have emphasized my undogmatic approach to Christianity because I hope for this book to be an inquiry into the truth, not just a statement of truths already known, I have emphasized my orthodoxy because of the kind of truth I wish to inquire into—truth that is authentically Christian. We live in a time of profound confusion. Disagreement and doubt are pervasive in almost all nations. Few societies or individuals enjoy untroubled certitude, and judging from the disorder of the world, few societies or individuals are in touch with the truth. At the same time, the Christian understanding of things has to an astonishing degree been forgotten. Even among professed Christians, not many are very sharply aware of the most distinctive Christian insights into human nature or political life. Do not many Christians, for example, suppose that their faith requires them to make light of the evil in human beings or to face optimistically the immediate historical future? Probably a great many do, and on both points they are deeply in error. One of the main assumptions underlying this book is that our confusion and our Christian forgetfulness are connected. There are insights in the Christian tradition that we cannot afford to neglect whether we are Christians or not. If we become incapable of recalling them, we shall suffer from a spiritual impoverishment that will be reflected not only in inner turmoil but in outer, political turmoil as well. I have stressed my adherence to traditional Christian principles because I want to be in a position to help in the task of recollection and reconsideration that I believe our Christian past and our tumultuous present put before us. The ideas we shall reflect upon in the following pages are truly Christian, I believe, or at least in harmony with true Christianity.

Whether ideas are not simply true but also truly Christian obviously matters greatly to those who wish to be truly Christian themselves. This has become a difficult and confusing undertaking, partly because of spiritual circumstances, such as the prestige of science, which tells us nothing of God and thus can easily be understood as telling us that God does not exist, but partly also because of the deep political divisions among Christians. Some Christians assert that Christianity entails a commitment to free enterprise, others that it implies a kind of socialism; some think that it means reverence for tradition and established authority, others that it demands revolution. Conscientious Christians are bound sometimes to be confused, and when they are, it is not only the wisest course of public policy that is in doubt but the very meaning of their faith. I hope to do something through this book to lessen such confusion.

I believe, however, that Christian ideas are properly of concern to people who are not Christians and even to people who are entirely closed to the possibility of becoming Christians. This is simply because of the wisdom—the deep and credible good sense concerning life, as distinguished from the revealed truth concerning God—that those ideas contain. This is wisdom pertinent to public as well as personal life, and one does not have to be a Christian to accept it. For example, according to Christian principles, people are deeply and persistently selfish. There is a good deal of evidence indicating that this is so. If it is, then it is essential to our public life that the evidence not be ignored or denied, unpleasant as it is, but faced. In a matter of this kind, Christianity can help to highlight reality even for those who are not Christian.

I write, therefore, with the hope of finding non-Christian, as well as Christian, readers. Is this not reasonable? It is taken for granted that non-Marxists should read and learn from Marxist writings; people who reject the atheism and materialism of Freud readily consult the writings of Freud and his followers. It seems arbitrary and hazardous to be less open-minded toward Christianity.

Prologue: The Prophetic Stance

"God so loved the world," according to the Gospel of John, "that he gave his only Son, that whoever believes in him should not perish but have eternal life."[1] This short statement summarizes Christian faith: God has come to human beings, creatures alienated from the source and end of their lives and existing therefore in need and desperation, and has transformed their situation. In the mystery of Christ's crucifixion and resurrection, all of the guilt and hatred dividing human beings from God and from one another have been overcome.

The political meaning of Christianity is implicit in this faith. God has established his solidarity with the human race and with all of its members; in consequence, every person is exalted and glorified. God's love is not like the feeble and often futile affection bestowed on one another by human beings. It transfigures its recipients, rendering them worthy—by destiny, by what they are called upon and enabled to become—of the love of the Creator of heaven and earth. The dignity of the individual, often ineffective and even trite as a human ideal, becomes the law of all being and history. It is thus the source of all political obligations.

The first thing we see when we examine these obligations, however, is that they are ambiguous. Although every individual is exalted, in the Christian view, society is not. On the contrary, every society is placed in question, for a society is a mere worldly order and a mere human creation and can never do justice to the glory of the human beings within it. The glory of the individual requires relationships of a kind that are unattainable by human beings as they now are and in the circumstances they have created on earth. It calls for the deep and flawless community symbolized in Christian scripture and theology as the Kingdom of God. The life and death of Christ transformed the human situation by making the Kingdom of God not only possible but in some sense necessary. But society is very unlike the Kingdom of God. The exaltation of the individual reveals the baseness of society.

Hence the ambiguity of our political obligations. If we recognize what God has done—so Christian principles imply—we shall be limitlessly respectful of human beings but wary of society. Yet human beings live in society, and we meet them there or not at all. We cannot stand wholly apart from society without failing in our responsibilities to the human beings whom God has exalted. So far as we are responsive to God, we must live within human kingdoms as creatures destined to be fellow citizens in God's Kingdom. This obligation gives rise to a political stance that is ambiguous and, in a world of devastatingly unambiguous ideologies, unique: humane and engaged but also hesitant and critical. We must assume the posture that I refer to in the following pages as the prophetic stance.

The idea of the prophetic stance is the central concept of this essay. I believe that the primary political requirement of Christianity is not a certain kind of society or a particular program of action but rather an attitude, a way of facing society and of undertaking programs of action. Christianity implies skepticism concerning political ideals and plans. For Christianity to be wedded indissolubly to any of them (as it often has been: "Christian socialism" and Christian celebrations of "the spirit of democratic capitalism" are examples) is idolatrous and thus subversive of Christian faith. Political ideals and plans must vary with times and circumstances. Christianity can indicate only how to stand in the times and circumstances in which—Christians believe—God places us. But that is a great deal. It can enable us to embrace political ideals and plans, which always reduce many people to the status of means in relation to governmental ends, without betraying individuals exalted through Christ. It can show us how to live in temporal society as citizens of an eternal society.

It is essential to the prophetic stance that it is maintained only by individuals. It is not a standard for group action. A prophetic attitude might for a time be dominant within a group, but it necessarily causes every member to stand off from the group. Maintaining a prophetic attitude means looking beyond every historical relationship and remembering that nothing in history, nothing human, can be absolutely relied upon. It depends on a guarded attitude toward even the best of groups. Individuals must assume responsibility for their own prophetic orientation, and very often this responsibility will have to be exercised without the support of the world around or even in defiance of it.

The objection may be made that the prophetic stance is therefore a recipe for weakness. I fully agree, if we are speaking of human strength and human weakness. A single, detached individual is nothing against the forces of history. Standing prophetically means being not only without set plans but also without power. The individual is solitary and exposed. Political organization and action are not ways of surmounting this condition, however, for the sense of solidarity and power thus gained is in truth illusory. This has been shown again and again in the tragedies that fervent political movements have brought not only on nations but on their own participants. It is the Christian view that since God's love has raised us above history, yet has left us for the time being within history, we are as individuals inescapably solitary and exposed. True political consciousness enables us not to change this situation but rather to inhabit it lucidly and responsibly.

Yet a prophetic attitude is not one of anxiety and desperation. The very term *prophetic* signalizes confidence in the future. To stand prophetically is to rely, in one's own weakness, on the strength of God. Christians believe that the coming of God into the world was not a mere gesture, which may prove finally to be inconsequential, for it expressed the intention of one who is not subject to irresolution or defeat. The exaltation of the individual became the ruling purpose of history, an end to be accomplished, without fail, in a community unlike any society in history. The prophetic stance means offering one's own weakness as a medium for the sovereignty of God in history. A human being may feel as inadequate to the demands of historical circumstances as five loaves and two fish to the hunger of many thousands of people; such incongruities—according to Christian faith—can be left in the hands of God.

The idea of the prophetic stance entails quite a different political attitude from those that are common in public life today. The attitude it calls for is neither conservative nor revolutionary. It is not cynical; nor is it, in the usual sense of the word, idealistic. It is different even from attitudes prominently displayed by many professed Christians. It is distant, for example, from the faith that Christian standards are represented unambiguously in the free market and the bourgeois family; but it is equally distant from the idea that the political implications of the life of Christ can be adequately realized through revolution. It requires human beings to be politically serious yet forbids them to join unreservedly in any of the collective activities that make up the visible political life of the human race. The spirit of the prophetic stance was indicated by Paul when he said that "the appointed time has grown very short" and called on those who "deal with the world" to live as though they "had no dealings with it. For the form of this world is passing away."[2]

The concept of the prophetic stance, then, is grounded in the Bible and in the basic principles of Christian faith. At the same time, however, I believe that it responds to some of the most pressing political needs of our time.

Uppermost among these needs is one that is deeply personal—for everyone, I believe, though it is not recognized by everyone—and is at the same time political: to know how to live in the public world in times such as ours. We inhabit an exceedingly discouraging period of history. There have never before been wars as destructive as those of our century; there have never been tyrannies so frenzied and all-consuming as those of the Nazis and Communists. Never until our day, apparently, has there been a need for the word *genocide*. At the present moment, most of the human race lives in crushing poverty; the rest, in societies where industrial abundance is devoted to creating an atmosphere of material comfort and spiritual inanity. Surrounded by such conditions, how should one feel and behave? How can one be as steadily critical as our historical circumstances require us to be without living in embittered solitude? How can one be fully cognizant of the human depravity and the terrifying dangers our historical situation so starkly display without falling into despair? Where can one stand between cynicism and sentimentality, apathy and fanaticism? Unless we have answers to such questions, it is hard to see how many of us can remain truly human, even if we avoid nuclear war and remain alive. It is in this sense that our global circumstances are deeply personal.

They are at the same time political, however, for there can be no decent polities unless there are many citizens who are discriminating and independent, capable of aloofness and defiance, yet communicative and responsible, disposed to join with others in the consideration and management of common affairs. Mass society and fascism are both examples of what is likely to happen when nations become populated predominantly by people incapable of citizenship.

Christianity offers the only general view of life, so far as I know, that answers to these needs. Unlike almost every other creed offered in the intellectual supermarkets of our time, Christianity tells us that human beings are profoundly selfish and can be exceedingly destructive. Humanity, in Christian terms, is a fallen race. Nonetheless, Christianity not only makes hope possible; it requires it, at least of believers, for the central proposition of Christian faith is the inevitable coming of the Kingdom of God. In between cynicism and sentimentality, Christianity calls for penitent submission to the judgment of God; in between apathy and fanaticism, a determination to seek out and do God's will.

Trying to take into account both the profound evil in human nature and the immense hope in the human situation leads inevitably to what reformers and radicals are apt to regard as fatal equivocations. It leads, as I have already indicated, to a critical spirit and to qualified commitments. It would be easy to charge that such a posture reflects the self-interest and complacency of those who do not suffer from the injustice characterizing existing structures. Equivocation, it may be said, is one of the luxuries of bourgeois life in the industrial world. I cannot entirely repudiate such a charge; in dealing with political issues, no one can claim to be free of the influence of circumstances. But circumstances do not necessarily produce false conclusions.

It seems to me that the circumstances of most writers in industrialized nations offer, at least in some ways, a fuller view of the human situation than those prevailing in the Third World. Facing scandalous poverty and flagrant injustice, Third World writers understandably find it hard to do anything but demand immediate and sweeping change. To ponder the difficulty of such change is like temporizing with evil; to be greatly concerned with its dangers seems callous. Yet the difficulty and the dangers always are great, for they are rooted in nothing less fundamental and irremediable than human avarice and pride. For an economically secure writer in a wealthy nation to see this is not a source of moral credit. It is, however, it seems to me, to see something that is true, of great importance, and typically neglected by humane and intelligent Third World writers. Let me be more specific.

A Christian in the United States, without being particularly discerning or morally sensitive, can see at least two things not so clearly visible to Third World Christian writers (I am thinking particularly of liberation theologians). One of these is the universal disaster of revolution. There is perhaps not a single example in our time of a determined effort to produce immediate and sweeping change that has not ended in tyranny; and these efforts often result in abominations, such as those witnessed in Cambodia, immeasurably worse than those perpetrated by the old social order. Third World Christian writers manifest little awareness of this fact, a fact so reflective of the omnipresence and power of human selfishness and cruelty.

The second thing a Christian in a prosperous industrial nation can see is visible because it is near at hand and all about. It is the fact that life can be culturally vulgar, morally degraded, and spiritually vacuous even under conditions of substantial justice. Not that justice has been fully achieved in nations such as the United States. But it has been approximated closely enough for us to begin to gauge its significance. We can begin to see that justice does not necessarily mean an entirely good society. The masses in the United States enjoy historically unprecedented prosperity, in stark contrast with the masses in the Third World. Accompanying this prosperity, however, are signs too numerous and well known to need mentioning, of moral cynicism, spiritual frivolity, and despair. If revolutions make plain the power of sin—its ability to captivate idealistic reformers—mass society displays the ingenuity of sin. Human beings in their passion for justice have not devised institutions that, in their pride and selfishness, they cannot outwit.

The moral naïveté (as I think it can fairly be called) of liberation theologians is far from depriving their writings of all value. Indeed, it has inspired them to perform an important service for Christian political thought. They have dramatized elements of hope and historical dynamism that belong to the essence of Christianity but are often neglected by Christians in more privileged nations. By taking too little account of human fallenness, however, they have provided an unbalanced version of the political meaning of Christianity. Hope is present in their thought, but not the *paradox* of hope. The concept of the prophetic stance represents an effort to work out a political viewpoint that, if not less hopeful, is better balanced.

The need such a viewpoint would fulfill—that of knowing how to be both independent and engaged, free alike of fanaticism and of cynicism—seems to me universal. It is not a need that arises only in prosperous industrial societies. It must be granted that illusions about our capacity for swift and effective social transformation probably spark action at some historical moments. Can we think, however, that such illusions are in the long run truly beneficial? Surely the monstrous bureaucratic despotism prevailing today in the Soviet Union is strong evidence to the contrary. I envision the prophetic stance as suitable in all political circumstances and seasons. I would be less than a serious Christian if I did not, since that stance is based primarily on two basic Christian tenets, the selfish nature of humans and the hope that is present in Christ. I envision the prophetic stance as appropriate even in those tragic circumstances that necessitate revolution, for surely revolution is better undertaken in the company of truth, even when truth is sobering, than in the company of inspiring illusions.

To hold that the concept of the prophetic stance can answer to a universal need may seem dubious, however, in view of one consideration. This is the dependence of that concept on Christian principles—principles far from universally shared. How can counsels that are universally relevant be derived from principles that are only parochially affirmed? The answer, for Christians, lies in the nature of the truth Christians believe to be embodied in Christ. It is an ancient tenet of Christian faith that Christ is the Logos, the concentrated structure and meaning of all things. If that is so, then people who do not know Christ by name may nevertheless in some sense know him; everyone conscious of some part of the truth is conscious to that degree of Christ. It may be held, for example, that such is the case when a non-Christian senses that an individual human being, even a human being who can boast of no impressive achievements or distinguished qualities, has a peculiar dignity or when someone who has no conscious interest in Christ recognizes that society is somehow incommensurate with the moral majesty of even the least of its members. If Christ is the Logos, then a person may scorn Christian faith yet feel impelled to adopt a stance at once of engagement and of critical, perhaps rebellious, independence.

It may be helpful to mention at the outset, and answer briefly, two objections that the following argument is likely to call forth from readers. My effort to fuse engagement and independence relies heavily on the idea of awaiting the leadership of God in history. The spirit of such a politics was characterized by Martin Buber when he wrote that "there can be no forcing of YHVH's hand."[3] Buber calls our attention to the biblical anathema on those who say of God, "Let him make haste, let him speed his work that we may see it."[4] The principle of human dependence on the leadership of God makes it possible to be expectant (with those who affirm the liberating significance of history) yet also realistic (with theologians who stress human sinfulness), thus giving rise to a balanced sense of political responsibility. Here, however, politically sensitive readers are apt to hear two disturbing notes: quietism and individualism. Both are repudiated (and with good reason, I believe) by most Christian political thinkers today.

The note of quietism is easily heard. We should take care not to act against God's intent. This we may take as a primary principle of prophetic politics. Does it not, however, give religious sanction to conservatives who are unwilling to act at all? I shall have a good deal to say on this matter in the course of the essay. It seems in order, however, to say this much now: surely the time has come to think much more carefully and critically about *human* (as distinguished from divine) action than most writers today are willing to do. Some of the worst disasters and most flagrant atrocities of our century have resulted from uncritical confidence in our powers of action. Yet such confidence continues to reign among most Christian political writers, especially in America. Witness the complaint, in one of the most widely praised of recent theological works, concerning that fact that "there can still be heard those dark and foreboding proclamations of our need to be 'realistic' about the use of power in our fallen and sinful situation."[5] Might it not be said, in view of twentieth-century history and of Christian doctrines of human nature, that such proclamations are heard too infrequently?

And why should we fear them? Relying on the leadership of God does not spell inaction for those with faith in the God of the Bible, a God with historical purposes and engaged in historical action. For Christians, to think critically about human action is not to repudiate action but to reflect on its ultimate sources and proper conditions.

The note of individualism is perhaps less easily heard. It is there, however. It is present in the principle that determining the direction of God's leadership is, in the final analysis, the responsibility of each individual, singly. The initiative of God can never be equated with the initiative of any human leader or any historical party, nation, or movement. There is therefore an ineradicable element of solitary reflection and choice in our political lives. Although an individual is no more infallible than a group, an individual cannot allow a group to exercise any unconditional and uncritical authority. Each person must decide alone concerning his responsibilities in history.

It is good, certainly, that the kind of individualism commonly found among nineteenth-century liberals has been largely left behind. By Christian standards, it was radically false; I shall try to show why in the following chapter. But in this connection, too, it may be asked, as in the case of action, whether our repudiation of an erroneous view—here, individualism—has not been entirely too unguarded. It is vital to distinguish between true communities and monolithic societies and social groups. Authentic solidarity with others may carry the necessity of standing apart from the most compact and massive associations. The ancient Hebrew prophets were hardly individualists, yet they ordinarily had to live as solitary individuals; the same is true of Jesus. The tragedies of twentieth-century history are connected not only with uncritical activism but also with uncritical collectivism. Confidence in our powers of action has ordinarily been upheld by a tacit, if not overt, deification of a nation or party, a race or class.

But the concept of the prophetic stance is not an implicit attack on community any more than on action. On the contrary, it presupposes the essential communality of human beings; this is shown by its derivation from the Christian vision of the coming of the Kingdom of God. The note of individualism one can hear in it comes only from the notion that just as action requires a moment (in the Hegelian sense: an "aspect," which is also a stage of temporal unfoldment) of suspense, so community depends on a moment of singular personal decision.

In a word, this is a book about civility, or at least a certain sort of civility. It is an effort to discover the nature and conditions of humane relationships in the grand collectivities that structure our lives in history. It is particularly concerned with the question of how civility can be defined and defended in an uncommonly chaotic and demoralized—hence uncivil—age. The main thesis of the book is that Christianity points to a concept of civility that corresponds closely with our needs. To practice this concept is to adopt the posture I call the prophetic stance.

I have tried in the preceding pages to provide an introductory sketch of this prophetic civility. Perhaps an example will be more effective than the necessarily swift and imprecise lines I have drawn. My example is fictional. In Ignazio Silone's great novel *Bread and Wine*, Pietro Spina, a one-time Communist, returns to his native Italy, which is under the rule of Mussolini. Pietro is institutionally, and literally, homeless. He is an enemy of the established government. He refuses to be associated with the Church—beyond the symbolically significant act of wearing priestly robes as a disguise—because of the ecclesiastical support Mussolini receives. He resigns from the Communist party in order to assure that his thoughts and actions are entirely his own. He has no home, no property, and no position and is hunted by the police. He is solitary. He has returned to Italy, however, to affirm his solidarity with the peasants of his native land and with oppressed people everywhere. Not only is he solitary, he is condemned to inaction; alone and powerless, he has no means of action. Still, every hour of his life is a protest against despotism and injustice. Pietro is not an avowed Christian and does not profess a belief in God. But his life is based on the faith that there is a mysterious significance in the course of events and that the silent sacrifice of an individual's life and comfort has historical consequences. Pietro exemplifies, in spite of his lack of explicit faith, my understanding of the prophetic civility implicit in Christianity.

In understanding this civility more fully and exactly, we must begin by considering Christian values and the way in which these values are subverted by sin. Christianity has no place for the current popular notion (embodied, for example, in the work of John Rawls) that civility is based on rational self-interest and that the particular values one happens to embrace are irrelevant. Civility is not merely prudential. Rather, it is based on allegiance to the things that— Christians believe—God has created and redeemed and thus made to be good.

One

The Exaltation of the Individual

Christian Love

The subject of love seems distant from that of politics, yet any discussion of Christian politics must begin by discussing (or at least making assumptions about) love. Love is the highest standard of human relationships, for Christians, and therefore governs those relationships that make up politics. Not that political relationships are expected to exhibit pure love; quite the contrary. But their place in the whole structure of human relationships can be understood only by use of the measure love provides. The prophetic attitude that defines the Christian view of politics is incomprehensible apart from the Christian concept of love.

This concept requires attention, however, not only because it underlies Christian political ideas but also because it is unique. Love as Christians understand it is distinctly different from what most people think of as love. In order to dramatize the Christian faith in an incarnate and crucified God, Paul spoke ironically of "the folly of what we preach,"[1] and it may be said that Christian love is as foolish as Christian faith. To mark the uniqueness of Christian love one does well to keep in mind its distinctive name, *agape;* this name sets it off from other kinds of love, such as friendship (*philia*) and erotic passion (*eros*). Among non-Christians, the uniqueness of Christian love is often not fully understood; and among Christians, it is sometimes forgotten, with the result that the dialectical tension and prophetic power of Christian political ideas is lost. A swift review of its main characteristics seems thus to be in order.

We need not worry about the precise boundary lines dividing *agape* from the other major kinds of love, such as *philia* and *eros*. It will suffice to distinguish Christian love from the worldly love to which the ordinary impulses of our nature lead us. The latter is a love everyone experiences. Indeed, it is probably, in the minds of most people, the only kind of love there is. Its main characteristics are these: (1) It is aroused by certain qualities in the one who is loved. For someone to ask why you love a particular person would seem intrusive but not irrational; it would be a question with plausible answers. You love a person because of the beauty, intelligence, vitality, thoughtfulness, or other such qualities you see in that person. "What does she see in him?" "What is the attraction?" Such common expressions of incredulity assume that love is called forth by lovable characteristics and that where those characteristics are lacking, love is senseless. (2) Worldly love answers to certain needs in the one who loves. Thus, in answer to the question, "What does she see in him?" it might be said not only that she prizes his firmness of character and steadiness of purpose but that factors such as instability in her own family background cause her particularly to *need* such qualities. In short, worldly love arises where something is supplied on one side that is wanted on the other. (3) Finally, worldly love is a source of satisfaction or enjoyment. Love is presumably pleasant. People who cling together even though they bring pain to one another are assumed to suffer from psychological disorders of some kind.

The Christian concept of love, in contrast, is based on the nature not of human beings but of God. We humans are weak and often perverse, and our love reflects all of the defects of our nature. Hence it is not human love, Christians believe, but God's love that tells us what love really is. The very heart of Christian faith is expressed in John's statement that God "first loved us."[2] This, and not the erring impulses of human nature, is why love is the highest standard of human relations. John makes the connection clear when he writes, "If God so loved us, we also ought to love one another."[3]

Human love, then, should be patterned after divine love. But divine love, in comparison with the worldly love we have just examined, is strange. (1) No human charms or virtues moved God to enter into history in our behalf; our moral degradation is shown in our crucifixion of Jesus. No human excellence, but only divine compassion, lies at the source of the Incarnation. To ask why God loves human beings has no answer. In his sovereign freedom, he simply does. (2) It is doubtful that God is in need of human beings or of anything that human beings can supply. His love comes from *our* need, not his. This point, admittedly, is not uncontested in Christian writing. The Christian God is sometimes contrasted with the independent, self-absorbed deity of most other religions; and creation and redemption, it is argued, both reflect a divine need for companionship. Such assertions are not entirely implausible or unappealing. Still, it hardly seems that God would be God were he in need of others, as we are. Hence, Christian theologians have typically held that creation and redemption were acts of pure generosity. (3) God's love, which was not called forth by qualities in those who were loved or by needs in the one who loved, did not lead to satisfaction or enjoyment. It led to the Crucifixion. Christians believe that God entered into the deepest agonies of human existence. When John writes that "God so loved the world that he gave his only Son," he illuminates the sacrificial character of divine compassion.

These are the marks of *agape*. If one could love others without judging them, asking anything of them, or thinking of one's own needs, one would meet the Christian standard. Obviously, no one can. Many of us can meet the requirements of friendship or erotic love, but *agape* is beyond us all. It is not a love toward which we are naturally inclined or for which we have natural capacities. Yet it is not something exclusively divine, like omnipotence, which human beings would be presumptuous to emulate. In fact, it is demanded of us. *Agape* is the core of Christian morality. And even though we cannot aspire to and attain it, as we can a virtue such as temperance, it appears occasionally in many lives. Parents sacrifice themselves for children and children for parents, and not wholly from biological instinct. Friends sometimes help one another without selfish motives, and there are even moments of peculiar moral brightness when someone risks his life for a stranger. Perhaps *agape* has to be given by God, by grace. If so, there is more grace in human relations than one might at first suppose, and it is not Christians alone who receive it. Nor is *agape* confined to personal relationships. As we shall see, it is a source of political standards that are widely accepted and even widely, if imperfectly, practiced.

Christian love can be briefly defined simply as unselfish love. This ordinary and unassuming phrase, however, makes it sound far more commonplace and far easier than it is. Other loves, such as friendship, aim at fairly definite values. Those values are always *my* values and are ultimately selfish, even when they are noble values, such as truth and courage, and even when they are values that unite us with other human beings. For Aristotle, the ultimate aim of friendship is self-realization, an aim few would criticize, but basically selfish. *Agape,* it might even be said, in order to mark the contrast sharply, is aimless: it aims at nothing designed to enhance my own life.

Is not such a love absurd and irrational? In an effort to make sense of *agape,* some suggest that Christian love is as purposeful and self-interested as any other love, with the difference being simply that Christian love aims at values held to be eternal rather than temporal and worldly. I sacrifice my worldly happiness in order to gain ever-lasting happiness. *Agape* is rational (on Christian presuppositions) and ultimately selfish, according to this interpretation. It is distinctive only in its farsightedness. Is this so?

It is a very puzzling question. Paul indicates that he would sacrifice even his own salvation if that would procure the salvation of his fellow Jews.[4] How is one to understand such a statement? Does it express the height—the absolute unselfishness—of agape? On the one hand, it seems that it does. Paul's fervor and sincerity, in the passage cited, are too manifest to be questioned. On the other hand, it is hard to make sense of such a love. Jesus says without qualification that our first duty is to love God. To love human beings is in some sense, apparently, a derivative duty. Our love of God's human creatures expresses our love of the Creator; such, at least, is seemingly implied by Jesus' statement. But to sacrifice personal salvation, as Paul proposed to do, is to accept eternal separation from God; and to do it for others, who are loved for God's sake, is to do it from the love of God. That seems absurd. If we conclude that it is absurd, however, where does that leave us? Was the first and greatest of Christian thinkers simply confused?

The trouble with this whole line of thought is that it misconstrues *agape* at the outset. It assumes it to be a calculating love, a love alert to results. It is not, however; hence, all calculations that would justify it go awry. What, then, is the source of agape? I have already suggested the answer: not reason, but grace. If *agape* is a response to grace, it is not governed by calculations nor subject to the test of reason. At no point—not even in terms of eternity—do I ask, What is in it for me? I do not seek eternal happiness, but neither do I give it up. I do not think of it. When one is moved by *agape,* the left hand does not know what the right hand is doing. This does not imply that *agape* is impulsive. Jesus' crucifixion, the classical act of *agape,* represented a mature and enduring purpose on the part of Jesus and, Christians hold, an eternal purpose on the part of God. But any such act on the part of an ordinary human being must be the fruit not of calculation but of a necessity experienced as grace. Jesus' words in approaching the Crucifixion were, "Not my will, but thine, be done."[5] There is no reckoning of consequences.

Thus, *agape* is irrational but not absurd. It would be absurd in a universe in which an act must represent a rational relationship of means to ends in order to be meaningful. But that is not the universe of Christian faith.

The sense in which *agape* is irrational may be better understood through consideration of a concept closely connected with it, that of forgiveness. According to Christian understanding of divine mercy, it seems that God is willing to forget a variety of human defects— physical weaknesses, intellectual imperfections, and so forth. Above all, however, God is willing to forget our moral defects, our subservience to lust and pride. Divine love is manifested principally in forgiveness, and *agape* is merciful. Nowhere does Christianity depart more radically from Greek antiquity than here. Even moral goodness is not a condition of love. This principle wrought a revolution in human relationships—a revolution even Christians have had trouble comprehending and accepting. For the ancient Greeks, such as Plato and Aristotle, the ultimate aim of all relationships was the cultivation and sharing of a virtuous life. One of the most reprehensible of failings, if not the source of all other failings, was neglecting virtue. Forgiveness, however, is a way of doing precisely that. Needless to say, Christianity does not maintain that the moral law can be ignored or casually broken. If it did, the doctrine of forgiveness would be pointless, for there would be nothing serious to forgive. But Christianity does tell us that we must be prepared to disregard infractions of the moral law, not because they are unimportant but because God, in the mystery of his merciful entry into history, has disclosed his own willingness to disregard them.

Here the "folly" of Christian teaching stands out starkly. Although the idea of forgiveness is familiar, the practice of it is exceedingly difficult. It collides with our retaliatory instincts; it offends us deeply when people commit evil deeds and never suffer for them. Further, it seems unsafe; presumably, crimes that are unpunished are likely to be repeated. Finally, for evil deeds to be set aside and forgotten seems unfair. Does not justice require that wrongs be requited in proportion to their gravity? In short, forgiveness as an act and not a mere sentiment strikes us as disagreeable, imprudent, and unjust. Perhaps Christian principles allow the stipulation of reasonable conditions, such as repentance. The New Testament does not clearly say that every sin must automatically be forgiven. But it lays down no definite limits on forgiveness, and there is a note of recklessness in Jesus' preaching on this theme; you must be ready to forgive "seventy times seven" times someone who persists in sin.[6] To those concerned above all that society be organized in a just and rational way—to all "Greeks"—the Christian doctrine of forgiveness violates good sense.

But *agape* requires forgiveness, and this illustrates the gratuitousness of *agape*. It is a love given without manifest reason or justification. It is reckless, like forgiveness, for it precludes the calculation of consequences. Politically, it is dangerous because it challenges what we might call political rationality—the practice of judging human beings and distributing honors and powers, rewards and penalties, in ways calculated to maintain effective government and the peace and order of society. Not that Christian political thinkers have been indifferent to political rationality. Christianity does not call on us to disregard the social and political realities that concern reasonable people. Christians, too, can be reasonable people. But among all of the terms of praise that might be applied to Jesus, "reasonable" is not the first that comes to mind, and Christian doctrine casts doubt on any conception of human life that sets reasonableness as the highest standard. It does this out of faith in a God who bestows on human beings an unjustified, and in that sense unreasonable, love and commands human beings to treat one another with similar mercy. Hence, though Christians can be reasonable people, this involves severe tensions, tensions of a sort that those untroubled by faith can largely escape.

Let it be noted that we stand here at the parting of the ways followed by the two traditions of Christian thought pointed out in the Preface. In defining *agape* as antithetical to all worldly loves, I have taken the "Reformation" way. The "Catholic" conception of *agape* comprises elements of friendship and erotic striving; and in doing this, it leads to an appraisal of society, state, and action less pessimistic than that expressed in this essay. The "Reformation" outlook, locating the center of *agape* in selflessness, cannot avoid the conclusion that there are elements of radical evil in worldly order and political action, however necessary both may be to our lives in history. Given the scope of this essay, all I can say here in defense of the pathway taken is that it has, so to speak, been legitimized by a number of great Christian thinkers and, moreover, that it seems to me to follow more closely than the other pathway the directional signs inherent in the life of one who said that the fullest love was giving up your life for your friends and who died at the hands of men of power.

Agape is a prophetic love. It refuses to equate anyone with his immediate observable being. A human being is not deeply and essentially the same as the one who is visible to the employer, neighbor, salesman, policeman, judge, or even the friend or spouse. A human being is destined to live in eternity and is fully known only to God. This, at any rate, is the Christian view. Because *agape* recognizes the prophetic mystery in which every person is enshrouded, it is, as Paul said, a love that "bears all things, believes all things, hopes all things, endures all things."[7]

In its prophetic character, then, *agape* is anticipatory and otherworldly. But it is also immediate and worldly. It requires observance here and now. It cannot be fully obeyed, partly because of our moral deficiencies and partly because of the constraints of worldly reality. But it cannot be ignored, and thus it has implications for politics and government.

The Exalted Individual

The life of every society is a harsh process of mutual appraisal. People are ceaselessly judged and ranked, and in turn they ceaselessly judge and rank others. This is partly a necessity of social and political order; no groups whatever—clubs, corporations, universities, or nations—can survive without allocating responsibilities and powers with a degree of realism. It is partly also a struggle for self-esteem; we judge ourselves, for the most part, as others judge us. Hence, outer and inner pressures alike impel us to enter the struggle. When we do, we anxiously strive to evade the adverse judgments of others. But we are inclined to subject others to our own adverse judgment, partly because sometimes we must and partly because in adversely judging others we seem to exalt ourselves.

The process is harsh because all of us are so vulnerable. All of us manifest deficiencies of natural endowment—of intelligence, temperament, appearance, and so forth. And all personal lives reveal moral deficiencies as well—blameable failures in the past and vanity, greed, and other such qualities in the present. The process is harsh also because it is unjust. Not only are those who are judged always imperfect and vulnerable, but the judges are imperfect, too. They are always fallible and often cruel. Thus, individuals are never rated exactly, and seldom even approximately, as they deserve.

There is no judgment so final and no rank so high that one can finally attain security. Many persons are ranked relatively high; they are regarded as able, or perceptive, or courageous. But such appraisals are never unanimous or stable. A few reach summits of power and honor at which it seems for a moment that their victory is definitive. It transpires, however, that they are more exposed to judgment than anyone else, and often they have to endure torrents of derision.

Agape means refusing to take part in this process. It lifts the one who is loved above the level of reality on which a human being can be equated with a set of observable characteristics. The *agape* of God, according to Christian faith, does this with redemptive power; God "crucifies" the observable, and always deficient, individual and "raises up" that individual to new life. The *agape* of human beings bestows new life by accepting the work of God.

The power of *agape* extends in two directions. Not only is the one who is loved exalted; so is the one who loves. To lift someone else above the process of mutual scrutiny is to stand above that process yourself. To act on the faith that every human being is a beneficiary of the honor that only God can bestow is to place yourself in a position to receive that honor. (That is not the aim, of course; if it were, *agape* would have been turned into a way of serving oneself and would thus have been nullified.) *Agape* raises all those touched by it into the community brought by Christ, the Kingdom of God. Everyone is glorified. No one is judged and no one judges.

Here, we come to the major premise of the prophetic stance and, indeed, of all Christian social and political thinking—the concept of the exalted individual. Arising from *agape,* this concept more than any other shapes Christian perceptions of reality and Christian delineations of political goals.

Fully to grasp the idea of the exalted individual is not easy. That is not because it rests on a technical or complex theory but rather because it is beyond the realm of theory. It refers to something intrinsically mysterious, something one cannot see by having someone else point to it or describe it. It is often spoken of, but the words we use—"the dignity of the individual," "the infinite value of a human being," and so forth—have become commonplace and no longer evoke the mystery that called them forth. Hence, we must try to understand what such phrases mean. In what way, from a Christian standpoint, are individuals exalted? In our efforts to answer this question, the concept of *destiny* may provide some help. This concept, as a representation of the principal value other than God in the Christian universe, will be important throughout this essay and must therefore be fully defined.

In the act of creation, God grants a human being glory, or participation in the goodness of all that has been created. The glory of a human being, however, is not like that of a star or a mountain. It is not objectively established but must be freely affirmed by the one to whom it belongs. In this sense, the glory of a human being is placed in the future. It is not a mere possibility, however; nor does it seem quite sufficient to say that it is a moral norm. It is the most fundamental of imperatives, even though all of us, in our sinfulness, in some degree refuse it. This fusion of human freedom and divine necessity may be summarily characterized by the statement that the glory of an individual, rather than being immediately given, is *destined.*

It must be noted in passing that nothing is said here of sin, which I shall discuss in the following section. It is not sin that renders human glory the result of a spiritual process rather than a simple natural quality. Rather, it is our freedom. Sin, it may be said, tragically complicates but does not constitute the task of affirmation that is laid upon us. Sin is not the occasion of destiny but rather requires the form that destiny is given through Christ: dying to the mortal and inglorious selfhood chosen in rebellion against God, and rising into eternal life.

The "dignity" and "infinite value" of a human being, then, as understood in Christianity, arise from the destiny bestowed in creation and restored and reformed in Christ. It will be apparent that destiny is not the same as fate. The word does not refer to anything terrible or even to anything inevitable, in the usual sense of the word, but to the temporal and free unfoldment of a person's essential being. My destiny is my own selfhood, given by God, but given not as an established reality, like a rock or a hill, but as a task lying under a divine imperative. Not only is selfhood unlike any natural reality, however; its achievement is unlike any natural process of growth, such as that of a plant. A destiny is a spiritual drama.

A destiny is never completely fulfilled in time, in the Christian vision, but leads onto the plane of eternity. It must be worked out in time, nevertheless, and everything that happens to a person in time enters into eternal selfhood and is given meaning and justification there. My destiny is what has often been referred to as my soul. It is of no avail to gain the whole world and fail my destiny, for then I have lost my very being.

Realizing a destiny is not a matter of acquiescing in some form of relentless causality. If it were, there would be no sin. A destiny can be failed or refused. That is why it is not a fate. True, the very word *destiny* is indicative of necessity, but the necessity of a destiny is not like the necessity that makes an object fall when it is dropped. Rather, it is the kind I recognize when I face a duty I am tempted to evade and say to myself, "This I *must* do; I can do nothing else." Yet my destiny has a weight unlike that of any particular duty, since it is the life given to me by God. As is recognized in words like *salvation* and *damnation*, the call of destiny has a peculiar finality.

Although a destiny is worked out in time, it is not entirely visible. Ever since the beginnings of human thought, some have argued that a human being is nothing more than what is empirically evident—a biological organism, perhaps, or a social function. The full human being is reduced to certain objective characteristics. Both Marx and Freud, in different ways, and with genius, carried out such an act of reduction. Christians—and adherents of other religions, too—refuse to do this and look with Paul, "not to the things that are seen but to the things that are unseen."[8] They insist that a human being in essence is not something here and now in front of us, which we can examine and understand, as we might an automobile or a building, but is something that has yet to be discovered and realized; this, they believe, can finally be accomplished only beyond the limitations of space and time. Destiny is the drama of discovery and realization.

The core of Christian faith can be expressed in these terms. Christ was pure destiny. With most of us, because of both outward limitations and inward resistance, much comes into life that is fate rather than destiny. Christ was not untouched by fate, for he was crucified. His fate was transformed into destiny, however, by the Resurrection; and since his fate was death—the hardest and most final blow fate can deliver—fate was definitively overcome. Because Christ was both God incarnate and archetypal humanity, fate was thus potentially overcome in every human life. Christ in his destiny marks out and ordains human destiny as such. He reveals the human future as leading, through the forbidding doorway of death, to limitless life. Faith is acceptance of that revelation, and living with faith is opposing fate and, in God's good time, overcoming it.

The ancient conception of Christ as the Logos means not only that Christ is the word, or speech, of God but also that Christ is the underlying principle and significance of all reality. To understand Christ would be to understand the purpose of all that is real and all that happens. But Christ is the destiny of every person. Thus, the vast universe, apparently indifferent and brutal, is in truth subordinate to the ultimate ends of each one of us. This may sound extreme.

It is implicit, however, in the faith that God, the Creator, has given every person a destiny; it is a measure of the exaltation of the individual. And it is not as far from common intuitions as one might suppose. If, as we so frequently say, every individual is an end and not merely a means, then the universe either serves the true ends of every person or else is absurd. Neither the intellectual Ivan nor the saintly Alyosha, in *The Brothers Karamazov,* would accept any final and universal harmony, however glorious, that depended on the torture of just one innocent child. This is the attitude of Christians. They are confident, as Paul put it, that in spite of appearances "all things work together for good to them that love God."[9]

A destiny is intensely personal, uniquely one's own. It is also, however, universally human. It is difficult to explain conceptually how this can be. It is certain, however, that we are deeply interested in the lives and destinies of others, and not merely from idle curiosity. In reading letters, diaries, memoirs, and autobiographies, we feel that the lives thus revealed are of compelling concern. This reflects an intuition that the destiny of any human being is mysteriously pertinent to the destinies we ourselves must live. In some sense, all destinies are one. The unique importance of the novel as a form of literature may lie in its expression of this intuition. The novel not only pictures destiny unobscured by the accidental circumstances that nonfiction writers are compelled to record; it also exhibits destiny as at once universally human and intimately personal.

The mystery and dignity of human destiny are suggested in the Gospel of John. One who is "born of the Spirit"—called by God to a destiny—is likened by John to the wind. You "hear the sound of it, but you do not know whence it comes or whither it goes."[10] To be conscious of one's destiny is to feel called out of the world into an eternal commonwealth. It is to realize that a human being is born to the task of journeying beyond mortal time and space—born to die and in this way again to be born. But a being who does not belong in the world cannot properly be treated merely as something to be appraised objectively and used as social needs and circumstances dictate. A citizen of the Kingdom of God must be treated with a deference akin to that shown any member of an august association, with the proviso that every worldly association is paltry in comparison with the association ordained, as Christians believe, by God through Christ.

Agape can readily be understood in these terms. The *agape* of God consists in the bestowal of a destiny; and that of human beings, in its recognition through faith. In the ordinary life of the world, constituted as it is by the process of mutual judgment, anyone with a destiny is, so to speak, invisible. But everyone has a destiny. Hence, the process of mutual scrutiny is vain, and even the most objective judgments of other people are fundamentally false. *Agape* arises from a realization of this and is therefore expressed in a refusal to judge.

Maintaining the prophetic stance is awaiting destiny—the destiny that is mine and, in the solidarity recognized by *agape,* the destiny of all humanity. If I am sure of destiny, I am not afraid of the fate embodied in my personal circumstances and historical situation. Listening for the divine commands through which destiny takes the form of moral requirements and political obligations, I can be resolute even though I am weak and uncertain.

The nobility granted in Christianity to even the most degraded individuals would have been incomprehensible to the ancient Greeks, for they envisioned neither God nor the universe in a way that would have permitted them to think of divine *agape* as the ruling force in all nature and history. Individuals were variable, and ultimately insignificant, reflections of cosmic order. Considering the long ages after Christ during which slavery, serfdom, and other drastic inequalities endured almost undisturbed, it cannot be claimed that Christians based their conduct on the concept of the exalted individual or even that they thoroughly understood it. But the seed had been planted.

It is surely one of the most potent seeds ever to lodge in the human mind. One is reminded of the mustard seed to which Jesus likened the Kingdom of God: "it is the smallest of all seeds, but when it has grown it is the greatest of shrubs and becomes a tree, so that the birds of the air come and make nests in its branches."[11] People were envisioned in relation to an eternal glory that God had defined as their ultimate possibility and mission. Social and natural determinations—rank and nationality, sex and color, intelligence, beauty, and charm, all of the qualities by which we judge and which in judging we accentuate and confirm—fall away. The Lord of all time and existence has taken a personal interest in every human being, an interest that is compassionate and unwearying. The Christian universe is peopled exclusively with royalty. What does this mean for society?

To speak cautiously, the concept of the exalted individual implies that governments, and all persons with power, must treat individuals with care. This can mean various things—for example, that individuals are to be fed and sheltered when they are destitute, listened to when they speak, or merely let alone so long as they do not break the law and fairly tried if they do. However variously *care* may be defined, it always means that human beings are not to be treated like the things we use, discard, or just leave lying about. They deserve attention. This spare standard has, of course, been frequently and grossly violated by people who call themselves Christians. It has not been without force, however. Even in our own secularized times, individuals who are useless or burdensome, individuals who are hopelessly ill or guilty of terrible crimes, are sometimes treated with extraordinary consideration and patience.

The modest standard of care implies other, more radical, standards. Equality is one of these; *no one* is to be casually sacrificed. No natural, social, or even moral differences justify exceptions to this rule. Of course, people are made not equal but, rather, incomparable by their destinies; equality is a measurement, and dignity is immeasurable. But in Christ—according to Christian claims—every person has been immeasurably dignified. Faith discerns no grounds for making distinctions, and the distinctions made by custom and ambition are precarious before God. "Many that are first will be last, and the last first."[12] Even if some are eternally condemned (a proposition to which few Christian theologians today would unreservedly assent), they are recipients of a kind of terrible dignity. Moreover, no human beings and no social authority can know who the condemned are. Hence, not only love but humility as well—the humility of not anticipating the judgments of God—impels us toward the standard of equality. This, like the standard of care, has been flagrantly violated but not wholly ignored. Echoes of Christian egalitarianism can be heard in numerous present-day practices—in governmental arrangements that allow everyone to speak and to vote, in welfare programs set up to ensure that everyone has food and shelter, in judicial reforms enacted so that even the most disadvantaged would be equal to others before the law. The principle of the exalted individual has had a part in the advances made by American blacks and in the uprising of nonindustrial peoples.

No one, then, belongs at the bottom—enslaved, irremediably poor, consigned to silence. This points to another standard: that no one should be left outside, an alien and barbarian. *Agape* implies universality. Greeks and Hebrews in ancient times were often candidly contemptuous of most of the human race. Even Jesus, although not contemptuous of gentiles, conceived of his mission as primarily to Israel. However, Jesus no doubt saw the saving of Israel as the saving of all humankind, and his implicit universalism became explicit, and decisive for the history of the world, in the writings and missionary activity of Paul. Christian universalism (as well as Christian egalitarianism) was powerfully expressed by Paul when he wrote that "there is neither Jew nor Greek, there is neither slave nor free, there is neither male nor female; for you are all one in Christ Jesus."[13]

Christian universalism was reinforced by the universalism of the later Stoics, who created the ideal of an all-embracing city of reason—*cosmopolis*. Medieval Christians cast their universalist visions in Hellenic terms. Thus, the two streams of thought, from Israel and Greece, flowed together. As a result, the world today, although divided among nations often ferociously self-righteous and jealous, is haunted by the notion of a global community. War and national rivalry seem unavoidable, but they burden the human conscience. Searing poverty prevails in much of the world, as it always has, but no longer is it unthinkingly accepted in either the rich nations or the poor. There is a shadowy but widespread awareness, which Christianity has had much to do with creating, that one person cannot be indifferent to the destiny of another person anywhere on earth.

In summary, the principle of the exalted individual implies that governments must, as far as circumstances and imagination permit, be considerate, egalitarian, and universalist. It is hardly too much to say that the idea of the exalted individual is the spiritual center of Western politics. Although the principle is often forgotten and often grossly violated, were it erased from our minds, our politics would probably become altogether what it is at present only in part—an affair of expediency and self-interest.

The exalted individual is not an exclusively Christian principle, as I have already implied in noting that destiny is not an exclusively Christian intuition. If it were, it would be difficult for Christians to take part in public affairs. They would have no moral principles in common with those not sharing their faith and thus could not engage in general political discourse, which implicitly or explicitly always involves moral principles. There are two ways in which a non-Christian may sense the infinite worth of an individual. One is love. Through personal love, or through the sympathy by which personal love is extended (although at the same time weakened), we sense the measureless worth of a few and are able to surmise that what we sense in a few may be present in all. In short, to love some (it is impossible, as Dostoevsky emphasized, to love everyone) may give rise to the idea that all are worthy of love. Further, the exalted individual may become a secular value through reason, as it did with the Stoics. Reason tells me that each person is one and not more than one. Hence, my claims upon others are rightfully matched by their claims upon me. Simple fairness, which even a child can understand, is implicitly egalitarian and universal; and it is reasonable. Both passion and intellect, then, provide intimations that the value of a person is beyond all measure. This is important, for otherwise the prophetic stance could be expressed in the world only in dogmatic assertiveness. As it is, Christians can appeal to the moral insight of everyone and can articulate their political convictions in the public realm.

Will passion and intellect suffice to undergird our politics if faith declines? That is doubtful. Love and reason are suggestive but not compelling. Christianity alone offers a world vision that commands absolutely the strange act of disregarding the natural limitations and moral defects so evident among human beings and treating every individual as noble. It cannot be denied that professed Christians often have behaved abysmally. It still is arguable that the moral sparks that come from love and reason are fanned into flame only by Christ. Greeks of the Periclean Age, living at the summit of the most brilliant period of Western civilization, never entertained the notion that every individual ought, as modern usage has it, to be treated as an end and not merely a means. Today, why should those who assume that God is dead entertain such a notion?

This is the question Dostoevsky posed when he asserted that if there is no God, "all is permitted." It may be the most fateful question facing the highly secularized civilizations of the twentieth century, and we shall return to it. But first we must note a paradox at the heart of the Christian view of the individual—a paradox unparalleled in secular outlooks but crucial in Christian political wisdom.

The Fallen Individual

The fallen individual is not someone other than the exalted individual. Every human being is fallen and exalted both. This paradox is familiar to every informed Christian. Yet it is continually forgotten, partly, perhaps, because it so greatly complicates the task of dealing with evil in the world and, no doubt, partly because we hate to apply it to ourselves; although glad to recall our exaltation, we are reluctant to remember our fallenness. It is vital to political understanding, however, to do both. If the concept of the exalted individual defines the highest value under God, the concept of the fallen individual defines the situation in which that value must be sought and defended and in which the prophetic stance must be maintained. Hence, as in the preceding section, a swift review of fundamentals may be in order.

The principle that a human being is sacred yet morally degraded is hard for common sense to grasp. It is apparent to everyone that some people are morally degraded. It is ordinarily assumed, however, that other people are morally upright and that these alone possess dignity. From this point of view, all is simple and logical. The human race is divided roughly between good people, who reflect the infinite worth we attribute to individuals, and bad people, who do not. The basic problem of life is for the good people to gain supremacy over, and perhaps eradicate, the bad people. This view appears in the most various forms: in Marxism, where the human race is divided between a world-redeeming class and a class that is exploitative and condemned; in some expressions of American nationalism, where the division is between "the free world" and demonic communism; in Western films, where virtuous heroes kill the bandits and lawless Indians.

This common model of life's meaning is drastically irreligious because it places reliance on good human beings and not on God. It has no room for the double insight that the evil are not beyond the reach of God's mercy nor the good beyond the need for it. It is thus antithetical to Christianity, which maintains that human beings are justified by God alone and that all are sacred and none are good.

The proposition that none are good does not mean merely that none are perfect. It means that all are persistently and deeply inclined toward evil. All are sinful. In a few, sin is so effectively suppressed that it seems to have been destroyed. But this is due to God's grace, Christian principles imply, not to human goodness; and those in whom sin has been suppressed testify emphatically that this is so. Saints claim little credit for themselves.

Nothing in Christian doctrine so offends people today as the stress on sin. It is morbid and self-destructive, supposedly, to depreciate ourselves so. Yet the Christian view is not implausible. Twentieth-century history, not to speak of earlier ages (often assumed to be more barbaric), has displayed human evil in extravagant forms. Wars and massacres, systematic torture and concentration camps, have become commonplace in the decades since 1914. Even in the most civilized societies, subtle forms of callousness and cruelty prevail through capitalist and bureaucratic institutions. Thus, our own experiences indicate that we should not casually dismiss the Christian concept of sin.

According to that concept, the inclination toward evil is primarily an inclination to exalt ourselves rather than allowing ourselves to be exalted by God. We exalt ourselves in a variety of ways: by trying to control all of the things and people around us—by power; by accumulating an inequitable portion of the limited goods of the world—by greed; by claiming to be wholly virtuous—by self-righteousness; and so forth. Self-exaltation sometimes is carried out by individuals, sometimes by groups. It is often referred to, in all of its various forms, as "pride." It is evil because human beings thus put themselves in the place of God, as both capitalists and Communists, exhilarated by technology, often have done. Pride is unwillingness to acquiesce in finitude or in the necessity that goes with finitude—that of sharing life with others. In ways immeasurably subtle and ingenious, proud people evade the consciousness of their creaturely nature and limitations. All of us are proud people, according to Christian doctrine, and what we do in our pride, essentially, is refuse to trust God, finding ourselves in consequence impelled to affirm our own being aggressively and incessantly.

This refusal has a secondary form. If the yearning to be more than a finite being is severely checked, one may settle for being less. One may reject finite selfhood through the self-forgetfulness that is found in sensual pleasure, intense busyness, or thoughtless routine. Let us use a term of Pascal's and set an inclination to "diversion" alongside "pride." Pride comes first; we would all be gods if we could. When pride is defeated, we fall back on diversion in order to avoid the conscious dependence on God that is faith.

Most people, of course, are not so bold as to pursue the ways of pride until utterly crushed nor so abandoned as to devote themselves unreservedly to diversion. They judiciously mix pride and diversion, often in ways that enable them to appear to others, and to themselves as well, as moderate and well balanced—as virtuous.

When it comes to virtuous appearances, our ability to deceive ourselves—and our willingness to be deceived—should not be underestimated. Our principal strategy is simply neglecting to inquire into motives, our own or others'. Thus, we commend behavior we would scarcely admire if we examined it critically and comprehended its sources—for example, devotion to scientific or literary goals inspired by a thirst for fame; unflagging work impelled by a fear of thinking about one's life; commitment to social reform arising from self-righteousness and resentment. Seen in their full reality, many activities that are commonly respected are not morally admirable.

But are these respectable activities so bad? Does Christianity ask for too much? It asks for love, as we have already seen. Pride and diversion make love impossible, for both reflect unwillingness to be one finite being among many. Even in a society as deeply secular as the United States, activity carried on without love is not usually commended.

The Christian concept of sin is not adequately described, however, merely by the statement that people frequently commit evil actions. Their predisposition toward such actions is so powerful and unyielding that it holds them captive. As Paul said, "I do not do what I want, but I do the very thing I hate."[14] This does not imply, of course, that I am entirely depraved. If I disapprove of my evil acts, then I am partly good. However, if I persist in evil in the face of my own disapproval, then I am not only partly evil but also incapable of destroying the evil in my nature and enthroning the good. I am a prisoner of evil even if I am not wholly evil.

This imprisonment is sometimes called "original sin," and the phrase is useful, not because one must take the story of Adam's disobedience literally but because it points to the mysterious truth that our captivity to evil originates in a primal and iniquitous choice on the part of every person. I persistently fail to attain goodness because I have turned away from goodness and set my face toward evil.

Neither society nor nature can be blamed. A Christian cannot blame society, even though society manifests and reinforces the primal commitment to evil, for that would relieve the individual of responsibility and thus of the need for divine forgiveness. And a Christian cannot attribute original sin to nature, for nature is created by God, and God found his creation good. We are therefore, in our captivity to evil, our own captors. Otherwise, it would make no sense to speak of original *sin*.

The weakness of the concept of original sin is that it fails to explain the origins of sin. It tells us, in effect, that the source of sin is sin. The strength of the doctrine, however, is great. It takes into account, to begin with, that human evil does not consist merely in evil acts. Evil acts presuppose an evil disposition. Distinguishing the two levels is indispensable to moral understanding, for it precludes the superficial notion, beloved by the self-righteous, that goodness is mere avoidance of sin. And it stands in the way of judgment of others—one of the worst acts of pride—and reminds us that some who are outwardly virtuous may be inwardly worse than some whose behavior is vile.

The doctrine also elucidates our real inner state. Careful introspection will show that we are often impelled to do something we condemn in advance; a seemingly unavoidable act is a source of remorse. The notion that we are at once prisoners and authors of evil is an accurate psychological observation, not just a morbid fantasy.

Of greatest importance politically, however, is that the doctrine of original sin recognizes our evil tendencies as something other than a problem we can rationally comprehend and deliberately solve. To say that the source of sin is sin is to say that sin is underivable and inexplicable. A sinful person is not like a malfunctioning machine, something to be checked and repaired. Human control is thus drastically limited; this is one reason people are so offended by the idea of original sin. In our pride, we persistently look for a morally pure vantage point that will make us independent of God and give us access to God's cosmic sovereignty. This search often is political. Thus, Plato claimed a morally pure vantage point for philosopher-kings, and Marx tacitly did the same for the working class. But Christianity tells us that no such moral sovereignty is available to human beings. It denies us something we fiercely desire and are offered, in one form or another, by the great political ideologies and also by almost every popular doctrine of the day—the power of managing our lives all on our own.

To say that we cannot do what sin leads us to attempt—that we cannot be masters of our existence—does not suffice, however. It suggests merely that sin creates practical problems. The truth, emphasized in Christianity, is that sin alters our entire situation; this is what is meant by fallenness. Sin is ironic. Its intention is self-exaltation; its result is self-debasement. In trying to ascend, we fall. The reason for this is not hard to understand. We are exalted by God; in declaring our independence from God, we cast ourselves down.

In other words, sin concerns not just our actions and our nature but also the setting of our lives. By sin, we cast ourselves down into a degraded sphere of existence, a sphere often referred to as "the world." It must be immediately noted that the world is not equivalent to what we may conveniently call "the earth." The former is a product of sinful humanity; the latter is created by God. The world is man's sinful distortion of the realm of realities—light, sky, sea and dry land, fish and birds, trees and plants—formed by God for human habitation and use.

We may define the world most simply as the dimension of being that is made up of objects, or things—realities that are purely spatial and temporal, sensibly perceptible in their entirety, and fully understandable in terms of causal relationships. The world is altogether impersonal. Human beings, although persons, belong to the world through sin. They observe one another objectively; they manipulate, mutilate, and kill one another. In diverse ways, some subtle and some shocking, some relatively innocuous and some devastating, they continually depersonalize. They behave as inhabitants of the world they have sinfully formed rather than the earth created by God.

From within, the world looks like all there is. It continually presses into our minds the prejudice that every true reality is a thing and that any purported reality that is not in its totality spatial and temporal, empirically observable, and causally explicable is not a reality at all. From this, it follows, of course, that neither God nor destiny is a reality and that the exaltation of the individual is an illusion.

Common experience, however—not to speak of revelation—shows that we are not naturally and inevitably confined within the world. Appearances are ambiguous; the data our senses offer us so profusely during our waking hours can be interpreted in various ways. This can be seen in mythology, poetry, and visual art. Painters like Cézanne and Matisse display a sphere of being not composed wholly of the plain facts that constitute the world. They enable us to see reality, but the reality they reveal is informed with grace and meaning. They show us the earth.

The world is something we are continually constructing and maintaining. This is due partly to the nature of reason. We take in sights, sounds, and other data of the senses in a manner that satisfies reason only when we group them together in the form of objects—things causally interrelated in space and time. Sensuous experience prompts us continually to ask questions such as, What is that? Why is it behaving as it is? To answer these questions, we ceaselessly build the world around us. The methods by which this is done are exhaustively analyzed in Immanuel Kant's *Critique of Pure Reason*.

It is not only the nature of reason, however, that gives rise to our world-building activities. Convenience also plays a part. We can deal deliberately and assuredly only with those realities that are things. Action is performed upon objects. Hence, to have food and shelter and to be safe from others, we must fit the realities around us into the world. And we do this not only through perception and understanding but also through action. We force realities to conform with our worldly expectations and needs. We turn fields into shopping centers, trees into boards, and unpredictable human beings into compliant consumers or, perhaps, prisoners of the state. The product of these activities is simply society.

If only reason and convenience were involved, however, we would not be confined to the world as we are. We would still build up the world, both to satisfy our rational faculties and to meet practical needs. But we would easily and frequently transcend the world because we would feel more at home in other realms of being. It is sin that causes us to consolidate the potentially incomplete and open world into something all-inclusive and closed.

Pride strives for mastery, for command over all reality. This is its very nature. Assured and confident mastery depends on rational understanding, which is not only necessary to confident and effective action but is in itself a kind of mastery. Hence, pride is intolerant of the mysteries that break into the world, as when we experience beauty. Pride is only at home where reason is at home, and it uses reason to force all realities into the world. Diversion, too, extends and empowers the world. It does this by allowing one's own personal being, the self, to be a mere thing in the world—an organism searching for sensual satisfaction, perhaps, or a mechanism automatically performing the actions prescribed by society.

Sin, then, is worldliness. Original sin is the quiet determination, deep in everyone, to stay inside the world. Every sinful act is a violation of the personal being that continually, in freedom, vision, and love, threatens the world. The archetype of sin is reduction of a person to the thing we call a corpse.

Worldliness means that all sequences are conceived of in terms of causal regularity. A mind at home in the world cannot recognize the mysterious sequences that form destinies or the dignity that destinies bring to individuals. Persons must be thought of as objects, a principle illustrated by capitalism, bureaucracy, propaganda, and other highly developed forms of modern worldliness. Whether in the form of pride or diversion, worldliness depersonalizes.

Denying destiny, worldliness inevitably empowers fate. It tends to make events irresistible, inescapable, and destructive. This is not accidental. It is inherent in worldly strategies. Seeking mastery, pride sets up chains of causal consequences. Not all chains of consequences, however, are either calculable or benign; hence they are often experienced by those who initiated them as arbitrary and hostile—as fate.

When pride is enhanced by science and equipped by technology, it can set up vast and highly destructive chains of consequences. Nuclear energy is only the most conspicuous contemporary example. Our times are fateful in many ways. In our scientific and technological pride, we are self-assertive; but, conscious of fate, we are also fearful. Today, we know that we are powerful beyond all historical precedent, but we also know that we are so vulnerable that we could snuff out civilization in a reckless hour.

The nature of the world is reflected in death. It is sometimes suggested that all scientific resources be focused on the problem of extending life further and further until death is overcome. As an assessment of real possibilities, such an idea is incredible; as an aspiration, however, it is understandable. Death reflects a fundamental derangement of being: our nature is incongruous with our dignity. Even as an aspiration, however, the idea has a fatal fault. This is the assumption that death is rooted in biology and not in the nature of the world. To live in the world is to be touched by death every day. It is to find every value limited in degree and duration. It is to be continually dealing with realities that are not personal and, in that sense, are dead. It is again and again to be depersonalized by others. If these experiences are fully comprehended, to live in the world is to realize that death is not an absurd interruption of worldly life but its logical culmination. Death shows forth our fallenness.

Sin, then, accomplishes the opposite of what it intends. It begins in self-exaltation. It ends in indignity and death. It seeks human supremacy but in fact imprisons us in the world. In this sense, sin is necessarily and naturally punished unless it is forgiven by God, who restores the dignity and life we have deliberately surrendered.

To speak of forgiveness is to remember the paradox that determines our nature and situation—that the individual who is fallen is nevertheless exalted. This is because the God who is able to forgive with a force that transfigures life has forgiven us. This is the basic proposition of Christian faith.

As a way of understanding this proposition, especially in its political significance, I have suggested the concept of destiny. The divine transfiguration of our lives—lives carried on in time—is a reshaping of human destiny in response to sin. The principal condition of destiny, as I have argued, is not sin but freedom; because we are free, our glory as creatures of God, and the only creatures made in God's image, is not possessed as a natural characteristic but must be deliberately affirmed. In this way the glory of our divine likeness is given to us as something that lies before us, in the future. But we have rejected the future thus put before us and cast aside the divine likeness offered us. This is our primal sin—the refusal of our original destiny. God's mercy lies, so to speak, in allowing us to reconsider. Human destiny has been renewed and recast rather than being eternally lost. Now it necessarily takes the form of redemption. In this form, it has been defined and established by the death and resurrection of Christ; and it is fulfilled only as we ourselves, following Christ, die to the world created by our pride—and die also to the doomed and inglorious selfhood we have substituted for God's image in us—and enter into authentic life, into eternity. As in the beginning, the glory of our divine likeness still lies before us. Although fallen, we are still exalted—not as we are but as, through grace, we shall be. This, at any rate, is the Christian conception of the human state.

Our nature and destiny, thus understood, cannot possibly be grasped by anyone who believes that the world is the totality of being. Our exaltation depends on the mercy of God, who is not a being in the world, and is reflected in destinies that lead us beyond the world. Exponents of worldly philosophies, denying God and unconscious of destiny, move back and forth between two contrasting misunderstandings. Trying to maintain the dignity of human beings, they affirm their goodness; that is the only possible source, for them, of their dignity. When they discover that most human beings display little goodness, they are forced to question their dignity. Thus, they fluctuate between complacency and cynicism. Only those conscious that the world is transcended, and that our lives in the world lead beyond the world, can say that a human being is morally perverse yet of measureless value, fallen yet sacred.

Agape is simply the affirmation of this paradox and of the destiny underlying it. *Agape* looks beyond all marks of fallenness, all traits by which people are judged and ranked, and acknowledges the glory each person—as envisioned in Christian faith—gains from the creative mercy of God. It sets aside the most astute worldly judgment in behalf of destiny. *Agape*, then, is a love that rises above, without abolishing, the consciousness of human perversity. Thus, it allows for a realistic understanding of human failings and of the worldly imprisonment to which they give rise but does not finally judge human beings on the basis of such an understanding. *Agape* means approaching people with radical and unqualified love but without illusions.

The power of affirming people paradoxically, the power in which *agape* consists, is of great importance politically. It sets humane standards but rules out dreams of harmony without government and coercion. Through *agape*, Christians can be both compassionate and realistic. This brings political balance of a kind that secular creeds find unattainable.

This political balance is at the heart of the prophetic stance. But before defining the prophetic stance—the main task of the following chapter—we must pause long enough to examine more fully the difficulty secularism encounters in attaining political balance and the consequences of this difficulty. By doing this, we shall gain a much clearer view of the prophetic stance than would otherwise be possible.

The Man-god versus the God-man

When the paradox of simultaneous exaltation and fallenness collapses, it is replaced by either cynicism or (to use a term that is accurate but masks the destructive character of the attitude it refers to) idealism. Cynicism measures the value of human beings by their manifest qualities and thus esteems them very slightly. It concludes, in effect, that individuals are not exalted, because they are fallen. Idealism refuses this conclusion. It insists that the value of human beings, or of some of them, is very great. It is not so simplistic, however, as to deny the incongruity of their essential value and their manifest qualities. Rather, it asserts that this incongruity can be resolved by human beings themselves, perhaps through political revolution or psychotherapy. Human beings can exalt themselves.

We shall dwell in this discussion on idealism, partly because idealism is much more tempting and therefore much more common than cynicism. Idealism is exhilarating, whereas cynicism, as anything more than a youthful experiment, is grim and discouraging. We shall dwell on idealism also because it is so much more dangerous than it looks. The dangers of cynicism are evident; that a general contempt for human beings is apt to be socially and politically destructive scarcely needs to be argued. But idealism looks benign. We must understand why its appearance is misleading.

Idealism in our time is commonly a form of collective pride. Human beings exalt themselves by exalting a group. Each person, of course, exalts the singular and separate self in some manner and degree. In most people, however, personal pride needs reinforcement through common ideals and emotions, such as nationalism. Hence the rise of collective pride. To exalt ourselves, we exalt a nation, a class, or even the whole of humanity in some particular manifestation, such as science. Such pride is alluring. It assumes grandiose and enthralling proportions, yet it seems selfless, since not one alone but many others as well are exalted. It can be at once more extreme and less offensive than personal pride.

To represent the uncompromising and worldly character of recent and contemporary idealism, we may appropriately use the image of the man-god. This image is a reversal of the Christian concept of the God-man, Christ. The order of the terms obviously is crucial. It indicates, in the case of the God-man, the source of Christ's divinity as understood in Christian faith. God took the initiative. To reverse the order of the terms and affirm the man-god is to say that man becomes divine on his own initiative. Here, pride reaches its most extreme development. The human, whether represented by many or by only a few, becomes divine. The dignity bestowed on human beings by God, in Christian faith, now is claimed as a quality human beings can acquire through their own self-creating acts.

In using the concept of the man-god, I do not mean to suggest that divinity is explicitly attributed to certain human beings. Even propagandists, to say nothing of philosophers, are more subtle than that. What happens is simply that qualities traditionally attributed to God are shifted to a human group or type. The qualities thus assigned are various—perfect understanding, perhaps, or unfailing fairness. Illustrative are the views of three great intellectual figures, familiar to everyone, yet so diversely interpreted that the fundamental character of their thought—and their deep similarity—is sometimes lost from sight.

Friedrich Nietzsche sets forth the ideal of the man-god more literally and dramatically than any other writer. Nietzsche's thinking
was grounded in a bitter repudiation of Christianity, and he devoted
much of his life to scouring human consciousness in order to cleanse
it of every Christian idea and emotion. In this way, his philosophy
became a comprehensive critique of Western civilization, as well as
foreshadowing an alternative civilization. It is, as practically everyone now recognizes, remarkable in its range, subtlety, and complexity; Nietzsche is not easily classified or epitomized. It can be argued,
nevertheless, that the dramatic center of his lifework lay in the effort
to cast down the standard of Christian love and to wipe out the idea
that every human being deserves respect—leading Nietzsche, in the
field of politics, to attack such norms as equality and democracy. If
Christian faith is spurned, Nietzsche held, with the courage that was
one of the sources of his philosophical greatness, then Christian morality must also be spurned. *Agape* has no rightful claim on our allegiance. And not only does *agape* lack all moral authority, it has a destructive effect on society and culture. It inhibits the rise of human
beings to the heights of glory, which, we realize at last, are not in-
habited by God. By exalting the common person, who is entirely
lacking in visible distinction and glory, *agape* subverts the true order
of civilization. The divine quality Nietzsche claimed for humanity
was power—the power not only of great political leaders like Julius
Caesar but also of philosophers, writers, and artists, who impose in-
tricate and original forms of order on chaotic material. Such power,
in the nature of things, can belong only to a few. These few are human gods. Their intrinsic splendor overcomes the absurdity that
erupted with the death of the Christian God, and it justifies human
existence.

Karl Marx is perhaps not only as well known but also as influential
among Christian intellectuals as are even the most celebrated theologians. The familiar saying that "we are all Marxists now" dramatizes the fact that Marx's views on such matters as class and capitalism are part of the furniture of the modern mind. Christian writers
are not exceptions; spontaneously they think in some measure as did
Marx. A considerable number of them can even be called "Marxist
Christians"—an appellation fully justified in the case of most libera-

tion theologians. Marx has in that sense become a familiar member of the Christian household. Having thus domesticated Marx, however, we may tend to forget what he really thought and felt. We may forget that he was as apocalyptically secular and humanistic as Nietzsche, even though he disdained the kind of elevated and poetic rhetoric that abounds in Nietzsche's writings. He called for the entire transformation of human life by human beings, and this, in Marx's mind, included the transformation of nature as well. The universe was to become radically—in its roots, in its sources and standards—human. True, like the Christians he scorned and unlike Nietzsche, Marx was egalitarian. The transformation of humanity and being was envisioned as the work of multitudes—the proletariat—and not of exceptional individuals, and ahead there lay justice and community rather than glorious solitude. Nevertheless, Marx tacitly claimed for the proletariat qualities much like those attributed in the Old Testament to God—omniscience, righteousness, and historical sovereignty, all devoted to avenging past wrongs and transfiguring human existence.

Sigmund Freud, of course, avoided not only the rhetoric of redemption but the thought as well. He regarded any great change in the character of human beings or the conditions of human life as unlikely; and by intention, he was a scientist, not a prophet or revolutionary. He belongs among the heralds of the man-god, however, by virtue of the conviction that underlay all of his psychological investigations. Disorders of the soul—which for Christians derive in one way or another from sin and which in their ultimate origins are thus mysterious— Freud believed to be scientifically explicable. From this conviction, it followed that the healing work Christians believe dependent on divine grace Freud could assign altogether to human therapy. The soul thus was severed from God (for Freud, a childish illusion) and placed in the province of human understanding and action. Not that psychoanalysis and Christianity are in all ways mutually exclusive; the many Christians who have learned from Freud testify to the contrary. But with Freud and his major followers, psychoanalysis is a comprehensive faith, not merely a set of useful hypotheses and techniques. As a faith, it attributes to man alone powers and responsibilities Christians regard as divine. Human beings are exalted by virtue of purely human faculties. Freud's attitude of resignation was a matter mainly of temperament; his methods, theories, and basic assumptions have reinforced the efforts of man to seize the universal sovereignty that Christians assign exclusively to God.

Nietzsche, Marx, and Freud represent a movement by no means restricted to those who consciously follow any one of them or even to those familiar with their writings. Not only are we "all Marxists now," as is often said; with nearly equal justification it could be said that we are all Nietzscheans and Freudians. Most of us have come to assume that we ourselves are the authors of human destiny. The term *man-god* may seem extreme, but I believe that our situation is extreme. Christianity poses sweeping alternatives—destiny and fate, redemption and eternal loss, the Kingdom of God and the void of hell. From centuries of Christian culture and education, we have come habitually to think of life as structured by such extremes. Hence, Christian faith may fade, but we still want to live a destiny rather than a mere life, to transform the conditions of human existence and not merely to effect improvements, to establish a perfect community and not simply a better society. Losing faith in the God-man, we inevitably begin to dream of the man-god, even though we often think of the object of our new faith as something impersonal and innocuous, like science, thus concealing from our own eyes the radical nature of our dreams.

The political repercussions are profound. Most important is that all logical grounds for attributing a peculiar dignity to every individual, regardless of outward character, disappear. Some individuals may gain dignity from their achievements in art, literature, or politics, but the notion that all individuals without exception—the most base, the most destructive, the most repellent—have equal claims on our respect becomes as absurd as would be the claim that all automobiles or all horses are of equal excellence. The standard of *agape* collapses. It becomes explicable only on Nietzsche's terms: as a device by which the weak and failing exact from the strong and distinguished a deference they do not deserve. Thus, the spiritual center of Western politics fades and vanishes. If the principle of personal dignity disappears, the kind of political order we are used to, one structured by standards such as liberty, equality, and the supremacy of law, becomes indefensible.

Nietzsche's stature is due to the courage and profundity that enabled him to make all this unmistakably clear. He delineated with overpowering eloquence the consequences of giving up Christianity—and every like view of the universe and humanity. His approval of those consequences and his hatred of Christianity give force to his argument. Many would like to think that there are no consequences—that we can continue treasuring the life and welfare, the civil rights and political authority, of every individual without believing in a God who renders such attitudes and conduct compelling. Nietzsche shows that we cannot. We cannot give up the Christian God—and the transcendence given other names in other faiths—and go on as before. We must give up Christian morality, too. If the God-man is an illusion, so is the immeasurable worth of every person.

It is true, as we have seen, that love and reason provide intimations of such worth. But intimations alone; they provide no grounds for overruling the conclusions of our eyes and senses. The denial of the God-man and of God's merciful love of sinful humanity is a denial of destiny, and without destiny there is only life. But life calls forth respect only in proportion to its intensity and quality. Except in the case of infants and children, we ordinarily look on those lacking in vitality with pity or disgust. Respect we spontaneously reserve for the strong and creative. If it is life we prize, then institutions that protect and care for people whose lives are faltering are worse than senseless. It is hard to think of anyone else, with the single exception of Dostoevsky, who understood all of this as profoundly as did Nietzsche.

Marx certainly did not. His mind was on matters of a different kind, matters less philosophical. The result in his case was an illogical humanitarianism. He was incensed by the squalor in which the common people of his time were forced to live and by the harsh conditions and endless hours of their work. Marx sympathized deeply with the downtrodden and disinherited. But this was due to his personal qualities, not to his philosophy or faith. His philosophy was a materialism that can be interpreted in differing ways but that implied, at the very least, that reality was not created and is not governed by God; his faith was in science and human will. He provided no philosophical or religious grounds whatever for the idea that every individual must be treated with care. In spite of Marx's humanitarianism, therefore, there is a link between Marxist thought and the despotic regimes that have ruled in his name. It is perfectly true, as his defenders aver, that Marx adhered to political principles quite unlike those manifest in the purges and prison camps of the Soviet Union. That such practices should claim the authority of his name is thus outrageous in a sense. Nonetheless, the connection between Marx himself and modern Marxist despots is not entirely accidental. They share the principle that a single individual does not necessarily matter.

If the denial of the God-man has destructive logical implications, it also has dangerous emotional consequences. Dostoevsky wrote that "a man cannot live without worshiping something."[15] Anyone who denies God must worship an idol—which is not necessarily a wooden or metal figure. In our time, we have seen ideologies, groups, and leaders receive divine honors. People proud of their critical and discerning spirit have rejected Christ and bowed down before Stalin, Mao, or some other secular savior.

When disrespect for individuals and political idolatry are combined, the results can be atrocious. Both the logical and emotional foundations of political decency are destroyed. Equality becomes nonsensical and breaks down under attack from one or another human god. Consider Lenin: as a Marxist, and like Marx an exponent of equality, under the pressures of revolution he denied equality in principle—except as an ultimate goal—and so systematically nullified it in practice as to become the founder of modern totalitarianism. When equality falls, universality is likely also to fall. Nationalism or some other form of collective pride becomes virulent and war unrestrained. Liberty, too, is likely to vanish; it becomes a heavy personal and social burden where no God justifies and sanctifies an individual in spite of all personal deficiencies and failures.

The idealism of the man-god does not, of course, bring as an immediate and obvious consequence a collapse into unrestrained nihilism. We all know many people who do not believe in God and yet are decent and admirable. Western societies, as highly secularized as they are, retain many humane features. Not even tacitly has our sole governing maxim become the one Dostoevsky thought was bound to follow the denial of the God-man—"everything is permitted."

This may be, however, because customs and habits formed during Christian ages keep people from professing and acting on such a maxim even though it would be logical for them to do so. If that is the case, our position is precarious, for good customs and habits need a spiritual base; and if it is lacking, they will gradually—or perhaps suddenly, in some crisis—disappear. To what extent are we now living on moral savings accumulated over many centuries but no longer being replenished?

To what extent are those savings already severely depleted? Again and again, we are told by advertisers, counselors, and other purveyors of popular wisdom that we have a right to buy the things we want and to live as we please. We should be prudent and farsighted, perhaps (although even those modest virtues are not greatly emphasized), but we are subject ultimately to no standard but self-interest. If nihilism is most obvious in the lives of wanton destroyers like Hitler, it is nevertheless present also in the lives of people who live purely as pleasure and convenience dictate.

And aside from intentions, there is a question concerning consequences. Even idealists whose good intentions for the human race were pure and strong would still be vulnerable to fate because of the pride that causes them to act ambitiously and recklessly in history. Initiating chains of unforeseen and destructive consequences, they are vulnerable to fate in spite of the humane character of their designs. Modern revolutionaries have willed liberty and equality for everyone, not the terror and despotism they have actually created. Social reformers in the United States were never aiming at the great federal bureaucracy or at the pervasive dedication to entertainment and pleasure that characterize the welfare state they brought into existence. There must always be a gap between intentions and results; but for those who forget that they are finite and morally flawed, the gap may become a chasm. Not only Christians but almost everyone today feels the fear that we live under the hand of forces that we have set in motion—perhaps in the very process of industrialization, perhaps only at certain stages of that process, as in the creation of nuclear power—that threaten our lives and are beyond our control.

There is much room for argument about these matters. But there is no greater error in the modern mind than the assumption that Christ, the God-man, can be repudiated with impunity. The man-god may take his place and become the author of deeds wholly unintended and the victim of terrors starkly in contrast with the benign intentions lying at their source. The irony of sin is reproduced in the irony of idealism: exalting human beings in their supposed virtues and powers, it undermines them. Exciting fervent expectations, it leads toward despair.

The concept of the prophetic stance represents an effort to understand the human condition and gain hope in a different way.

Two

Prophetic Hope

Community and Society

The world is not a fitting home for the exalted individual. It knows nothing of beings with a value entirely beyond observation, measurement, and the comprehension of reason. Thomas Hobbes spoke for the world when he said that "the value, or worth of man, is as of all other things, his price."[1] The idea of something that has value but no price and that, properly speaking, is not even "something"—not a thing among other things—is nonsensical from the standpoint of the world.

This is one way of describing the situation created by the paradox that an individual is at once exalted and fallen. Described in these terms, the prophetic stance is a way of facing this situation—of trying to treat individuals with respect in circumstances (which they themselves have created) that tend continually to debase them. It is a way of living in a deeply ambiguous universe.

We must be wary, however, of reading into the concept of the exalted individual something that is not there—an individualism very common in modern thought but false by Christian standards. We must interpret our situation in accordance with our communal nature. To do this, we can find no more useful concept, I believe, than the antithesis of community and society.

The exaltation of individuals implies not separation but the contrary. The very concept of the exalted individual was derived, in the preceding chapter, from that of a relationship—*agape.* Individuals are exalted by God's love and accept their own exaltation by accepting the exaltation of others. The exalted individual thus does not exemplify the lonely splendor of the Nietzschean man-god but rather the common humanity recreated in Christ. If I am to realize my own exaltation, I must live within and cultivate that humanity. I must seek relationships.

The idea of the exalted individual leads, in this way, directly to the ideal of community. It calls for sustained efforts to perfect human relationships, and what we mean by *community* is simply a set of perfected relationships. Community is authentic unity among human beings—authentic in the sense of uniting people in their true being rather than in the being given them by terror, ignorance, lust, or some other sinful cause. The early Platonic dialogues and the sermons of Jesus can give us a sense of what community is; an armed platoon or a totalitarian state indicates what it is not. A community is a setting in which individuals are exalted.

Community is such a setting, but society is not. It may be that no other distinction in the area of social and political theory is quite as important as this one. If community is what arises when we recognize one another as having a value beyond price, society is the kind of unity that comes about because of the necessities of life in the world. These necessities are, above all, economic and military; and they require that the value of an individual be assessed on the basis of social utility—as a laborer, technician, manager, teacher, consumer, soldier. Even when society is relatively cooperative and benign, even when it recognizes standards such as equality and social justice, it is based finally on mutual need rather than mutual respect. Individuals are used rather than exalted. Society is the form we give to the world to make it humanly habitable. That form may be modified by a recognition of the transcendental worth of an individual, but the pressures of life—of the need for food, clothing, shelter, and safety from attack—necessarily govern.

Society is not merely a product of physical necessity, however. Christian principles indicate that it arises ultimately from human sin and is shaped by sin throughout. The very fact that we live under a more or less continuous threat of physical deprivation reflects our fallen condition. And were we not fallen, we would cooperate spontaneously and would not need the pressures and contrivances that constitute society. Finally, because we are sinful beings, we gladly adopt social modes of thought and feeling, and we extend them much further than necessity requires. We take proud pleasure in judging others, and we seek ascendancy and power more for the sake of self-exaltation than for the service of common necessities.

Clearly, it is beyond human powers to erase the antithesis of community and society. It originates in human finitude and sin. Society cannot be formed in accordance with sacred norms (thus, presumably, making it a community), as some Christians have desired, and if the attempt to do so is made, the result will be less a sacralization of society than a degradation of the sacred. Nor can society as a coercive order judging and using individuals be abolished, as envisioned by Marxists; attempts to do this have everywhere led in the opposite direction, toward totalitarianism.

The ineradicable distinction between community and society constitutes the ambiguous universe in which the prophetic stance is maintained. And the prophetic stance may be understood as communal openness and availability maintained in the midst of, and against, the pressures of society. Before moving further toward a definition of the prophetic stance, however, we must pause and ask whether the antithesis of community and society is really as sharp as I have made it appear to be.

Any one of several questions might occur to a reader and give rise to doubts. Are not some societies better than others? Are not the better societies better by virtue of uniting people more authentically—by being more communal? Are not community and society, then, often fused? And is not the difference between community and society, therefore, one of degree rather than kind?

There is no doubt that the picture I have drawn needs shading. That some societies are better than others is manifest; and the point is important, for if societies were uniformly evil, moral standards would be irrelevant in the political sphere, and political activity guided by such standards would be futile. Politics would be inalterably base, and there would be little reason for inquiring into the political meaning of Christianity.

It does need to be noted, in passing, that one of the main ways in which some societies are better than others is in their granting and safeguarding of liberty. In doing that, they recognize the very theme I have been arguing—their imperfection. Liberty is life unregulated by society. The passion for liberty is a tacit acknowledgment of the deep and ineradicable flaws of society. To say this, however, does not dispose of the matter. A good society (that is, a society substantially better than the worst of societies) does more for its members than meet their most pressing material needs.

Very simply, it provides traditions, beliefs, and ideals. Although not communal bonds in themselves, these constitute raw material from which communal bonds are constructed. Every society, of course, brings people into *physical* proximity with one another, and even that is an indispensable contribution to community. Ancient Athenians congregated around the Acropolis for the sake of military security, but in doing that they laid the basis for the celebrated communality of the Athens of Pericles. As the example of Athens illustrates, however, the better societies bring people not only into physical proximity but, in a manner of speaking, into *spiritual* proximity as well. They do this by upholding and setting before them the high values in whose sharing community consists. This is apparent in primitive societies in the centrality of ritual and myth and in modern societies in the prominence of cultural and educational institutions. An art gallery or a university is not in itself a community, but without art and truth to be shared, community could not come into existence.

Society, then, can do more for community than merely meet economic and military necessities. It can preserve and make available values, such as truth, art, and historical memories, without which community could not exist. Although distinct from society, community is not a visibly different set of relationships subsisting apart from society. Rather, it is an interpersonal realization and creative elaboration of values affirmed by society. Thus, Socrates' conversations embodied a rationality that came down from an ancient Greek tradition; and his conversations were creative explorations into a set of values, such as justice, courage, and friendship, that were commonly prized in the Greek cities. The better societies, it might be said, are those that offer superior communal opportunities.

Christianity, then, requires acceptance of society, and such acceptance cannot be a matter simply of bowing to bitter worldly necessity. It is more appreciative than that. Even if society is not community, it serves community in various and essential ways; and a responsible person will feel obliged to defend society when it is threatened, sometimes even if that means putting temporary restrictions on liberty and communication. The student rebels of the 1960s were shortsighted when they idealized community but acted in ways that furthered social disintegration.

What happens to the antithesis of community and society, however, in consequence of qualifications such as these? Is it seriously weakened? I do not think so. A "good" society is not a blend of society and community. Rather, it is a society that offers numerous communal opportunities. As a society, it is essentially different from a community. It is occasioned partly by the fact that we are physical creatures continually more or less threatened by the loss of the things we need in order to live. And it is also occasioned by our willful yet irremediable (so far as human resources go) state of separation from God and hence from one another. Community, on the other hand, comes from the grace that lifts us out of our fallenness; it is essentially different from society. "Good" societies, then, are not communities, not even inferior communities. They are worldly settings favorable to the rise of community.

The communal moments that occasionally occur in societies do not change them in essence. They remain subject to the conditions that called them into existence. They are still economic and military organizations, and they are rooted in sin. Economic and military exigencies must generally take priority over cultural and educational aims; and the quest for status and power will predominate over the quest for community. Even within their own spheres, culture and education are continually invaded by objectifying modes of thought, in which human beings are appraised in relation to the needs of society. This is partly because even institutions that serve community cannot dispense with calculation and contrivance (communal moments in the classroom do not free teachers from the necessity of grading their students); it is partly because of the mental habits that, in our sinfulness, we acquire from society; and it is partly because we delight in appraisal and domination.

As a result, society always more or less betrays the values it formally affirms. For those values to be taken with utmost seriousness, as they are when human beings are striving to meet one another on the deepest levels of being, is threatening to society. Community arises from moral purity and unmixed truth, whereas society depends on compromise and works best where superficiality is not considered intolerable. Athens could not allow Socrates to live, even though Socrates, with his courage, gregariousness, and love of reason, was a quintessential Athenian. And though the sermons and parables of Jesus were thoroughly Hebraic—a communal realization of ancient traditions—the spiritual leaders of Israel felt driven into instigating the Crucifixion.

It is not difficult to find scriptural support for what I have tried to say in the form of rational argumentation. Societies are not loved and redeemed by God; only individuals, in the Christian vision, receive this mysterious glorification. If what is important is what God cares for, rather than what is revered by human beings, then a single human being is more important than a nation or an empire. Only individuals are exalted, not societies.

Moreover, the individuals exalted by God are crucified by society. Jesus in his uncompromising love exemplifies community in its purity. He was rejected and condemned by the principal spiritual society of his time, Israel, and he was put to death by the principal political society, Rome. The state, the one human agency with the right to kill, is not the antithesis of society, as is sometimes suggested, but its fulfillment. It is the fulfillment of society when it pursues economic and military ends, appraising and using human beings as means to those ends. And it is the fulfillment of society when its offices are the highest summits sought by pride and personal ambition.

And if society is a crucifier of men, it is also opposed to God. It is telling that the words *society* and *world* are often used more or less interchangeably. Of course, every society has religious institutions. But these tend to be brought into the service of social ends; illustrative is the nearly invariable wartime chauvinism of priests and pastors. A human arrangement for attaining human purposes, society tends to exclude all that cannot be grasped by natural intelligence and subordinated to human purposes. But God, above all, cannot be used in this way. "For my thoughts are not your thoughts, neither are your ways my ways, says the Lord."[2] The God encountered in the Bible confounds our preconceptions and deranges our plans. He cannot, in his own authentic reality—as distinguished from lifeless religious forms and symbols, which obscure his reality—be welcome in the world of social designers and men of power.

The Kingdom of God therefore comes as a judgment on human societies. God's final and complete act of self-disclosure was accomplished in the person of one who brought to a climax a long history of prophetic denunciation of social idolatry and injustice and who, in consequence, was rejected by society; furthermore, it was focused in the culminating event of rejection, the Crucifixion. Christian faith is centered in the antithesis of God incarnate and human society. The coming of God and his Kingdom is coincident with a condemnation of worldly institutions.

The building of the Kingdom of God, which Christians believe is mysteriously carried forward in the course of history, reflects this condemnation. It does not occur only through improvements in society, although such improvements as increases in justice and freedom presumably are not unrelated to God's intentions; it occurs through the singling out of individuals by grace. In the Old Testament, a decisive role is played by minorities ("remnants") that did not succumb to the sins of their Jewish brothers and sisters. Christianity as a world religion began with a man who was singled out, on the road to Damascus, from among the most fervent Jewish opponents of Christianity. And to our own day, the spirit of love has been borne and movements leading to the improvement of social institutions have been called forth by individuals, such as Martin Luther King, set apart from society and finally crucified.

Many suppose that not society as such but only society that has not reached its full technological and industrial development is discordant with humanity. Supposedly, as man's scientific and practical genius unfolds and the poverty of the human race is overcome, society will cease to be oppressive. This conviction underlies both Marxism and the kind of Americanism that rests on confidence in the prowess and beneficence of American industry.

It is astonishing that such a view should be as widespread as it is. Not only is it unsupported by experience, it is not even very plausible in theory. Technology is highly refined objectification. For it to flourish, objectifying intellectual habits and skills are needed; hierarchies of technicians and managers must be established; riches and pleasures are offered that render people more satisfied and dependent, and thus more compliant, than when they were poorer; and media of quick and far-reaching propaganda, devices for surveillance, and other means of obliterating personal privacy become available to dominant groups. Are conditions such as these likely to bring a withering away of society and state?

No more plausible is the common view that only large societies obstruct community. It is true that a small society facilitates personal relationships of a kind that cannot pervade a large society. But the personal warmth of a small society is not the same thing as community, and in important ways a small society is apt to be antithetical to community. Cultural riches and diversity will ordinarily be lacking; ancient Athens and Renaissance Florence were far from typical among small societies. And as village and small-town life has so often shown, the liberty that enables communal individuals to resist society may be lacking, too; custom is more uniform and common censure more intrusive.

The truth is that the inhuman and threatening character of society manifests our fallenness and not the limitations of particular circumstances or historical eras. Representatives of the "Catholic" tradition, who do not see society as manifesting our fallenness and thus as essentially and always more or less base, seem to me to take too little account of one or both of two conditions: the functions of society, which require objectification of its members, and the alacrity with which sinful human beings enter into these acts of objectification, trespassing much further on *agape* than social responsibilities require. Proponents of the "Catholic" view seem to regard human fallenness as less profound and irremediable (by human action) than is indicated either by the unceasing tragedies of history or, to refer to the very core of Christian faith, by the hatred and bloodshed attending the event that Christians regard as God's decisive act of salvation. Formed so that we can live safely in the world, society reflects the conditions of worldly action—the ascendancy of the few and the objectification of the many. Also, society reflects our pride and (since human beings will not only to rule but also, in some circumstances, to cast away their liberty and be ruled) our inclination to self-abandonment. Society will not merge with community—it will not disappear—until human nature is transformed, and that cannot happen without so altering the conditions of life that history is ended.

The political meaning of Christianity, then, does not lie in the ideal of a Christian society, for no such society can exist. Christianity calls for *agape* and *agape* for community—the unity of individuals in their exaltation. Society is the unity of human beings in subjection to one another and to the worldly necessities underlying custom, law, and governance. The terms *Christian* and *society* cannot logically be joined.

This, it must be granted, is not the unanimous verdict of the Christian tradition. Many Christians have sought the unity (although rarely the total fusion) of Church and state. They have envisioned a unified Christian order of life, implicitly denying the antithesis of community and society. It is natural for this to happen. If you feel deeply in touch with the truth—as any Christian must—you naturally and properly want it everywhere known and fully lived; you envision it in an order of life. But the truth with which Christians are in touch is not one they possess. It is not a truth they can adequately embody even in the infinitely pliant and receptive material of words; much less is it a truth they can embody adequately in the intractable and rebellious material that constitutes a society.

Today, however, relatively few Christians aspire to a Christian society. Far more common among Christians is an ideal shared with many others. Since this ideal contradicts the view of society presented here—a view vital to the concept of the prophetic stance—we must consider it briefly before defining the prophetic stance.

The Ideal of the Just Society

Streams of thought flowing from diverse sources—secular liberalism, Marxism, and democratic socialism, as well as traditional Christianity—mingle in the conviction that a just society can and must be created. The preceding argument, however, implies that a perfectly just society is not a feasible human project. This implication contradicts many common assumptions and common aspirations. How can it be defended?

The impossibility of a just society is partly due to the physical necessities underlying society. Perfect justice would require considering every person exclusively as an end, not a means, and to do that would be incompatible with maintaining and carrying on the work of society. The practical aims of society—military and economic efficiency—necessitate infringements on justice. This is illustrated by a discovery made in recent years in many socialist societies—that markets are indispensable. Markets are needed for creating wealth even though they inevitably lead to inequities and by their very nature involve the reduction of human beings to producers and consumers—that is, to means.

The human impossibility of justice results from another circumstance as well, however. The very standards of justice are in mutual conflict. The first principle of justice is equality. This is clearly implied by the concept of the exalted individual and is embodied in such institutions as equal suffrage and equality before the law. Nevertheless, in effecting a just distribution of values, such as wealth and honor, the actual inequalities of human beings cannot be ignored. Some people have contributed more than others to the welfare of society, and it would be unjust for such people not to be rewarded. Some are more intelligent, more virtuous, more gifted, or more highly disciplined than others; although such qualities do not dim the equal and transcendental dignity inherent in mere humanity, for them to go entirely unrecognized would be not only unjust but subversive of any sound scale of values. Thus, the ancient argument, going back to the times of Plato and Aristotle, that justice entails inequality cannot be simply set aside in behalf of the Christian principle of infinite personal worth. The pursuit of justice is consequently subject to two irreconcilable demands. These were in contention when oligarchs and democrats fought one another in the city-states of ancient Greece and again in modern times when the bourgeoisie rose up against the feudal aristocracy; they are in contention today in the conflict between protagonists of the free market and the welfare state. It is in the nature of the human situation that we cannot be just in one way without being unjust in another.

Similar conflicts become evident when we consider the principles that must govern our response to crime. Here, *agape* is expressed primarily in the principle of mercy. A criminal must be allowed and helped to change. The principle of mercy is apt to come into conflict, however, with the principle of retribution; repentance and reform call for opportunities that strict insistence on matching the punishment and the crime will often foreclose. Yet the claims of retribution are not slight. Vengeance, by most people properly deplored, has no necessary role in it. The principle of retribution is based simply on justice in the narrowest and strictest sense of the term. Exacting an eye for an eye is a public reaffirmation of a moral law that has been flagrantly defied. Thus, society cannot ignore the requirements either of mercy or of retribution; a conflict of standards is inevitable. This conflict is greatly complicated, moreover, by the intrusion of a third principle, one often incompatible with both mercy and retribution—the protection of society. Here, the physical insecurity that occasions the very rise of society enters into the question; one of the main reasons we punish criminals is simply to defend ourselves. Yet if we thought only about our physical security (which necessarily includes the security of our property), we would execute embezzlers and cut off the hands of petty thieves. We would abandon both mercy and justice.

It seems that the phrase "just society," as common and apparently unchallengeable as it is, does not represent a coherent and practicable ideal. The term *just* comprises discordant standards or else comes into conflict with different, but no less compelling, standards; the term *society* designates a source of practical necessities incompatible with justice. Christianity leads to this conclusion by affirming the simultaneous exaltation and fallenness of every individual. Our self-contradictory nature gives rise to conflicting imperatives.

To speak of our fallenness, moreover, may remind us of another point that ought to be noted in connection with the ideal of the just society. Even if equal justice were a practical and coherent aim, it would not be generally perceived or supported. To be fallen is to be in some measure captured by injustice—to be unable to see what justice requires, to be unwilling to perform what it requires. This is far from being a merely academic consideration. If justice is not spontaneous, it depends on force. We have seen again and again that an unyielding determination to achieve perfect justice leads to the use of force on such a scale that the ends are swallowed up in the means. It has been assumed by protagonists of the just society that human nature would in certain revolutionary circumstances swiftly change; this is illustrated by the Marxist principle that competitiveness does not underlie, but is produced by, capitalism and with the fall of capitalism will disappear. But such changes have not come about—for reasons brought out in the preceding discussion of original sin. Hence, the quest for justice has given rise to violence and with violence to terrible new forms of injustice.

To argue, as I am doing, that we must give up the ideal of a just society is to assault prevailing habits of thought in a way that is likely to offend modern readers. Let me hasten, then, to warn against exaggerating the scale of assault. Nothing I have said implies that particular injustices do not exist, cannot be identified, or should not be fought. Even the best of modern societies are filled with instances of unjust wealth and deprivation and of undeserved power and suppression. The number of such instances can be significantly reduced, and society becomes more just when this happens. I assume that the effort to live with prophetic hope requires one to watch for and resist these injustices. Otherwise, this book could not include a chapter on social transformation.

Even with this qualification, however, my argument here obviously invites opposition. At the same time, it is closely connected with the concept of the prophetic stance. It may not be superfluous, then, to state it again and differently.

Justice is admittedly a commanding ideal. From the time of Plato to the present it has, in the eyes of many, been both the center of political philosophy and the aim of political action. There is, I believe, a certain truth in this attitude but also a serious error. The truth and the error may be defined and distinguished by the observation that there are two quite different reasons why justice has been so compelling an ideal, one of these valid, the other not. Let us now consider the latter.

One reason for the powerful appeal of the ideal of justice lies in the vision it represents—a vision of perfect worldly order. In a just society, human relations would be informed with the same harmony that is thought to prevail in the cosmos as a whole. A glowing example of this vision is contained in the political philosophy of Plato. Philosophers are qualified for kingship by virtue of their understanding of the order of being itself. Under their governance, the polity would become a reflection of the harmony present among the timeless forms constituting ultimate reality. Cosmic order, reproduced in the polity, is justice. For Plato, a just polity is a mirror of eternity. Few can entirely resist the appeal of such a vision. Hence, it continuously reappears in the history of political thought. It can be seen in Augustine (a Platonist of a sort) and in Aquinas; in modern times it is discernible, as mediated by the dialectic, in Hegel.

It is this vision that I intended to attack in the preceding pages. Even though Christians have shared it, it is essentially Hellenic, depending on the sense that being is primarily order rather than history (I shall elucidate this distinction in the following section of this chapter), that understanding the order of being is the proper work of the intellect, and that reconstructing it, in the world around, is within the scope of human powers. These premises are in conflict with the Christian understanding of things. The key point is our fallenness. The original harmony of creation has been destroyed, and we have the capacity neither for understanding nor for reconstituting that harmony. The conditions of our existence not only are in conflict with the perfect practice of justice but preclude our framing an altogether coherent conception of justice. And even if we could conceive of perfect justice, and circumstances were not in the way, we would not have the moral power and purity to practice it.

Some may deplore so negative a view of our nature and situation; surely it instills discouragement. I would argue, however, that a falsely positive view of our situation cultivates hopes that cannot be fulfilled and in this way makes for disappointment and despotism, the latter arising from a desperate effort to conquer the conditions producing the former. In the history of modern Marxism, on the side both of practice and of theory, signs of such a development are too well known to need illustration.

As I have said, however, there is another reason why justice has so commanded human attention and concern. It has represented, rather than a vision of perfect order, the intense desire that particular, immediate wrongs be righted. The cry of justice has been a summons to piecemeal action. The spirit has been not visionary but practical, and the aim less the attainment of imagined perfection than the elimination of palpable and present imperfections. Christian principles provide no grounds for criticizing a concern of this kind; they imply, on the contrary, that it represents an essential expression of *agape.*

The prophetic stance, accordingly, presupposes a disposition to attack concrete, visible injustices. To pursue the ideal of perfect justice is to ignore our fallenness; but to attack injustices in the world around us—injustices we must either attack or tacitly accept—is essential to the integrity of prophetic hope. Although transformation of our fallen situation is beyond us, resisting particular evils in that situation is not. To fail to resist social evils that we are able (by grace, Christians believe) to see—and to see within the scope of our powers of resistance—is seriously, even fatally, to compromise the hope we profess. The attitude I would like to evoke is perhaps best described by Albert Camus, who draws a distinction between revolution and rebellion.[3] Revolution tries not merely to remove or alleviate particular social wrongs but to destroy the common root of all social wrongs. Its goal is comprehensive and lasting social harmony. Rebellion, in contrast, arises when we see social circumstances so manifestly hurtful to fellow human beings that we are driven to fight against them. Rebellion is a refusal (almost, for Camus, an inability) to acquiesce in present, palpable injustice. It seeks only the end of that injustice, however, not a sweeping transformation of our condition. Rebellion is a realization of our shared humanity; as Camus says, paraphrasing Descartes, "I rebel, therefore we are." Camus was attempting to frame a political ethic that was humble (Camus preferred the word *modest*) but not conservative. He spoke, I believe, in a way that is deeply congruent with Christianity. A person motivated by prophetic hope would not be revolutionary (for reasons I shall bring out more fully in the chapter on social transformation) but would, in the fashion of Camus, be rebellious.

A final note, designed to guard against the mistake of thinking that criticizing the concept of a just society lays a basis for political apathy, is this: we are talking about human powers and not about historical possibilities. To assert the *human* impossibility of justice is not to place prior limits on historical progress, for human limits do not imply divine limits. How far God intends, within history, to change human nature and the human situation Christian principles do not permit us to infer. Hence, to stand prophetically is not to close one's mind toward the future. It is rather to avoid presumption in order to serve the Lord of history.

Nevertheless, in behalf of the ideal of the just society, an objection may be raised. In a country with settled constitutional traditions, such as the United States, it may be said, the ideal of perfect justice involves negligible dangers; moreover, it encourages progress, since most people in an affluent democracy will be inclined to do nothing unless aroused by the illusion that they can do more than in·fact they can. But aside from the broad question of whether we should, or even can, entertain illusions for the sake of their practical benefits, there is a point to be made that bears significantly on the overall argument of this essay. To think that a just society is a present human possibility tends to incapacitate us for lucid historical life. It tends in this way to undermine prophetic faith and hope. If history is (or could be) moving under the guidance of human plans toward the establishment everywhere of just societies, then it is simply a process, definable in terms of finite goals and essentially comprehensible by reason. It is not a mystery and does not invite us to ask about human destiny. It is akin to natural and economic processes in which we routinely participate, such as those followed in agriculture and manufacturing. It calls less for hope than simply for rationality. For a participant in history thus conceived, the prophetic stance would be quixotic.

This may be the most serious consequence of the ideal of the just society. It rationalizes and oversimplifies our view of history. In this way, it jeopardizes the political wisdom that we can draw from Christianity and that, I believe, is necessary if we are to preserve and deepen our humanity as we pursue our way amid the tragedies of history. "To preserve and deepen our humanity" may sound to pragmatic American ears like too vague a standard to be worth maintaining. But a major tenet of my argument in this essay is that it is, so to speak, not practical to be practical in the narrow and willful fashion of most secular reformers. The quality of our humanity surely will prove at least as important as our practical skills in determining our success in pursuing justice.

We are led back to the idea of the prophetic stance. It seems that the fundamental question before us is not the one addressed by the major ideologies clamoring for our attention. It is not how we should go about creating an ideal society. Rather, it is how we should bear ourselves in the face of the paradox, arising from our simultaneous fallenness and exaltation, that we are confined to society but destined, and thus bound to hold ourselves available, for community.

The Prophetic Stance Defined

The prophetic stance has been partially defined in preceding pages: as leaving the initiative in history to God, as recognizing simultaneously the exaltation and the fallenness of individuals, as maintaining communal openness within society. These are ways of briefly characterizing the prophetic stance. The time has come to attempt a systematic definition. Three propositions are requisite for such a definition.

1. *Holding to the prophetic stance means waiting for God in history.* I stress the term *waiting.* Human beings must wait because they are finite and fallen and confined within society; because community, in which they search out and live their common exaltation, is a gift, not something deliberately constructed; because, above all, they are in every detail of their existence subject to God. They are not only forced to wait, however, but allowed to. Waiting expresses hope. We hope for two things: to see meaning in events (and in such meaning manifestations of the presence and power of God) and to know our historical responsibilities. These two things are not separate. A perception of historical meaning entails historical responsibilities, and a perception of particular responsibilities is implicitly an insight into the meaning of surrounding circumstances and events.

The major premise of the concept of the prophetic stance is the notion of destiny. By having a destiny, an individual is exalted; because one's own destiny is a share in human destiny, individuals are bound to one another in community; and owing to the universal reality and power of destiny, history has meaning. In a word, the reality and power of destiny enable us to live with hope. Hope is manifest in many ways. *Agape* is a kind of hope, maintained in relation to individuals in their fallenness; community is the fruit of hope, which is not defeated by society; waiting for God in history is only possible, in the face of the horror and apparent senselessness of so much that happens, if through faith we have hope. The notion of destiny is a way of formulating the view of man and history that underlies hope.

Through faith that events are informed with destiny, initiative is left to God.

2. *The prophetic stance entails solitude and inaction.* This was intimated in the Prologue in connection with the modern and American distaste for individualism and quietism. There can be no genuine prophetic hope without solitude and inaction—not as final or exclusive determinants of one's attitude but as elements of it (or, as I suggested earlier, Hegelian moments in its development). Human beings live in history with hope only so far as they recognize how unsatisfactory their existing situation in history is; but this situation involves essentially the fact that none of the groups or powers that define it—none of the nations, parties, movements, or leaders constituting man's historical circumstances—can be altogether trusted. Hence, in every act of historical responsibility, one must judge for oneself; one is finally alone. The modern world has been enthralled by such ideas as solidarity and commitment. Taken literally, these ideas are misleading and dangerous, for they obscure the fact that lucid historical (that is, political) responsibility imposes an unavoidable moment of solitude.

And what can one do in solitude? One can observe, and reflect, and pray, but not, in the usual sense of the word, act. That necessitates sacrificing one's solitude and joining with others. To maintain prophetic hope, therefore, one must for a moment step back into the powerlessness and inactivity inherent in being merely one individual among the billions of individuals populating the earth.

Solitude and inaction are difficult and therefore demanding. This should be carefully noted. They are not consequences of personal weakness—of indecisiveness, fatigue, irresponsibility. On the contrary, as elements of prophetic hope, they can come only from strength. It needs strength to live in full consciousness of the tragic character of history, the fallibility of the best historical agents and the demonism of the worst, and the consequent responsibility that singles out each individual in all of the weakness and vulnerability inherent in being merely one solitary human creature among human creatures as multitudinous as grains of sand on the seashore.

3. *The prophetic stance also entails attentiveness and availability.* These attitudes qualify prophetic solitude and inaction. Prophetic solitude is not a state of self-confinement. It is, rather, acceptance of

the distance from society that is needed for entering into relationships that are free and personal and avoiding relationships into which one has been hurried or forced by society. It is watchfulness—of individuals and of the things they do and suffer in history; that is, prophetic solitude is attentiveness. It is also availability, by which I mean readiness for relationships; thus, one's distance from society becomes merely provisional. Similar comments pertain to inaction, so far as it is prophetic. It is not a state of apathy but of responsibility. It arises, indeed, from a distinctively religious sense of responsibility; one steps back from all human leaders in order to follow the leadership of God. If solitude and inaction are ways of recognizing that God has the initiative, then attentiveness and availability express the faith that such initiative will in one way or another surely be taken and that we must therefore be watchful and ready.

Waiting, then, is prefatory to communication and action, not a way of avoiding them. Communication, or the search for community, is, as I have argued, required by our essential humanity; and communication, under the conditions of fallen existence, inescapably leads into action, into efforts to alter outward circumstances. But communication and action are continuously threatened by the evil in human nature and conditioned throughout by our dependence on God. This point cannot remain a mere thought. It must shape our lives, and it does this in the political realm when we implant at the center of all deliberations and activities a moment of solitude and inaction, a moment that not only prepares the way for communication and action but remains as a spirit informing all that we do. We must listen and speak out of valleys of solitude, and we must act, as the *Bhagavad-Gita* enjoins, in a spirit of inaction. In Deuteronomy, God warns that you should, as your possessions increase, take care in case "your heart be lifted up, and you forget the Lord your God." "Beware," God says, "lest you say in your heart, 'My power and the might of my hand have gotten me this wealth.'"[4] It can be plausibly claimed that with the progress of industrialism and the growth of industrial abundance, our hearts in the Western world have been lifted up; in consequence, we have recklessly committed ourselves to grandiose goals and now are in danger of seeing fulfilled the prophecy accompanying the admonitions in Deuteronomy—that those ignoring God's warning "shall surely perish."[5] Solitude and inaction can be seen as ways of drawing back—not into isolation and passivity, but rather into openness and faith, into a spiritual realm where we prepare to speak and act in awareness of our creaturely fallibility and sinful imperfection.

In the light of this definition of the prophetic stance, it will be apparent why I suggested early in the essay that maintaining a prophetic attitude is practicing civility. Allowing our hearts to be lifted up, we have fallen into savage conflict. If we learn the art of historical waiting, however, we will have learned to approach one another differently, in communication more inclined to listen, in action more tentative. To stand prophetically is to try to keep one's mind and spirit poised for the more-than-human work of carrying on together our common history.

The idea that waiting is the appropriate human stance is repeatedly, and in various ways, affirmed in both the Old and the New Testaments, and considering the historical consciousness that pervades ancient Jewish thought and spiritual experience, one can assume that biblical writers were thinking ordinarily of *historical* waiting. The following are a few among many examples. "Wait for the Lord; be strong and let your heart take courage; yea, wait for the Lord!"[6] "Be still, and know that I am God."[7] "I wait for the Lord, my soul waits, and in his word I hope; my soul waits for the Lord more than watchmen for the morning, more than watchmen for the morning."[8] Martin Buber identifies as "the core" of Isaiah's "theopolitical teaching" the doctrine that "Israel must keep still, as YHVH keeps still."[9] As for the New Testament, one of the most firmly established facts about the historical Jesus is that he proclaimed the imminent coming of the Kingdom of God. This, for Jesus, implied a posture of expectancy. The men and women of Israel, and indirectly human beings everywhere, were called upon to turn their lives into a concentrated act of waiting for a community that would be created not by political leaders but by God. "Watch, therefore . . . be ready; for the Son of man is coming at an hour you do not expect."[10] Jesus' words echo and re-echo in Paul: "Be watchful, stand firm." "The day of the Lord will come like a thief in the night . . . let us keep awake."[11]

It may seem that waiting of this sort rests on a faith possessed only by Christians and religious Jews. If faith is a fully articulated state of mind, perhaps this is so; if it is a way of standing amid confusing and alarming circumstances, however, I doubt that it is. It is possible for anyone to recognize that human beings are weak and imperfect creatures and that circumspection befits us when it comes to actions of historical scope. But is this enough? What can prophetic hope mean, for unbelievers, beyond mere sensible caution? Here, I wish to suggest something that is far from incontestable but that, I suspect, many will grant: that history has meaning; that, although often obscure and always defying literal description, this meaning sometimes is sensed by people who lack any religious or metaphysical assumptions to explain it; and that it sometimes carries indications of specific historical obligations. In sum, a person without explicit religious faith may in some historical circumstances feel that certain actions are unconditionally required. For a Christian, such a person is moved by the Logos, which is fully revealed only in Christ. Concerning Christ, however, believers and unbelievers need not quarrel. What is important politically is the possibility of a common civility. I have shown in detail what this civility means for Christians and for Jews. For unbelievers, I suggest, it means hopeful modesty (to borrow Camus' term), manifest in a willingness to wait and to watch for signs of what in existing circumstances must unfailingly be done.

In the Prologue, I cited as an example of the prophetic stance the attitude of Pietro Spina in Silone's *Bread and Wine*. Let me here offer another example, a nonfictional one. This is Dietrich Bonhoeffer, the German pastor and theologian who died in the anti-Nazi resistance.[12] On the surface of Bonhoeffer's life, action is more conspicuous than waiting. Bonhoeffer had an uncommon capacity for commitment, and this was repeatedly shown in his unceasing and resourceful opposition to the Nazi tide in Germany and in the German Church. But Bonhoeffer went through long periods of uncertainty, waiting for signs of what he should do; and he went through these periods with little human company, for not many Germans, even among Christians, were as clear-sighted and independent as Bonhoeffer in facing the events of the early 1930s. Thus, Bonhoeffer was sometimes reduced to inaction and often driven to solitude, in spite of his immersion in the events of his time. He was also steadily attentive. For example, he saw what was happening to the Jews and resisted, when even humane and honorable Germans, many of them Christians, were acquiescing in Nazi anti-Semitism. He was attentive toward God as well as toward human beings. The basis for this was expressed in the ethical principle, sharply enunciated before Hitler came to power, that the one final rule of action in all circumstances is to do God's will. That Bonhoeffer was available as well is shown by his fervent devotion to theological reflection and writing, parish and ecumenical work, and political action. Indeed, one may see the strength that enabled Bonhoeffer to follow the course that led him into prison and then to his death as originating less in a powerful will than in a staunch availability. This is suggested by Bonhoeffer's remarkable ability to be at once uncompromising and open, both steadfast and dialogical.

Underlying Bonhoeffer's prophetic faith was one of the key ideas of this essay. After more than a year in prison, and while nearing the end of a life that had been continually thrown into disarray by the political events of his time, Bonhoeffer repeatedly and strongly expressed his belief in destiny. Writing to Eberhard Bethge, after nearly a year in a Nazi prison, he said, "I'm firmly convinced—however strange it may seem—that my life has followed a straight and unbroken course, at any rate in its outward conduct. It has been an uninterrupted enrichment of experience."[13] Ten days later, he wrote that "everything seems to have taken its natural course, and to be determined necessarily and straightforwardly by a higher providence."[14] And finally, several weeks later: "I believe that nothing that happens to me is meaningless."[15]

It may bring the concept of the prophetic stance into clearer focus to take brief note of some of its primary sources in Western intellectual and spiritual history. This seems particularly important in view of its dependence on those sources. I do not regard the concept of the prophetic stance as particularly original (and would probably have little confidence in it if I did). At most, it brings together certain lines of thought that for a long time have been clearly convergent.

The most important source by far, aside from Jesus and the orthodox Christian understanding of Jesus, is the Old Testament. It may be worth quickly reviewing what the prophetic outlook means in the Old Testament, for it differs fundamentally from the way most people today look at the political world and, correspondingly, from the main modern ideologies, such as socialism and conservatism.

At issue is an ancient cultural and philosophical split. Most people today base their political views on conceptions, of one sort or another, of good order—a state of affairs they assume we can finally reach, whether by revolution, gradual reform, or respecting and maintaining continuity with the past. The tendency to think in terms of order derives mainly from Greek antiquity. The major political thinkers of ancient Greece concentrated on defining the ideal polity, in relation either to ideal circumstances or to typical, more or less unfavorable, circumstances. Practical politics consisted, as they saw it, in striving to embody the ideal in social reality. This view of politics expressed a view of the universe. Being was envisioned as a vast, all-embracing order, a cosmos; this order could be known by reason; and humans, possessing rational knowledge of the cosmos, could live well by establishing the patterns of cosmic order alike in their personal lives and in the polity.

Much of this outlook has passed into the modern mind, which helps explain our absorption today in the realization of the good society. If anything, modern man pursues the concept and reality of ideal order more relentlessly than his ancient counterpart. Inspired by the doctrine of progress and by the powers seemingly offered by technology, he has been less inclined toward contemplative withdrawal and more confident in action.

The idea of the prophetic stance (and, of course, its Christian presuppositions) derives from a tradition fundamentally different from the Hellenic tradition. The general differences between the Hebraic and Hellenic traditions are familiar to everyone. Yet we tend to neglect them and to look at things in ways derived from the Greeks— ways that obscure Christian understanding. For the ancient Hebrews there was no cosmos, in the sense of an invariable and eternal order embracing all things. There was, of course, an order of creation. But transcending this was the Creator and the human beings created in his image and likeness. God could speak and listen; he could lovingly guide human history or "hide his face" and leave human beings to disasters of their own making; he could be angry and merciful, he could pass judgment on men and then relent. Men and women possessed a similar freedom, a freedom real enough to enable them to defy God and oppose God's will. More important than all else, perhaps, was the fact that God and human beings could enter into communal relations with one another, into "I-Thou relations."

In short, the Hebraic universe was basically personal. The personalism of the Hebrews had profound consequences. There could be no impersonal, changeless order governing all events. Ultimate reality belonged to the events themselves, to all that happened between God and the human race. Reality therefore had to be understood as history. To comprehend what was and had been, it would have been futile to look for a causal law; it would have been necessary rather to remember and tell what had happened. Reason, the faculty that finds the universal in the particular, could not be as important as it was for the Greeks. With the universal subordinate to the particular—a particular God and particular human beings, such as Abraham—reason was necessarily subordinate to the human capacity for hearing God's revelatory and sovereign words.

In politics, Hebraic attitudes preclude a preoccupation with ideal order. If our supreme obligation is to hear and respond to God, we must be wary of firm commitments and set plans. The kind of political and social order we try to create will depend more on God than on changeless principles, and what we do will be determined more by our understanding of God's will than by prior plans. Yet there is nothing apolitical in these reservations. The contemplative withdrawal that tempted the Greeks has no place in the Hebraic vision of life. God is not an object of contemplation, as the cosmos is; God speaks to us and, moreover, speaks to all of us together. We must respond; and we must do so collectively as well as personally. We must live *responsively*, toward God and human beings, in history.

It cannot be denied that Christianity weakened the prophetic attitude that it inherited from Israel. One reason for this no doubt lay in the refusal of most Jews to accept Jesus as the Christ. As a result, Christians could not regard Israel as still God's unique medium of revelation. The tendency now, in spite of the rise of the Church, was to assume that God addressed individuals, not peoples or groups. Personal salvation became the primary concern. The individual, so to speak, veered off from history in the direction of eternity.

The Christian weakening of the prophetic attitude, however, was not only a loss—a temporary loss—but also an important spiritual advance. It marked the exaltation of the individual. It became clear that every human being was of concern to God—not just as a member of a certain nation, Israel, but in the individual's own singular identity. Consequently, Christian individualism (which is situational and provisional and which we might call "prophetic individualism" in order to distinguish it from the false, ontological individualism of modern liberalism) is a second major component, along with the Hebraic view of history, in the concept of the prophetic stance. This stance is maintained by individuals who stand apart from society; and it is defined by reverence for individuals exalted, by God's grace, above society.

This prophetic individualism gives a modern tone to the concept of the prophetic stance. Although the individual was exalted from the earliest beginnings of Christianity—indeed, from the moment when Christ was "lifted up" on the Cross—it was left to the modern world to bring out, in thought and action, many of the implications of the idea of individual separateness and dignity. Thus, Christian in-dividualism is expressed with particular sharpness in the Lutheran tradition, by Luther himself and later (and more uncompromisingly because with less deference to the Church and nation) by Kierkegaard. The idea of the prophetic stance is in part an effort to interpret politi-cally Kierkegaard's intense centering of spiritual life in "the existing individual." And it must be added that even secular liberals, in par-ticular John Stuart Mill, although losing all sense of the relationship of the individual to eternity and affirming an ontological individu-alism, have deepened our understanding of the meaning and glory of singular personal existence.

But how can a stance that is individualistic, in the Christian sense, still be prophetic? Does not the Christian exaltation of the individual preclude Hebraic historical consciousness, rendering it a stage in our spiritual history that we have definitively left behind?

The key intellectual act underlying the idea of the prophetic stance is the effort to affirm and keep together both elements—Christian re-spect for individuals and Hebraic awareness of the significance of his-tory. The link is destiny. Even if the track toward personal salvation does not coincide entirely with the track of empirical history (as it certainly does not), what happens in history cannot be meaningless in a universe ruled by God; nor can historical events be a matter of indifference to creatures who perforce share with one another the for-tunes of history and are bound to one another by love. The individual has a fundamental interest both in eternity and in history.

I do not mean to suggest that I think of the effort to hold together Christian individualism and Hebraic historicism as original—except perhaps in my emphasis on the connection. The individual and history have, of course, never been entirely separated in the Christian tradition. Although personal salvation was from the beginning the central concern in Christian faith, history did not lose all meaning. The historical consciousness of the Jews persisted among their Christian heirs. Although there have been great Christians, such as Thomas Aquinas, in whom this consciousness was weak, there have all along been others in whom it was very strong. Paul and Augustine, both exercising an incalculable influence over succeeding centuries, illustrate this. In the twentieth century, Nicolas Berdyaev and Reinhold Niebuhr are two eloquent writers who have united individual and history in a prophetic Christian vision.[16] More recently, this has been done by various liberation theologians, who have emphasized the continuity between the New Testament and the Old and have seen the key to Jesus' life in the liberation of the ancient Hebrews from Egypt. Indeed, one of the most indisputable contributions of liberation theology has been to help us realize that the Christian God is a God engaged in history, and not only in the history of the Church but in the history of all peoples. From the outset, then, Christianity has embodied the paradox of a responsibility, inherent in the task of working out one's own salvation, that is intensely personal and at the same time—in view of God's universal sovereignty and the love that unites all human beings—sweepingly historical.

The concept of the prophetic stance does little more than make this paradox explicit, bringing out in particular its political implications. The personal character of responsibility is implied by the concept of the exalted individual and plainly stated in the proposition that waiting for God involves moments of solitude and inaction. The historical scope of responsibility is implied by the concept of destiny and made plain in the first proposition defining the prophetic stance: that we must wait for God in history.

Finally, to fill out this sketch of the intellectual backgrounds of the idea of the prophetic stance, we must note that the paradox of a responsibility at once deeply personal and comprehensively historical is matched in the Hellenic tradition. Greek thinkers clearly envisioned the individual, alienated from all actual communities, living as a citizen of an ideal community. This we might call the paradox of "solitary communality." My understanding of the prophetic stance owes a great deal to it. The paradox was perhaps first enacted rather than enunciated—by Socrates, condemned to death by his native city and yet refusing to escape because of his loyalty to the laws that in his view had nurtured him and, up to the final minutes of his life, bearing himself as a communal being, concerned with serious conversation above all else. No doubt inspired by Socrates, Plato defended a form of solitary communality in *The Republic*. Facing the improbability that an ideal city would ever actually exist, Plato asserted that the philosopher, the only one fitted by nature and training for ruling such a city, must inhabit and rule his own inner city. The philosopher would, so to speak, be a solitary citizen and king. A broadly similar idea was present in Stoicism. The Stoic sage was envisioned as a citizen of the world, united with all humanity through obedience to universal moral law. Finally, in modern times, a concept of solitary communality was formulated by Immanuel Kant (formally a Christian but philosophically Hellenic) in his *Fundamental Principles of the Metaphysic of Morals*. There, he argued that by acting according to maxims that are purely moral and unrelated to personal interests, one rises above nature, where every reality can be regarded as a means to some end, and enters the "Kingdom of Ends"—a hypothetical commonwealth made up of all moral beings. For Kant, one might be actually solitary yet transcendentally at one with all humanity.

The basis of the Greek view, then, is the polarity of individual and community, or of worldly isolation and transcendental unity. The corresponding Christian polarity is that of individual and earthly history. In both cases, the polarity is dialectical; the two terms are separate on the level of empirical history but at one on the level of fundamental reality. The idea of the prophetic stance, of course, embodies the Christian version. The Greek version is important, however, because it is so sharply defined—hence its utility in working out the concept of the prophetic stance. To my knowledge, no Christian theologian has in like manner worked out the relations of individual and world history.

In summary, it might be said that the concept of the prophetic stance is intended to articulate the convergence of certain spiritual trends. This convergence has been more or less in the minds of countless Christians since the time of Jesus. But it has not often, if ever, been plainly described. For us to do this today is appropriate, I think, not just because of our responsibility for developing and relating the insights of earlier times but also because of conditions peculiar to our age. There have been some (although not many) centuries as tumultuous and tragic as ours. But never before have great historical troubles been accompanied by so clear and widespread a feeling that great progress is possible and is demanded of us; today, multitudes of human beings, in all parts of the world, feel themselves engaged in a work of universal liberation and equalization. On one side, then, history alienates and threatens the individual; on the other side, it carries intimations of destiny and calls individuals to action. The idea of the prophetic stance is particularly suited, I think, to this ambiguous situation.

Christianity has from the earliest times given rise to a way of life in many respects the opposite of that required by the prophetic stance. This is the way followed by mystics and cultivated systematically in monasteries. Withdrawal and solitude are the rule, rather than historical involvement; various kinds of physical and psychological discipline, sometimes harsh, are imposed. The aim is not to await God's descent into the situations that, as creatures, we naturally inhabit. The aim is ascent and finally a rapturous state of union with God, a state to which many Christians have testified, even though all agree in finding it indescribable.

Many Christian writers have held that mystical rapture is the highest Christian experience and that the solitude and asceticism typical in the lives of mystics represent the fullest measure of Christian devotion. The idea of prophetic hope, however, indicates that these are questionable claims. Although the issue cannot be simply resolved, when the mystical ideal is pressed very far it endangers some of the most distinctive and important Christian insights: that as finite and responsible beings we are essentially historical; that love obliges us to stay in the world, where most of our fellow human beings are compelled by circumstances to stay; that by staying in the world we do not keep ourselves apart from God but rather become accessible to God, who entered into the world as Jesus Christ. "Even now, in sordid particulars," T. S. Eliot wrote, "the eternal design may appear."[17] Mystical disciplines carry a risk of spiritual presumption, of unwillingness to bear with "sordid particulars" and await God's own disclosure of "the eternal design."

It would be false to the nuances and complexities of Christian life, however, to suggest that the prophetic and mystical ways of seeking Christ are in irresolvable conflict. Many great Christian figures, such as Paul and Augustine, have spontaneously fused the two approaches. No doubt, mysticism must be regarded with reservations, from the prophetic standpoint; still, it need not be condemned absolutely. The withdrawal and solitude called for by mystics may help prepare one to enter into history thoughtfully and wisely; the disciplines of mysticism may enable one, if not to ascend to God, to wait for God patiently; and mystical rapture may color prophetic experience, as it did with the ancient Hebrews, led on their trek out of Egypt by a pillar of clouds during the day and a pillar of fire at night. If, as Eliot suggests, God's eternal purpose becomes evident occasionally in "sordid particulars," it seems that mystical and prophetic insight may coalesce. The one problem of life for a Christian is to be absolutely serious about God. Here, mystics such as the great twentieth-century monk and writer, Thomas Merton, set an example that is inspiring even to those wary of their methods. Mystics may be welcomed as allies even though not as guides.

The Individual and Prophetic Hope

The prophetic stance becomes real only by becoming deeply personal, a posture sustained in a mood of earnest responsibility and expressing the deepest concerns of the individual. This is simply because the values that require the prophetic stance—values such as truth and community—are not casual or ephemeral interests but are ultimate human concerns. In other words, the prophetic stance is not merely "political" in the sense often given to that word; it is not separate or detachable from the things within the "secret heart" (Psalm 51) of the individual. It is rather one's fundamental orientation toward the human and temporal world.

Today, we are strongly tempted to split the individual and history, the personal and the political, and then to discard one or the other. In this way, the individual person is mutilated, and history is turned into an alien and menacing abstraction. People in other times of bewilderment and disillusionment, such as the era of the downfall of the ancient city-state system, have been similarly tempted, and a standard of life first clearly enunciated by Epicurus in the aftermath of Alexander's conquests is still, in the twentieth century, extremely attractive. Epicurus's standard calls for withdrawal from public life and political activity. Personal life thus is set apart from the raging torrent of history. The private sphere contains all that is most important to a human being, such as friendship (for Aristotle, a relationship with political significance). Personal, individual being is in this way emphasized. It is also truncated, however. It becomes intimate and exclusive—in a word, nonhistorical. Authentic personal being is severed from the human situation, with its global scope and political contours. Contrasting with the ideal of withdrawal is that of absolute commitment. In recent times, many have been tempted to resolve the tension between their personal lives and the menacing conditions surrounding them by devoting themselves unreservedly to a vast political cause, such as communism. Personal life is submerged in the torrent of history. It is thus not merely truncated but is lost entirely, while history, deprived of personal roots, remains abstract and menacing. If these two ways of trying to heal existence are exemplified in ancient times by Epicurus and Aristotle, they are exemplified in modern times, I suggest, by two men whose names are rarely linked, Proust and Lenin.

At the core of my argument in this essay is the thesis that Christian principles—as well as principles recognized or tacitly accepted by many who are not Christian—are opposed to any such split. In its ultimate depths, the life of the individual is historical and political because it is indissolubly connected with the lives of all human beings. The exaltation of the individual is reflected in the microcosmic (or, more precisely, microhistorical) range of individual being. It cannot be denied that such dualities as the personal and political are valid and important in the organization of institutions. Premature efforts to unify life institutionally lead to violence and totalitarianism; much more will be said on this subject in coming chapters. But personal orientation is a different matter. The life of an individual is not subject to the same prudential restrictions that govern the institutional ordering of a polity; here, the dualities, which in our fallen

state protect us against society, need not govern. To live prophetically is to strive in one's own personal being for the unity that, in the
eschatological faith of Christians, at the end of time will characterize
the whole human race.

This means refusing to recognize any absolute dividing line between the political (that is, the historical, viewed as a matter of organized human responsibility) and the personal. The political universe
is authentically and truly understood only to the extent that it becomes concrete in my own life. The hope that shapes my attitude toward nations and parties must also govern my feelings for acquaint-
ances and friends; and it orients me toward coming hours and days as
well as toward coming centuries. I maintain the prophetic stance
only so far as I remember my own past when I study the history of
the world, imaginatively apprehend the conditions of my own existence when I ponder the political situation of my times, and surmount
personal fears when I shape images of hope for the human race. These
are not necessarily expressions of self-centeredness in the pejorative
sense of that term. If the hope I feel is truly prophetic, then it is universal, and I must try to read the experience of the human race in terms
familiar to me in my own existence. Not only must the historical be
translated into the personal, however; the personal must be recast, so
far as the limitations of love and imagination permit, as participation
in the experiences and trials of all human beings. "Do not be surprised
at the fiery ordeal which comes upon you to prove you, as though
something strange were happening to you."[18] Self-centeredness of the
kind rightly condemned—self-confinement—must be overcome, and
even the most intimate and seemingly incommunicable personal
problems must be incorporated into an understanding of the state of
humanity generally—an understanding that is political when linked
with the question of what we must do.

It follows that either I daily and hourly live the prophetic stance or
else I deny it altogether. I cannot accept it as a theoretical possibility
that happens not to apply to me in particular or only applies now and
then or at times when I would like it to apply. The truth of the concept of the prophetic stance is realized only to the extent that my life
is shaped by my apprehension not merely of the concrete here and
now but of the global situation and eternal destiny of the human

race. Such a unification of existence will be fully accomplished when love becomes all that it ought to be and there is no longer tension or even difference between love of self and others or between the love of personal friends and of all humanity. In organizing and maintaining the polity, it is vital to remember that love has not been thus perfected. But prophetic faith tells us that it will be and that this faith must form and direct our individual lives.

The personal and singular character of the prophetic stance, its essential individual embodiment, can be seen in two basic ways of waiting for God in history. One of these is familiar from earlier discussions—that of watching for signs of meaning in history. In *The Republic,* Plato speaks of the state as being the individual "writ large." In parallel fashion, a Christian might speak of history as the life of an individual written in global letters. Such a view is implied by the essential solidarity of the human race and by the sovereignty of God. If we could study history with perfect love and faith, we would see that the fiery ordeals of one person are not strange but in some sense pertain to us all. This is why each individual has a deep interest in history and its intimations of meaning. It is a very personal interest. If history has no meaning, neither has the life of any individual; but to gain a hint of meaning in surrounding events is to sense significance in one's own existence. This is why the philosophy of history, in spite of its forbidding scope, has been of such absorbing interest during most of the Christian era.

These statements, although based on Christian faith, are closer to the secular common sense of our time than one might at first suppose. Everyone can see that the loss of confidence in historical progress, the main key to the meaning of history for the modern age, constitutes a spiritual crisis in the lives of multitudes of ordinary people, giving them the impression of a universe without purpose and order. And numerous non-Christian novelists in recent times have dramatized the tenacious, often self-endangering, efforts of modern individuals—usually individuals without explicit religious faith—to find some meaning in history (for example, through revolutionary commitments) or else to live meaningful lives in the face of the apparent absurdity of history.

Although the involvement of the individual in history is not visible to Christians alone, however, it is deeply rooted in Christian principles. Christians believe that we know God in our finiteness and mortality, in our concrete lives, and not by ascending to the plane of eternity. We know God in our situation in time. In Jesus, God appeared in the form of a particular human being, shaped by social conditions, constrained by physical and historical circumstances, finally killed by dominant powers. We cannot and need not rise above the level of Jesus. The Christian outlook depends on a sense of "the infinite qualitative difference" between man and God. Man is not only finite but, through sin, has made finiteness a crippling and blinding disease. God, on the other side, is not a being whom man, even man free from sin, can investigate and explain. Any relationship between man and God must be established by God. Given our incapacity for entering into God's life, God must enter into ours.

The imperative of watching for meaning in history follows. If God comes to human beings in their mortality and finitude, then the circumstances of their lives are something more than impersonal, given facts; they are, so to speak, matter for the form that God may take in human existence. These circumstances are temporal and global—historical. In Jesus, Christians believe, historical circumstances became infinitely significant, and we await the initiative of God by watching for signs of significance in our own historical circumstances. Or, in accordance with Bonhoeffer's view of Christ as "the structure of reality"[19]—of historical reality—we watch for Christ in our own historical time and place and situation.

The task of watching falls ultimately on individuals, singly. Historical situations are experienced only in personal situations. The responsibility for interpreting these situations belongs inescapably to each person; even the least intellectual and least informed must decide, each one finally alone, what the circumstances of their times allow and demand. And each person has an urgent interest in reading these situations accurately. To catch all possible signs of the meaning of history, of the import and requirements of the circumstances I inhabit, is to discern indications of God's will and of what I must suffer and do, and why. Needless to say, many genuine Christians have given little conscious thought to history. But so far as they have seen the implications of their own faith, they have believed that the sufferings and tasks imposed on them by their times were mysteriously justified and acceptable.

The other basic way of waiting for God in history, reflective of the personal and individual character of the prophetic stance, has not been discussed so far in this essay. That way is eschatological.

The word *eschatology* is not used here, as it often is, to refer to the final state of human life—heaven and hell—but, in accordance with what is also common usage, to designate the unfoldment of history as determined by that final state. The word is used much as some theological writers use the word *apocalyptic*. An eschatological view of history holds that history will come to an end and that all events are moving toward that destined climax. Such a view differs from the cyclical view common in ancient times by holding that history has a goal and hence is not eternally repetitive. It differs from the modern doctrine of progress, which also attributes an overall direction to history, by holding that history will culminate in a state of life beyond all historical change. Human beings will not always live within time or in subjection to change. If we say that the prophetic stance is eschatological, we are saying that one must wait in history not only for signs of the meaning of history but also for the end of history.

We need not dwell on the conceptual difficulties that eschatology presents. The end of history in the sense intended by eschatology—as not merely a vast terrestrial disaster but rather a transformation of the very conditions that give rise to history—is inconceivable. Indeed, it is doubtful whether one can, without self-contradiction, speak of the end of history as a historical event. It does not follow, however, that it is meaningless. If it were, it would not have so aroused the imagination of great writers and artists throughout the centuries—of Augustine, Michelangelo, Verdi, and others. The idea of the end of history clearly is a symbol, or metaphor. The reason why metaphors must be used in theological discussion is familiar. Words and concepts are fitted mainly for speaking of things, of realities in space and time, and God is not a thing (otherwise God would be finite and, in principle at least, subject to calculation and control). Hence we can speak of God only metaphorically, and this is true when we speak of the relationship of God to history. Jesus himself suggested the metaphorical character of his eschatological proclamation when he said that the Kingdom of God is "not coming with signs to be observed."[20]

There are two reasons why it is necessary to speak of eschatology in the present context and to characterize the prophetic stance as eschatological. The first, a matter of common knowledge among students of theology, is that Christianity is thoroughly eschatological. Everything Jesus said and did was centered on the claim that the end of history was not only in store but was near at hand. The Kingdom of God was on the point of breaking in upon earthly affairs. The preaching of Jesus' early followers was likewise eschatological. For them, Jesus became not merely a herald but an embodiment of the *eschaton*. The Kingdom of God had already appeared momentarily and would soon appear conclusively. History would culminate, and its meaning become definitively manifest, in the person of Christ, who would come "in a cloud with power and great glory."[21]

But the New Testament vision does not enter into this essay as a foreign element, inimical to the ideas we have been discussing. This is the second reason why we are compelled to speak eschatologically. Eschatology expresses an indispensable insight into history—an insight closely related to the personal and singular character of the prophetic stance. The core of eschatology is the proposition that history leads into eternity.

What needs to be noted first of all is that only if this proposition is true can history be meaningful. Our ultimate concern is for things that do not vanish with the passage of time. The indefinite scope of human imagination, our capacity for perceiving the limits of every power and the inadequacy of every value, mark us as beings fitted for eternity. We cannot be at home within an endless succession of impermanent realities and temporal satisfactions. If history never ends, our lives in history are necessarily senseless. History has meaning only if it leads beyond history. Eschatology is the claim that it does, that it is the pathway on which human beings are led toward eternity. Strictly speaking, then, to watch for the end of history is not different from watching for meaning in history. Eschatology does not negate meaning in history but fulfills it. Hence every hint of meaning, deeply understood, is eschatological.

At first, eschatology may seem to have little relationship to the personal and singular character of the prophetic stance. It is difficult to speak eschatologically without using sweeping, even grandiose, terms, and these can evoke images distant from the particular and earthly individual. In truth, however, they are close to the individual, and this is because eternity is the source of the essential glory of the individual—a glory independent of all empirical, historical characteristics—and defines the individual's ultimate destiny. Eternity is the supreme interest, consequently, of every human being. Normally, of course, our minds are fixed on matters that seem nearer at hand. But normality, in this case, is determined by our sinful natures, by our worldliness; and Jesus' proclamation of the imminence of the Kingdom of God, accompanied by his call to repentance, was a way of saying that nothing is nearer at hand than eternity. Eschatology separates human beings from all secondary interests and in this way from all that diminishes their intrinsic glory. Although eschatology may lend itself to grandiose rhetoric, its essential truth lies in the fact that it fashions history on the scale of the concrete, existing human being.

My point can easily be restated in terms derived from chapter 1. Eschatology is history understood in accordance with the idea of the exalted individual. Measured against empires and centuries, a human being is almost nothing. On the other hand, if the God who exalts individuals is superior to the world and to history, as eschatology implies, so are individuals. As creatures beloved by God, they have destinies. Even one insignificant person is more significant than a great historical movement, and one unworthy human being has more worth than a nation. Eschatology is a metaphorical rebuttal of human pretensions, a humbling of deified heroes and idolized masses; and it is a metaphorical defense of the individual, one of a numberless multitude, who is devoured by history. In history, very few are remembered; in Christ, none are forgotten. That, at any rate, is the eschatological faith of Christians.

Not only does eschatology provide a vision of history consonant with the idea of the exalted individual, however; it provides at the same time a prophetic standpoint that is uniquely transcendental, yet situated in concrete human life. Only here can we begin to understand fully why the prophetic stance becomes deeply personal when it becomes eschatological. In being uniquely transcendental, eschatological faith undergirds individual integrity and independence; one gains a certain superiority to all of history. Yet only as an inhabitant of history can one claim and finally realize that superiority. Only within history can one live toward the end of history.

The unique transcendence implicit in eschatological faith is particularly evident when eschatology is presented in catastrophic colors. In the Revelation to John, such images as the pale horse and pale rider and the sun "black as sackcloth" are put before the reader on page after page. The book as a whole is a chronicle of condemnation and destruction, and there is much in it that is melodramatic and vengeful. But it starkly expresses the judgment on history and on all human works implicit in eschatology. In all historical acts there is sin, in all historical societies estrangement, in all historical truths errors and ignorance. Nothing that happens on earth, and not all things together that have happened and will happen on earth, are of absolute value or capable of making history meaningful. So history must be subordinated to something beyond history in order to have meaning; it must end. But so sweeping a judgment provides a standpoint (through faith, of course, not knowledge) beyond not only every party, nation, movement, and leader but beyond history in its entirety. The *eschaton* provides, for faith, ground on which the independence and integrity of the individual human being can be maintained regardless of historical circumstance and change.

Such a faith may seem abstract, negative, pretentious. Placing us in history, however, it leads toward face-to-face relationships. As already stated in chapter 1, the prophetic stance is a form of fidelity to the exalted individual. Since eschatological expectancy is faith in the sanctity and glory of human beings, it is lived through love. Paul, whose outlook was thoroughly eschatological, says that hope— eschatological hope—"does not disappoint us," and the reason is that "God's love has been poured into our hearts."[22] Hope is authentic—a vital orientation rather than mere sentiment—only when animated by love. If eschatology is alive within us, it is a sense of the destiny of every person and is awakened by every human encounter. Eschatological judgments and negations express a transcendent solidarity. But not just with humankind at large: rather, with concrete individuals, who are delivered from that supreme abstraction, the world, and affirmed as members of a peculiarly concrete and fundamental association, the one symbolized among Christians as the Kingdom of God.

Much that I have said might be summed up in the statement that eschatology is a refusal of historical idolatry—perhaps the most common form of idolatry in our time. It is widely assumed, even by many who do not consciously accept the assumption, that history definitively settles the fate of all things—men and women, works of science and art, nations and movements—and, moreover, is just. Whatever failed in the past presumably deserved to fail, and whatever we can see coming forcefully upon us is "the wave of the future," something that neither can nor ought to be resisted. Versions of such idolatry are provided both by Marx's dialectical materialism and by the liberal faith in progress. Another version is the popular assumption that the latest—in clothes, ideas, films, and all else—is the best; the most conclusive way of dismissing anything is to call it "out-of-date." History, seen as authoritative and irresistible, relativizes all that we think and do.

Eschatology relativizes history. It does this by saying that the meaning of history does not lie in history itself. Such a verdict is indispensable. It liberates the individual from the tendency—at once suicidal and murderous—to bow down to some historical god, whether this be an agency within history, like a nation, or history itself. By undermining historical idolatry, eschatology saves the concrete individual.

A final question remains to be addressed. Although the prophetic stance is a posture of communal openness and availability, the distinctive characteristic of this stance lies in the paradox of a communality that is compelled by the nature of the world to become solitary. Hence, along with communal openness and availability, I have also emphasized singular, personal responsibility. As a consequence, there may persist in the minds of readers a sense that the concept of the prophetic stance embodies an individualism at odds with the Christian tradition. Christians have always insisted that human beings are not to be called together only at the end of time. In at least one place, in the Church, they are together now, in history; the solitude of historical existence is already in some sense behind us. Does faith in the Church come into conflict with the idea of the prophetic stance? This question requires us to turn, in completing this definition of the prophetic stance, from the individual to the opposite pole in Christian social thought.

The Church and Prophetic Hope

The communality of Christian faith is strongly expressed in Christian attitudes toward the Church. Christians uniformly insist, as Karl Barth put it, that "there is no private Christianity."[23] Faith in the God who appeared in Christ places one in the company of all who profess this faith—in the Church. And the Church is not merely an accidental and miscellaneous set of social groups, existing alongside other groups. It has a peculiar dignity. Christian reverence for the Church seems unaffected by the fact that the Church is visibly a number of separate, differing—hence, presumably erring—churches. Institutions palpably plural are unified in name and faith. Associations displaying the universal failings of human associations are accorded sanctity.

Is community, then, to be realized only at the end of time, or is it realized already, in the Church? Can it be said that the exalted individual is incongruous with society as a whole, or does the Church provide a place where individuals meet one another in the fullness of their dignity? Does a Christian ever bear any strictly personal responsibility, or does responsibility always belong to Christians in a body?

To answer these questions, we must gain a sense of how Christian reverence for the Church might be valid. This is a perplexing question, as I have suggested, since the Church we see with our everyday eyes, whether we are believers or unbelievers, seems much like other social organizations, its members divided, often quarreling among themselves, ordinarily lukewarm in their support for group goals, sometimes prejudiced in matters such as race, not strikingly selfless, and capable of hatred. How can anyone say that the Church is sacred or that, unlike the other social groups it so much resembles, it is a true community?

Rather than searching for signs of sanctity in the Church as it actually *is,* I suggest that we begin by considering the Church as it *ought* to be; that is an easier matter for most of us to discuss, I think, and will provide a bridge to the harder matter. Asking what the Church ought to be, against the background of earlier discussions in this essay, is apt to call forth a simple, and certainly valid, answer: it ought to be a community. This means for Christians that it ought to speak to men about God and translate into human words the Word of God, which is Christ. That can be done in various ways, not only through preaching but also through doctrine and liturgy. Personal counseling is a form of communality; and the sacraments bring about symbolic or real reunions, anticipatory of the Kingdom of God. So far as its communal responsibilities are met, so far as God is truly heard and his Word is translated into human words that are true and are truly heard, the Church is a place where all come together—God and all humanity—in a single community. Human beings hear God, and they hear one another in speaking of God.

Such a community would not be merely one among numerous other communities. Community consists in sharing the truth, and degrees of community can be measured by the significance of the truth that is shared. A sharing of truth concerning the structure of the molecule might be truly communal, but not in the same degree as a sharing of truth concerning the structure of society. But there is, of course, for Christians, an object of truth more significant than molecules or societies, and that is God and his relations with men. Only theological truth (using this term to comprise liturgy and all other communal elements in the Church) can engage us in our full humanity; hence, it is the only truth in whose sharing our communality can be fully realized. Responsible for that truth, the Church clearly is a unique association. This, at any rate, is the Christian view.

It should be noted, further, that the communality of Christians does not comprise Christians alone. In Christ, God spoke to all human beings without exception. Accordingly, the unavoidable aim of the Church is to bring the entire human race into a single community. To lay the groundwork for community, the Church helps and comforts those who are ill, imprisoned, and destitute, and it does not ask which among them are Christians. And to bring community into existence, it speaks to all who will listen concerning the things it regards as supremely important. What has been whispered by the Holy Spirit, it "proclaim[s] upon the housetops."[24] So, at least, it ought to be.

But how does it help to speak of the Church as it ought to be, since we still have before us the Church as it actually is? True, there is a kind of dignity in having responsibilities so exalted; there is no exaggeration in saying that the Church ought to be humanity, reconciled in the truth. Still, it is not, not even approximately.

The core idea implicit in Christian reverence for the Church begins to emerge when we ask about the source of the communal responsibilities we have just discussed. In the eyes of faith, these responsibilities are not exalted just because they pertain to exalted
goals. More decisive is the fact that these responsibilities are imposed by God in furtherance of his redemptive purposes for the human race. Hence, we cannot think about them as we think about
ordinary responsibilities. The latter, we assume, can be failed and finally forgotten. Many tasks are taken up and later abandoned, un-
completed. But Christians cannot think of this happening with the
task of responding to Christ, for in Christ, they believe, God disclosed, and set on foot the accomplishment of, his supreme purpose
for the human race. The Church is called to the service of the Word,
which God will not allow "to return to him void." In Christian eyes,
the Church cannot fail.

In what sense can the Church not fail? A convenient way of answer-
ing this question is suggested by the concept of destiny. Community
is the destined end, as well as the responsibility, of the Church. The
sanctity of the Church is analogous to the dignity of an individual; it
is not owing to present actualities but to a future that rests in the
mercy and providence of God. The Church is an eschatological association. At the end of the ages, the Church and humanity will be indistinguishable. The destiny of the Church does not extenuate its
present failings; if anything, it renders them more grievous. Nonetheless, the Church is not merely one among the many groups that
fail to fulfill their functions. It represents, among fallen and warring
human beings, their destined exaltation and reconciliation.

This is to offer little more than a hint—a brushstroke intended to
suggest a painting. A theory of the Church based on this hint would
have to work out the implications of the concept of destiny for preaching, sacraments, and numerous other ecclesiastical institutions. The
distinction between the actual and destined Church, however, does
suggest a way of interpreting the traditional Christian evaluation of
the Church so that the personal and solitary responsibility inherent
in prophetic hope is not implicitly denied. The prophetic stance depends on a certain critical distance between the individual and every
social institution, and this critical distance is no less indispensable in

the case of the Church than of any other institution. Let us note, then, some of the principal criticisms of the Church that can be made, not from disbelief or disrespect, but on premises affirming the destiny of the Church.

1. The destiny of the Church—for Christian faith—is to bring human beings into the presence of God. In that sense, the Church is a place for deferring unreservedly to God, a scene of humility in glory. To say that in actuality the Church reflects the worldly necessities and human failings, above all the self-centeredness and self-assertiveness, that shape all social institutions is true but insufficient. As the only institution with a destiny, the Church gives rise to pride of a particularly grievous kind—a pride occasioned by responsibilities truly unique and causing those responsibilities to be unmet. Karl Barth speaks, in his *Epistle to the Romans*, of "the guilt of the Church."[25] Human beings must respond to the Word of God in Christ and therefore must live and work in the Church, according to Barth. They cannot do so adequately, however, for they are earthly and sinful beings and God is "the altogether Other, the Unknown and the Unapproachable."[26] For Barth, the Church is the greatest of human responsibilities but, for that very reason, also the greatest of human failures. In the terms I have suggested, the Church represents man's future with God; the tragic incongruity between destined future and present actuality is reflected in the irony of spiritual pride among leaders of a religion of humility.

2. The destiny of the Church is to bring human beings to agreement in the truth; and in that sense, the Church represents the truth within history. To say this, however, immediately reminds us that one of the most obvious characteristics of the Church is its fallibility. The fallibility of the Protestant churches is plainly manifest in their plurality; the fallibility of the Catholic Church is seemingly acknowledged by the many members who, since Vatican II, have called for decentralization and dialogue. Destiny, of course, concerns not only ultimate ends but also depths, and a Christian must think that the truth is in some sense present even now in the Church—but only in gleaming fragments and not in a vision lucid and entire, and not as a possession that can at will be passed on to others or securely kept.

3. The destiny of the Church, Christians believe, is to be the one perfect and authentic community. Lacking the truth, however, the

Church cannot be a full community, for community is a sharing of the truth. The Church cannot be home—a place where individuals can be fully themselves and at the same time intimately and securely at one with all others. Communal in its deepest purpose, existing in the world but upheld by grace, the Church would be that home if any institution could be. But it is not, as empirical observation indisputably shows. It reflects as sharply as any other institution the antithesis of community and society—more sharply, indeed, in the light of destiny, for the antithesis is not only between what is and what ought to be but also between what is and what finally, by God's command, shall be.

Such criticisms show, on the one hand, that the eschatological singleness of the individual is not compromised by any historical institution whatever. One must keep a measure of critical distance even from the Church. The Church in history is not the Kingdom of God, and the alienation inherent in living as a destined member of the Kingdom of God, within history, is inescapable. One can only give such alienation moral and spiritual form by using it as the basis for a prophetic relationship with the world around. And the Church is part of the world around. Hence, it is subject to prophetic criticism and appraisal.

On the other hand, however, to criticize and appraise the Church prophetically is to be aware that the Church is distinct from the world around even though part of it. The Church, as envisioned by faith, is essentially different from any other institution. Hence, critical independence of the Church is different from the critical independence that may characterize an individual's relationship to other social groups. Strictures on the historical Church can be true and justified only when originating, consciously or not, in the eschatological Church. To say, as I just have, that the Church provokes spiritual pride, is fallible, and is more social than communal does not presuppose merely standards of a kind any social critic might apply but also faith in what the Church will be at the end of time. When prophetic hope establishes critical distance between the individual and the Church, that distance lies within the Church, and an individual who opposes the Church as it is can be justified only if called into opposition by the Church as it is destined to be.

Underlying prophetic criticism of the Church, therefore, is a loyalty and respect not present in any other kind of social criticism. Although destiny points away from what is actual to what is ordained and in that way exposes the actual to critical observation, destiny also maintains the unity of the actual and the ordained. In that way, it requires our respect for the actual even when our criticisms of it are severe. Again, we see that a Christian's relationship with the Church is analogous to his relationship with individuals. We respect individuals in their destinies; yet we respect them in their present actuality, too, and do this without denying their fallenness. In similar fashion, personal independence of the Church is authentically prophetic only as a paradoxical form of loyalty to the Church.

It is not only the individual, however, who must take cognizance of the difference between the destined and actual Church; the Church, too, must do this. In recognition of its guilt, the Church must perform an act that is strange and difficult (how strange and difficult it is may be judged by the hearty approval non-Christians must accord the act) even though, habituated as we are today to the separation of Church and state, we take it for granted. It must accept the rest of society as a separate and independent area of life. This act would be innocuous if human beings were not sinful; it would be merely an acknowledgment of the intrinsic goodness of creation. It implies in our fallen state, however, acquiescence in the sinful determination of human beings to live apart from God. This is why it is strange and difficult. The natural and logical tendency of the Church is to take command of society and try to make it a sacred and sinless order. For Christians to recognize that they are not fitted for such a task, that they are sinful themselves, is an act of humility and cannot be easy. It expresses at once an admission of their own fallenness and resignation before the fallenness of the world around them.

If the Church suffers a kind of crucifixion by this act, the individual receives a kind of liberation—not from the Church in its destiny but from the Church in its sinful actuality. In accepting the secular realm, the Church grants the individual an independent sphere of existence. Society provides a place to stand outside the Church. But the converse also is true; the Church provides a place to stand outside of society. The individual thus is given the possibility of a life not belonging entirely to any worldly order.

Such liberation cannot be wholly enjoyable, however; it is indistinguishable, indeed, from alienation. This is partly hidden from us today by the fact of secularization; most people inhabit only one order of life, one that is secular and all-inclusive, and this is apt to be true even when they are members of a church. Thus, they escape the burdens of dualism. But to inhabit two separate orders of life lucidly and responsibly is to be, in some measure, a stranger in both. A serious Christian will experience estrangement with particular sharpness in the secular realm. Barth discusses the Incarnation as "the way of the Son of God into the far country."[27] The secular realm, it may be said, is the far country that a Christian must enter and inhabit. There, our human fallenness must be faced, and the suffering and death attendant on our fallenness must be borne. The prophetic stance might be characterized simply as the personal and political bearing of one who accepts without illusions, but also without despair, the hard liberation offered by the far country.

The difficulty of life in two realms is greatly enhanced by the lack of any overall principle for resolving tension between them. The relations of Church and society are bound to be normally unsettled. By granting sinful beings an independent order of life, the Church announces in effect that it will not, at every turn and with every resource, oppose evil. Yet Christians cannot grant evil an inviolable sphere. The concept of a "wall" between Church and society is as untenable as the concept of a unified sacred order. The uneasiness of this situation necessarily invades prophetic existence. A Christian inhabits and bears responsibility for the secular order. A Christian does this, however, necessarily as a Christian—a member of the Church. For a Christian to act is inescapably, in some measure, for the Church to act. When is this legitimate?

Christians can presumably speak in opposition to evil without wrongfully abridging the dualism of society; but society, in its secular distractions, is not likely to listen. Thus, Christians, and in Christians the Church, face the question of force. Society may betray humanity and the truth so radically, as in accepting and acting on superstitions of racial inequality, that forcible resistance—by Christians, by the Church—is unavoidable. Christians conspired to murder Hitler, and today they call on the state forcibly to limit abortions.

How can we decide whether such policies are legitimate? When is force justified?

In the absence of a principle for unifying the secular and sacred realms, one answer alone is possible for Christians. They can only rely on their sense of the commands of God—commands that pertain altogether to particular circumstances and are irreducible to general rules. It is a sign of our fallenness that we find ourselves in situations in which moral rules are in conflict. Christian acquiescence in the separate and independent existence of a secular realm gives rise repeatedly to such situations. Here, Christians can only do what they believe God requires of them (and unbelievers can only search out necessities that appear inherent in the situation itself). If they decide on force, they stand unjustified by moral principles. But they stand before God. They have carried out what Locke called, in characterizing revolution, an "appeal to heaven."

In the picture of an individual situated at once within the Church and within secular society, solitary yet engaged, determined by an eschatological faith but observant also of temporal responsibilities, and in maintaining so ambiguous a posture prepared to "appeal to heaven," we have a picture of the prophetic stance. Clearly, respect for the Church does not undermine prophetic solitude. As the destined community of all human beings, the Church is a judgment on all historical groups, including the historical Church, and on history in its entirety. Participation in the Church makes prophetic solitude necessary and possible.

Running through my argument there is no doubt individualism of a sort—an individualism that will be rejected by many Christians, moved by their conception of the Church, and by many others who are influenced by the broad assault on individualism that has taken place in social and political theory during the past century or more. But my individualism is, as I have already noted, prophetic rather than ontological. Its major premise is that *individual separateness is imposed by our essential communality.* Many people today have become so committed to the goal of community that they have failed to notice the distinction between community and society. This helps to explain why our time, so communal in ideals, has been so ruinously anticommunal in many of its actions and commitments. Prophetic individualism is simply the notion that anyone who is steadily faithful to human beings in their destined exaltation, and to the truth in whose sharing community consists, is always going to be more or less alone, for society is not faithful to these things and cannot be.

It should be noted, moreover, that this idea is repeatedly affirmed in the Bible. Moses, the prophets, Jesus, Paul—all carried a heavy burden of singularity. When we are told that, before the Crucifixion, Jesus' disciples "all forsook him, and fled," we hear an insistent theme of both the Old and New Testaments.[28] When God bestows his grace, individuals are singled out—even from Israel and from the Church. They are singled out also from nations, parties, and political movements. To recognize this is indispensable in understanding the political meaning of Christianity. It is indispensable too, I believe, in maintaining civility and hope in times of tumult and discouragement. It is the paradox of the prophetic stance that we can live as good citizens in the world only if we are able to live, in faith, hope, and love, as what we inescapably are—strangers in the world.

We turn now to the political principles that guide prophetic conduct in the world. To be at once responsible and solitary, to be faithful both to one's human companions in history and to God, cannot be a task free of complexity and strain. Standards are indispensable. They enable one to associate with groups and movements discriminantly; they turn solitude into a vantage point from which society can be judged. Without standards, the prophetic stance could not be sustained. Prophetic criticism would be impossible, and hope would be impotent. These standards are discussed in the following two chapters.

It is vital, however, for these to be seen as guidelines for the shaping of political lives that cannot be altogether circumscribed by general rules. They are not intended as absolute imperatives or as outlines of an ideal society. Living politically is a creative task, involving unforeseeable variations of circumstance and calling. In recognition of the personal and creative character of political conduct, I have made my discussion somewhat unsystematic. Each of the two principal standards to be discussed—liberty and social transformation—

spected; to single out and accord limitless dignity to individuals is obviously not something that happens automatically in the evolution of society. It did happen, however, through Christianity.

Liberty is preeminently a prophetic ideal, for it honors individuals on the basis not of what they already are but of what they may yet become. The idea of destiny gives incalculable weight to the ideal of liberty by placing the future of an individual (the question of what an individual may yet become) beyond human reckoning and beyond the relativities of human evaluation. For Christians who adhere to the deepest implications of their faith, granting liberty is a way of providing space for the unfoldment of the drama of divine-human relations. It is, in this way, an act of hope.

In short, to maintain the prophetic stance is to will liberty for all human beings. This is one of the main themes of the present essay. Waiting for God in history means watching for signs of destiny among other people (that is, attentiveness) and holding oneself in readiness to respond to such signs (or availability). This is possible only where there is liberty. Just as loving God, whom we have not seen, requires, as John asserts, loving our fellow human beings, so waiting for God requires waiting for manifestations of destiny among our fellow human beings. Waiting, in relation to others, means leaving them free.

One should be careful not to put this condescendingly. Allowing others to be free is not something to be done proudly, as though making a concession, but penitently. Each of us is humbled before the other person in his exaltation. This is because the exaltation of a human being is owing—for Christians—to a destiny given by God and beyond our comprehension. Hence Jesus' injunction, "Judge not." Human sinfulness, as we have seen, consists in ignoring the mystery of the exaltation of others and presuming to judge, thus putting humans in the position of God. We affirm liberty in the right spirit only by doing so in recognition that we are finite and fallen and hence both continually tempted to judge and incapacitated for doing so.

To recall the character of society—the sphere of life created by fallen men—is simply to look at the matter from another angle. There are philosophies, even among those authored by the greatest modern thinkers, that attach a higher degree of reality and a higher value to society than to the individual. Liberty is not apt to be of supreme importance in such philosophies. When it is, it is reinterpreted.

Liberty is construed as something that may be realized through conformity with society and possibly even through state coercion. Liberty as most of us understand it is imperiled or denied. As brought out in chapter 1, Christianity logically entails a very different view. Society is the form sinful human beings give to the fallen world, under the spur of worldly necessity, and it is bound to be antithetical to the exalted individual. It is imperative that society and the state be curbed and that individuals be assured of the possibility of independent lives.

The word *independent* must be emphasized if Christian liberty is to be properly explained. It is a different word from *separate* or *isolated*. The latter words would suggest that an individual can live fully and well while disregarding the values that society transmits through tradition, teaches in schools, and in some fashion embodies in its way of life. But apart from those values an individual would not be human. To suppose the contrary would be to treat the individual as a god rather than a finite creature, a creature who cannot create values or build a life on vacant ground. The values of an individual are bound to be values drawn from the surrounding society. Liberty lies not in repudiating those values but in realizing them in a personal and creative way. To be protected from society is to be shielded from importunate and compulsory social requirements so that one can live social values in one's own way. Through liberty, individuals are enabled to transform society from fate into destiny. This qualification, however, clearly concerns the nature of liberty and not its value. The idea of liberty is an indispensable key to the political meaning of Christianity.

A broad answer to the issue posed at the outset of this chapter—that liberty permits, and will certainly be accompanied by, disbelief and sin—is implicit in the preceding paragraphs. On Christian principles, affirming liberty expresses trust in God and mistrust of human beings, particularly human beings as organized in society and the state. Human beings do not know how to create faith or eradicate sin. Christians believe that God does. Individuals are left free in order for them to be fully accessible to God. It cannot be denied that many Christians have despised or attacked liberty from a concern for faith and virtue. But did they not, in that way, manifest a confidence in state officials that might more appropriately, at least for Christians, have been placed in God?

This is only a broad answer to the doubts that hover about the idea of liberty, however, and it is an overly simple one. Prophetic liberality (to give this name to the support for liberty that is required by Christian principles) is a difficult and uneasy posture, not the untroubled endorsement of almost anything anyone wants to do. We have to understand not only why the prophetic stance is a will to liberty but also why it is always onerous, and sometimes impossible, to maintain this will consistently. To do this, we must examine some of the objections to liberty, especially objections that can be drawn from Christian doctrine. Is the Christian view of liberty quite so unequivocal as I have suggested?

There are several reasons why a skeptical reader might ask this question. One of the most obvious is the doctrine of original sin. Christians in the past have often been wary of liberty for fear of what human beings in their pride and selfishness might do with it. Liberty has looked like an invitation to chaos. Centralized and unchecked power has seemed, if not ideal, safe.

This issue involves prudential judgment and cannot be conclusively settled in principle. But Christianity casts doubts on the wisdom of favoring absolute power rather than liberty. If human beings are sinful, not only is liberty dangerous, so is power. It is perverse to deny liberty to almost everyone because of human faults and then grant to some, who are human and thus presumably affected by the same faults as all others, the limitless liberty inherent in absolute power. It is possible to construct a polity, as did the framers of the American Constitution, in which all have limited liberty and those who govern have limited power. That is not only the sensible answer to the dangers posed by original sin; it is also, as far as there is one, the Christian answer.

Another reason for questioning the Christian commitment to liberty lies in the typical Christian emphasis on inwardness. Christians indifferent to outward (that is, social and political) liberty have sometimes assumed that nothing can limit inward liberty—liberty of thought and belief—and that only inward liberty matters. Society and government supposedly can control your body but not your mind. It is unfortunate that this is false, for the political universe would be less complex and dangerous were it true. But the notion that political power cannot affect inward life is disproven by the dictatorships of our time. Although political power cannot control every thought and feeling, it can, by controlling the schools and mass media, easily cross the boundary line between body and mind. We have learned a great deal about this since Christianity began. For Paul, strong, centralized authority meant Rome, which even under the worst emperors was a government limited by law and primitive technology; it was also, in comparison with modern dictatorships, a tolerant government. Today, we know that strong and centralized authority can mean Stalin or Hitler. It is obvious to us that outward and inward liberty are not separable.

Regardless of what governments wanted or were able to do, however, was it ever legitimate to allow those in whom one recognized an inherent dignity and an inward liberty to be outwardly enslaved? Even if individuals could fully and uncompromisingly realize themselves without liberty—social and political liberty—is not a regard for someone's liberty an acknowledgment of his distinct and irreducible reality and an indispensable token of respect? That the Church for centuries affirmed in principle the dignity of individuals but in fact acquiesced in practices such as slavery was a perilous incongruity.

If the Christian concept of human character does not upset the ideal of liberty, however, what of the Christian concept of God? Is not God an infinite and irresistible power who demands detailed and unceasing obedience? Does not God himself set an example of authoritarian government?

No doubt, many Christians have answered affirmatively. Monarchy was commonly envisioned as the human form of a divine pattern. But such a viewpoint is very questionable. Even if the relationship of human beings to God is one of command and obedience, that relationship does not authorize dictatorial human relationships. Rather, it bars them, for it implies that God alone deserves unconditional obedience. Men can be accorded only conditional and critical obedience. Early Christians were sometimes persecuted by the imperial government in Rome because of a single requirement that they refused to meet even if it cost them their lives. They would not worship the emperor.

It is doubtful, moreover, that the Christian understanding of God's government can be adequately interpreted in authoritarian terms. The God of the Bible is not a cosmic dictator who seeks uncomprehending, speechless submission on the part of his subjects. He pleads and reasons with human beings. He seeks a relationship into which men and women enter as freely as he does himself. In his wrath, he tries to awaken, not to enslave. In his mercy, he forgets past acts of rebellion and refrains from vengeance. In his anger and forgiveness alike, there is human liberty. And at last, in Christ, he takes care not to burn up liberty in the fires of his revelation. He did not appear as a lord whose glory effaced every human doubt and every possibility of deliberation and choice but rather as a suffering and mysterious human being whose revelatory significance could easily be missed altogether, as it was by those who crucified him. Hence the accusation with which the Grand Inquisitor faces Christ: "Thou didst choose all that is exceptional, vague and enigmatic," thus placing on every person an awful burden of choice. "Instead of taking possession of men's freedom," he charges, "Thou didst increase it."[3]

The God who deprives human beings of their liberty is not the God revealed in Christ but one invented by human beings in the image of human despots. It is true that God issues commands, but the sum of divine commands is the duty to live our destinies, and that means to become unqualifiedly ourselves, the beings God intended us to be in the act of creation. Because God's commands are the requirements of destiny, of selfhood, they cannot be obeyed blindly and dumbly. Leading human beings toward the Kingdom of God, toward truth and community, they are truly obeyed only when they awaken understanding and love. They cannot do this by arousing terror. God's commands, and human destinies, have to be freely accepted, and not just once but daily and hourly. And it is the individual singly, not society, not even the Church, who must live this liberty. No wonder the Grand Inquisitor accused Christ of cruelty and of imposing a degree of liberty "utterly beyond the strength of men."[4]

Allied with the mistaken notion that Christianity turns human beings into slaves of God is the common charge that it turns them into slaves of the moral law. Supposedly, Christians are deprived of their liberty by having to live under a set of rigid rules enforced with threats of eternal damnation. Not only critics of Christianity but many Christians as well have accepted this interpretation.

The Christian view of morality is not so simple, however, as this accusation implies. Morality is unquestionably taken very seriously. "Till heaven and earth pass away," Jesus said, "not an iota, not a dot, will pass from the law until all is accomplished."[5] Nevertheless, it is entirely inadmissible to equate the task of being a Christian with the task of being moral. There are complexities in the Christian attitude toward moral law. These complexities do not represent mere afterthoughts or academic qualifications but are deeply rooted in Christian faith. Their effect is to leave human beings, in spite of the severity of the moral law, with the liberty that the Grand Inquisitor thought was too great for them to bear.

What is the nature of these complexities? In the first place, goodness does not consist of obeying the law, even though obeying the law is essential to goodness. Hatred, according to Jesus, is no less wrong than murder, and lust no less wrong than adultery. Goodness depends not only on outward behavior but on inner disposition. Goodness is a state of personal being. It requires, but is more than, conformity with the law. Hence, any project of making people good by forcing them consistently to obey the moral law would be absurd. Even drilling them so unflaggingly that they obey it habitually would not make them good, for goodness requires good motives and cannot consist in mere habit. If goodness is a state of personal being, it is inseparable from liberty.

Further, moral rules do not apply neatly and harmoniously to the situations in which we live. For example, how can we protect the innocent and defenseless without being ready, if absolutely necessary, to take the lives of the criminals and tyrants who threaten them? Does the commandment against killing forbid doctors ever to allow a life to end, whatever misery, futility, and expense its continuance might entail, so long as there are techniques and devices available for prolonging it? Because of the uniqueness of every situation, goodness is necessarily creative. Rules have to be adapted, reconciled, and sometimes broken. The commands of God and the requirements of our destinies are not formulae; they are new at every moment.

Finally, there is a much stranger way in which Christianity saves liberty from despotic moralists. God enables us to be in a certain sense unconcerned with the law and its illiberal guardians. The faith that this is so arises, surprisingly, from a kind of moral pessimism.

It is impossible to attain the goodness that the law intends simply by strenuous moral exertion. We repeatedly find ourselves either doing the wrong thing or else doing the right thing from the wrong motives. In fact, we uncover moral failures whenever we carefully examine our conduct and our minds. We perceive not only particular sins but original sin—not only occasional misdeeds but a settled tendency to commit misdeeds. Whatever we do reflects our primal selfishness. Perhaps we can keep from breaking the major moral commands; certainly we should try. But that will not make us good. In fact, it may make us bad, for in succeeding we may conclude that we are good when in truth we are not. Then we become guilty of moral and spiritual pride, which may be the most pretentious, and hence most egregious, form of selfishness. It must be remembered that Jesus' crucifixion was instigated not by petty, cynical, or openly irreligious men (the cynical Pilate would have let Jesus go) but by Pharisees, who were exceptionally earnest and righteous men. But they were *self*-righteous, too, and hence not truly righteous at all.

Does this not imply, however, that we are enslaved, if not by the law, then by sin? How can there be real liberty for creatures afflicted by a hopeless moral deformation? The Christian answer is that this deformation is hopeless only for human beings, not for God. Grace lifts individuals above their past failures by forgiving them and above their present perversities by making them morally better. God assumes the burden of moral responsibility and sets human beings free. He sets them free of the guilt inherent in their past acts, of the constraints of their sinful nature, and of the demoralization produced by a set of absolute moral demands that they are incapable of meeting. This does not authorize them to commit evil deeds in the confidence that God will forgive them. All Christians agree that faith is manifest in moral goodness. But it is also manifest in moral freedom—in freedom from anxiety regarding the exact demands of the law or one's own capacity for meeting them. The great Christians have not been obsessed with doing right and avoiding wrong. On the contrary, they have drawn from the confidence that God saves them from the crushing weight of the moral law a sense of liberty sometimes no less exultant than Nietzsche drew from the assurance that the moral law did not exist.

Liberty, then, is not insupportable; if it is "beyond the strength of men," it is not beyond the strength of God. Moreover, liberty seems clearly required by Christian principles; as we have just seen, objections to the Christian idea of liberty can be answered. Nonetheless, it would be seriously misleading to leave the impression that the prophetic affirmation of liberty is natural and easy. On the contrary, it involves substantial difficulties, and these affect the whole character of the prophetic stance, rendering it a demanding and uneasy posture.

This in part is because, affirming liberty for others, one must accept it for oneself. One must live one's own liberty, and though that does not mean being weighed down by moral cares, it is still a task—one not fulfilled by indulging momentary impulses or doing as one wishes. Being free is living a destiny. Hence, it presupposes disciplines, entails failures, and brings guilt inevitably. It involves tribulation, not just because living responsibly is difficult and trying but because tribulation, as the crucifixion of Christ reveals, is inherent in destiny. The liberty envisioned in Christianity is a long way from that urged upon us by advertisers and politicians. We are called to liberty by God, not by the spontaneous impulses of human nature. The very idea of "enjoying liberty" is dubious. No doubt, liberty brings joy, but not mainly by allowing us to do things we consider enjoyable.

Today, advertising and popular culture inculcate the impression that liberty is pleasant and natural. Primarily, it means consuming at will the material goods poured out by modern industry. It is not onerous, for it is merely a matter of choosing whatever promises to be pleasurable. But it is trivial. Nothing of great—much less eternal—consequence is decided. If it turned out that a dictator could make life more enjoyable (as in some circumstances would no doubt be the case), many people would have little reason to resist. In short, liberty is agreeable but not obligatory. This is the reverse of what Christianity tells us.

To accept and live one's own liberty, however, may not be as difficult and trying as accepting, and living in the presence of, the liberty of others. The latter has a large part in making prophetic liberality an uncomfortable stance. Human beings are dangerous, not just because they can wound and kill and withhold physical necessities but also because they can ignore and unfairly criticize one another; they can refuse to contribute to the common good and can oppose and sabotage common undertakings; they can close themselves off from God and create societies dominated by proud secularity. This, at any rate, is the Christian understanding of human nature. It implies that respecting and defending the liberty of others means working for conditions in which one's own physical and spiritual being are in peril. One may never be killed or physically wounded; one may even escape the moral and spiritual contamination with which secularism threatens everyone within its sphere. But inevitably, again and again, one will experience, in relations with others, uncertainty, opposition, disappointment, and humiliation. This is inherent in the liberty of sinful creatures.

My argument is at odds with attitudes common both on the left and on the right. On the left, it is widely assumed that we can steadily and deliberately eliminate the great evils afflicting human society; but little account is taken of what human beings are like when the spontaneous impulses of their nature are freed. The truth is that no common goal, such as justice or community, can be approached in accordance with human plans as long as there is liberty. This is why resolute determination to transform society leads everywhere to despotism. From the time of Lenin to the present day, those who hunger and thirst after perfect justice have almost always become, in action if not in principle, enemies of liberty. This theme was central in Dostoevsky and explains his hostility to socialism. Ivan Karamozov was driven to the edge of madness by historical impatience; a just society had to be created here and now, even if this entailed the universal enslavement imposed, in Ivan's fantasy, by the Grand Inquisitor.

On the right, many are incensed less by injustices than by infractions of traditional morality—by pornography, homosexuality, abortion, and so forth; they hunger and thirst after righteousness. Such people are sure to find liberty frustrating and trying. This cannot be blamed on their own misconceptions. To view liberty with wariness is entirely appropriate. Institutionalized liberty, it seems safe to say, has an inherent tendency to degenerate. Where liberty is prized, it is almost inevitable that it will come to be taken as a value in itself rather than, as it really is, a condition of every other value (since a value can be truly incorporated in a human life only by being freely chosen). But if liberty is a value in itself, it follows that all choices not destructive of liberty itself are legitimate. The moral law is forgotten.

The right is sensitive, then, as the left is not, to the connection between liberty and moral relativism; typically, however, it is less concerned than the left with liberty itself. Conservatives are inclined to think of righteousness as a problem of good laws and customs and are often willing for these to be backed with coercion. Although radicals, too, of course, resort to coercion, they regard it as only a temporary expedient, in conflict with basic principles and destined to be dialectically abolished. Among conservatives, the very principle of liberty is often in doubt.

The truth probably is, contrary to characteristic attitudes among radicals and conservatives alike, that the human race has to run the gauntlet both of injustice and of unrighteousness. Liberty has to be defended, even though it brings the injustice the left feels to be intolerable and the unrighteousness the right would suppress by law. From the prophetic standpoint, the concerns of both sides are entirely valid and understandable. In the Bible, God demands both justice and righteousness. Thus, liberty that allows these to be transgressed can be not only unpleasant but seemingly wrong. Yet if liberty is required by a respect for individuals and by trust in God, it is not an optional value, to be discarded in case of conflict with other values. It is the institutional form of waiting—for God's grace and the destiny in which grace is manifest.

The tension inherent in the prophetic stance is greatly increased, however, by the fact that liberty cannot be affirmed unequivocally. It must repeatedly and systematically be denied. Merely by accepting the state as a necessary institution, one acknowledges this. If liberty were not continually interfered with, there could be no *common liberty*—liberty that is available to all (not just to those who survive amid anarchy) and liberty of a kind that favors community (of assembly and speech, for example). To put the point more bluntly, if liberty were not continually interfered with, by public authorities, there would be much less of it. Thus, prophetic liberality is compelled to be inconsistent. Substantial concessions are made both to the left and to the right; without a measure of justice and righteousness, the realm of common liberty could not exist.

This obligatory inconsistency is made particularly trying by the fact that there is no rule to decide when liberty should be denied (in strict logic, were there a rule, there would be no inconsistency). Every act of coercion must be decided upon in the light of rules that at best are only conditional and of circumstances that can be variously interpreted. To consider one example alone, it is seemingly a sensible rule that a person's liberty can rightly be restricted when someone else would be harmed by it but not when the agent alone is harmed. In truth, though, any act that seriously harms the agent will harm others as well; that is assured by the interwovenness of our lives. Thus, committing suicide is not merely killing oneself; others are almost always severely hurt. Merely to do things to oneself that lessen one's effectiveness as a participant in common life is to injure others. In plain terms, liberty would be nonexistent were it not a right to harm other people. Thus, a seemingly sensible rule turns out to be seriously defective. Yet it is not entirely useless. In many cases, more harm falls on the agent than on others. Suicide is not the same as murder; risking one's own life, as in mountain climbing, is not morally equivalent to endangering the lives of others. Such differences are not irrelevant in deciding when coercion is justified. Thus, the rule that liberty can be rightly restricted only when harmful to others can be helpful, as can many other rules. But it is far too conditional, its proper application far too dependent on wisdom and prudence, to provide any moral security.

The fact that political responsibility is not attended by moral security shapes the prophetic attitude. Amid circumstances that are almost always tangled, humans are forced, as Christians see it, to look for the will of God, for the things our destinies require of us. Rarely is it clear *objectively,* to those who believe in liberty and also in justice and righteousness, what should be done. Only the arrogant can escape serious doubts. It is no wonder that tyranny is one of our ancient and enduring temptations, for it greatly simplifies political and personal life. But faith makes serious doubts tolerable. The prophetic stance is *prophetic* by virtue of the faith that tangled circumstances are not tangled in the eyes of God; underneath is destiny. It is a *stance* because of the capacity, created by this faith, for bearing the strains of liberty; with hope, one is able to wait.

From the outset, I have emphasized that the prophetic stance is not a possibility restricted to Christians or even to religious believers. The troubled and equivocal affirmation of liberty inherent in the prophetic stance might be called, in secular terms, a tragic liberalism. The word *tragic* is used partly in the ordinary sense—to refer to the evil men do; in the present context, it refers to the evil they do when possessed of liberty. The word also, however, is meant to refer to the mysterious sense of justification and hope that comes to a reader or spectator of tragic drama. That sense I take to be an intuition of the meaning that underlies and finally redeems all suffering, an insight into what Christians believe can be fully understood only as the Cross and the human destiny revealed in the Cross. It is a matter of record that non-Christians can be courageous defenders of liberty (indeed, often putting Christians to shame). No doubt, they are sometimes supported by falsely optimistic views of human nature. But need that always be so? One can imagine people who are not Christians, nor believers of any kind, tenaciously defending liberty not out of illusions about human nature but out of an enduring if inexplicable certainty that liberty and humanity are inseparable, however grave the difficulties that liberty brings. Such would exemplify a tragic liberalism.

For the tragic view of liberty to be fully elucidated and grounded, however, I believe that it must be made explicitly Christian. Only one great writer, to my knowledge, has done this. The writer is Dostoevsky. To what extent Dostoevsky consciously favored political and social liberty is, of course, in doubt; the answer depends partly on whether one seeks the answer in his journalism, where his views often seem quite reactionary, or in his novels, where there are indications of a liberalism so unqualified as to be anarchistic. As various critics have shown, however, Dostoevsky's novels are tragic dramas exhibiting the progress, in conflict and anguish, of destiny—explicitly in individuals like Raskolnikov and symbolically in the whole human race. Human beings are not like finished structures; they are rather in the nature of fire and tempest. Whatever Dostoevsky's political views, one sees the substance of liberty in his novels. The liberty Dostoevsky dramatizes typically brings crime and suffering but finally—reproducing the drama of all dramas, the death and resurrection of Jesus—peace and understanding.

We shall further explore the tragic—or, more precisely, Christian— view of liberty later in this essay. First, however, we must examine other aspects of liberty. In particular, it is necessary to take into account a proposition emphasized in the preceding chapters: that the individual is not exalted in solitary splendor but in community.

Liberty and Community

If Christianity is a communal faith, then liberty is not like a piece of private property, which belongs to one individual and to no one else.

I do not seek my own liberty as much as I seek the liberty that properly belongs to us all. Today, liberty is upheld in large measure by the activity of individuals claiming rights for themselves. There is danger in this—the danger of an individualistic distortion of the whole concept of liberty.

What is the connection between liberty and community? Jesus prays that his followers in every place and era "may all be one" and that "even as thou, Father, art in me, and I in thee, . . . they also may be in us."[6] If we are communal beings, destined for the mystical solidarity of the Kingdom of God, why be concerned with the liberty of each particular individual? Simply because liberty provides the only ground in which community can grow. Relationships must be entered into freely in order to be authentic and human. In respecting the liberty of other people, I allow the human world to be spread out around me like fertile fields ready for the tilling and sowing that bring community. To understand what this means, however, it is necessary to reflect on the nature of community.

What is community? There are numerous inadequate answers to this question. Let us glance at two of the most prominent and persuasive of them.

Christianity contains a tradition in which community is thought of in terms of organic interdependence. Paul speaks in this way of the Church. "Just as the body is one and has many members, and all the members of the body, though many, aré one body," so it is with Christians in relation to one another.[7] One enters into community by performing well the duties of one's station. The implications tend to be conservative. It is hard to think of an organic body as subject to deliberate reshaping. And it is difficult to conceive of it other than hierarchically, with some parts more significant and more honorable than other parts.

There is perhaps a kind of truth in the organic conception of community—a truth for which one searches in view of the authority of Paul and the important place this conception has had in the history of Christian thought. The truth it contains, I suggest, is of the kind contained in a symbol. A great organism made of human beings, in which every individual cooperates as spontaneously and perfectly with every other individual as does any member of a healthy physical organism with any other member, may serve as a vivid image of community, even though it cannot be taken as a literal description of community. The image becomes particularly apt in view of the fact that community is not altogether separate from society but is rather, as we have seen, an interpersonal realization of values and relationships that society provides. Community mines and utilizes social material. An image of community as an organically cohesive society is thus not entirely false to reality.

It is a dangerous image, however, for it is apt to blur, if not entirely obliterate, the distinction between community and society. It encourages the notion that a community is nothing more than a tightly organized and harmonious society. The inadequacy of the organic view was suggested by Paul himself when he said that there is "a still more excellent way"—by which Paul meant the way of *agape*.[8] Paul thus pointed to the most serious flaw in the organic conception of community.

Agape is love for what is deep and essential in an individual human being. It is precisely this that is apt to be lost when we think of community organically. A member of a physical organism—a foot, a hand, an ear—is not a person; to imagine human beings as members of an organism is thus to depersonalize them. An organism provides an example of unity that is intimate but impersonal. The primary challenge in defining community is that of defining perfect human unity in a way that does not, subtly or flagrantly, deny personality.

It is the failure to meet this challenge that renders inadequate another common idea of community, that of justice. It is easy to think of a just order as a community because it is presumably a perfect order. Human beings related to one another justly are related to one another as they ideally should be; hence, nothing beyond justice can be demanded of human relationships. Such a way of looking at community is exemplified by the first and greatest of political philosophers. Plato defined justice as giving each his due—to the wise, authority; to the courageous, military power; and to all others the duties and tools that befit their capacities. The abilities and natural qualities of every member of a just order are precisely understood and fully utilized by the governing authorities. Earlier, I defined community as the unity of persons in their essential being. On the face of it, Plato's ideally just order fully conforms with that definition. Even so, justice cannot be equated with community, and the reasons invalidating such an equation, it is easy to see, are roughly the same as those invalidating the equation of organic unity with community.

Justice is a state of society and cannot be equated with a reality—community—fundamentally different from society. This becomes apparent when we adopt the vantage point of *agape*. In Christian faith, *agape* establishes all authentic relationships; that is, *agape* establishes community. But it does not always seek justice. It is self-sacrificing; thus, someone moved by love does not seek justice for himself. It is merciful; thus, one who loves may refrain from imposing on a wrongdoer the penalties justice demands. Justice is a legal concept and pertains to the regularities of the outward order. It pertains to society.

In the same way, it is impersonal. Justice makes no exceptions. Wealth, power, and status count for nothing, and self-interest and passion are disregarded. This is its grandeur and also its great limitation. The equation of justice and community jeopardizes our awareness of the reality and value of individual human beings. It fails as definitely as the organic conception to define community in a way that does not implicitly deny personality. Plato's equation of justice and community arose from an impersonalism typical in Greek thought. The universal was prior in reality and value to the particular, even when the particular was a human being; such a view permitted a complete identification, in the case of a just society, of individual person and social function. The idea of justice, like that of organic unity, has its value. As I have argued earlier in this essay, the idea of justice provides a standpoint from which to identify and attack particular injustices. In doing this, since injustices always alienate human beings, it removes obstacles to community. We must look beyond justice, nevertheless, if we are to avoid compromising our consciousness of the ontological and moral ultimacy of the individual human being.

What is there beyond justice and beyond organic unity? What does *agape* call for? If we can arrive at an answer to these questions we shall have reached an understanding of how, from a Christian perspective, community may be defined without submerging persons in an impersonal unity.

Jesus showed concisely what love requires of human beings in the parable of the Good Samaritan, and we can hardly find a better basis for reflection than is provided by that parable. Here we need not go into details. Just two points seem essential in relation to our present concerns: the Good Samaritan did nothing particularly heroic or imaginative for the person he found lying wounded by the road but simply met his manifest needs; and the one whom he helped was no one in particular, not a friend or a figure of high repute or great wealth, or even a Jew, but simply "a man." Love, it seems, is simply helping your neighbor; help consists in responding to your neighbor's needs, and your neighbor is anyone in need whom you happen to encounter. In a few words, Jesus' parable transfixes both selfishness and abstract humanitarianism (which is often selfishness disguised). It would be hard to improve on this conception of love. But we do need to understand it, and I suggest that it has often been too narrowly construed.

The most obvious and pressing needs are usually physical—needs caused by conditions such as poverty and sickness. In most ages, poverty has been so profound and pervasive that physical needs have necessarily taken precedence over all others, and Jesus' parable encourages us to think of the neighbor in need as someone who, if not wounded by the road, is hungry, cold, or sick. Love accordingly is thought of as providing food, clothing, care. There is elemental truth in this attitude, truth that should not be obscured by more spiritual versions of need.

To understand community, however, we have to recognize that our needs are not physical alone and that love therefore must involve more than mere physical help. We provide that even for animals. We do not recognize the unique glory of human beings when we supply them only with things of the kind needed by all creatures, whether human or not. Physical needs are prior to all others in the sense that we cannot live unless they are met. But other needs are prior to physical needs in the sense that we cannot live *as human beings* unless they are met. What are these needs, the needs we have because we are not physical creatures only but are human? Christianity offers a simple answer to this question, one we have touched upon incidentally in discussing the Church.

All of our nonphysical needs are centered on one great need that we have simply in our humanity: truth, which is real only in the context of dialogue and is thus inseparable from community. Putting this in Christian terms, the truth is Christ, and human beings need above all to hear of Christ and to speak and be heard concerning Christ. It does not follow, however, that truth and community exist only among Christians. If Christ is the Logos, or destiny, all genuine truth concerns Christ. Many who consider faith in Christ a superstition are seriously concerned with the truth of human destiny. So it is with a number of Nietzscheans, Marxists, and Freudians. From a Christian standpoint, truth in its fullness can be found only in Christ, and no truth will ever be found that is not implicit in Christ; not to see this is hazardous. But God did not arrange the universe so simplistically that denying the name of Christ necessarily closes the door to truth. Truth is revered and sought in many places, and in all of these places there is ministry to our most pressing human need.

Here I think we find the answer to the question we have been asking. When urgent physical needs have been met, love consists in speaking the truth, as one understands it, and in listening to those who are speaking the truth as they understand it. When love performs these acts, it calls forth community. We began by asking, What is community? Can we not say that community is what comes into existence when people speak to one another, and listen, in an effort to discern the truth? Christians believe that the Church provides unique possibilities of community, for only in the Church is it recognized that the truth is Christ. But just as truth is revered and sought in many places, so community arises in many places, and sometimes, in the mystery of God's grace, community seems to be deeper and purer in places other than the Church.

In a moment, we shall be able to see what we have been looking for, the connection between community and liberty. But first, one aspect of community must be brought clearly into view. Community does not consist solely in the possession of truth but also in the search for truth. Thus, Socrates declared that his wisdom lay only in the realization of his ignorance, and it is suggested in the Gospel of John that claiming the truth as a possession blinds us.[9] If community consists in the search for truth, then communal relationships do not come about in holding to common dogmas, and much less in compelling others to accept such dogmas, but rather in inquiring together. Sharing uncertainty, so long as the uncertainty shared is hopeful and communicative, is more communal than sharing doctrinaire certainty. To put this in Christian terms, in revelation God simultaneously unveils and veils the truth. In Christ, the truth comes to us, but it comes as a mystery and not as a visible fact, plain to all. According to Christianity, then, we must inquire into Christ, into destiny. When we do this, we respond to God's command, "Seek ye my face."[10] We engage, at the same time, in communication of the most serious kind and create the substance of community.

Now we can begin to understand the role of liberty in community and the consequent importance of liberty. Liberty is the possibility of entering with others into the search for truth. It is the opportunity of inquiring in common into destiny. Our greatest need as human beings is to take account of the ultimate issues before us—death, evil, redemption—and to do this in the company of our fellow human beings. We need to be participants in searching conversations. When society assumes that our needs are merely physical, we are treated as nothing more than valuable animals. When someone recognizes our concern with the ultimate issues but does so only by commanding us to hold certain beliefs about them, we are treated as sophisticated machines, such as computers. We are treated as human beings only when we are invited to inquire with others into the meaning of our lives. But this can happen only where there is liberty.

It may seem that I have construed community and liberty far too intellectually and spiritually. Do we not enter into community when we work together? Is not liberty used significantly in choosing vocations, homes, and even hobbies and articles of consumption? I would assent in both cases and do not mean to suggest that we are present with others only when seriously conversing with them or that we are free only when thinking. But I do believe that we are not present with others if the things we do together are not frequently illuminated by serious conversation and that we are not free unless our activities are carried on thoughtfully. I also believe that when our lives are thus brought into the light of truth, all that we do and experience assumes the form of inquiry and that we take our lives seriously only so far as we live them inquiringly. Thus, one may find significant truth in the most insignificant event, and a Christian seeks the face of God, or Christ, in every detail of daily existence.

This is scarcely the prevailing view in modern society. Within the industrialized nations, governments have taken steps to see that basic physical needs are met as a matter of administrative routine. Although this effort has not fully succeeded, in many societies the people at large are adequately fed, clothed, and sheltered; they also are entertained. But they live in a spiritual void. Few serious words—sober and discerning words concerning human destiny—can be heard. The Church often fails to speak effectively, and its voice is often stifled or discredited by the pervasive secularity of democratic culture. Community is fragmentary and ephemeral, and liberty is debased.

This interpretation of community and liberty may sound more Socratic than Christian. That it is Socratic cannot be denied. Socrates died for the idea, which he unwaveringly practiced, that individuals and nations live serious lives only by examining again and again, in conversation and solitary reflection, the ends for which they live. But my interpretation is at the same time Biblical and Christian—more so, probably, than many Christians realize.

The God of the Old Testament is often thought of as wrathful and incalculable. Perhaps he is, at times. But if one were asked to characterize the God of Abraham and Moses in a phrase, one could hardly do better than to say that he speaks and listens. He is communal; and because he listens, as well as speaking, he is a God of liberty. Biblical figures not infrequently question him, and they even expostulate and bargain with him. The Old Testament is a record of divine-human dialogue, and the Jews were chosen not just as God's covenant partners but also as God's interlocutors. The words, "Come now, let us reason together," may sound like Socrates, in an early Platonic dialogue, but are, of course, God's words, according to Isaiah.[11]

The God of the New Testament is not less dialogical. His definitive act in relation to the human race, that of becoming visible and audible in Christ, was an act of communication. The communicative character of the Incarnation is dramatically expressed in the ancient Christian concept of Christ as God's Word. Through Christ, God spoke. Moreover, through Christ, God gave human beings time and room to listen thoughtfully and answer responsibly. This means that he allowed them to dispute his Word or simply not to listen; he did not speak in a way that forced them simply to hear and assent. Hence, the Grand Inquisitor's complaint that Christian revelation is "exceptional, vague, and enigmatic."

As we have seen, *agape* was taken by Christians as the supreme standard of human conduct because it animated the divine act of revelation in Christ. That divine *agape* took the form of speech seems particularly significant. God did not come to human beings to meet their physical needs. Christ refused the Devil's suggestion that he turn stones into bread and in his response—"Man shall not live by bread alone, but by every word that proceeds from the mouth of God"—explicitly recognized the dignity of speech.[12]

The Church symbolizes the communal character of Christianity. It is an association for conversing—in a wide variety of ways—with and about God. And such conversation depends on liberty. Although the Church has sometimes been hierarchical and repressive, it enacts its destiny only by calling its members to what Paul termed "the glorious liberty of the children of God."[13]

The prophetic stance can now be better understood. It means envisioning and inhabiting the world with a communal faith; everything is seen in the light of the Word. In attentiveness, one tries to catch the meaning not only of the things people say but, conscious of the communicative intent often present in human actions, of the things they do. Even in the solitude attentiveness imposes, one maintains an interpersonal area in which others can speak and act, and one thus supports their liberty. Availability is manifest not only in a readiness to speak when prompted by a care for others and for truth but also in a readiness to act, to *do* the truth. In these ways, one assumes a posture that must often be maintained among human beings who rarely speak seriously or listen with care—a posture commanded and upheld, however, as Christians believe, by one whose speaking is embodied in an omnipotent word and whose listening is unfailing.

The position in which the prophetic stance places one in relation to society can also now be better understood. Society, as I have argued, is anticommunal. This implies that society opposes truth. Every political observer knows that governments are continuously deceptive and frequently lie. This is not accidental. They are official agents of societies, and the purposes for which societies are organized are not necessarily furthered, and are often obstructed, by the truth. Just as society in essence involves inequality and manipulation, so in essence it entails the subordination of truth to social goals. In our time, the antagonism of society and community has been sharply delineated, for we have unprecedented powers of communication and yet, absorbed in commerce and consumption, have created societies in which serious communication is systematically discouraged. Prophetic hope requires resistance, although the resistance it requires is in its primary form very quiet—merely that of steadily, and in defiance of every social distraction, paying attention.

It would not be surprising if there were readers who could not reconcile the picture of Christianity being sketched here with a very different picture, one that shows Christians bound together by authority and dogma and ready, when they can, to subdue by force those who differ with them. Such a picture no doubt has historical justification. This makes it appropriate to consider the whole relationship of Christians to the multitudes who are opposed, or indifferent, to Christian truth.

Tolerance

To reflect on the implications of Christianity for tolerance is a particularly useful way of pursuing our inquiry into Christian liberty. This is first of all because tolerance means liberty. But further, tolerance can be understood primarily in terms of speech, or communication. From this standpoint, then, the two main concerns of this chapter, liberty and community, are fused.

Christianity does not appear to provide a good basis for tolerance, for it has never presented itself as merely one among various possible ways of approaching God and the truth. Far Eastern religions typically grant the existence of diverse and equally legitimate pathways to the divine. Here, Christianity differs from them fundamentally. Christian truth, it is claimed, is not a human pathway to God but rather is God's pathway to human beings. It is not a truth that human beings have discovered but one that God has revealed. And it is not one truth among others, incomplete and provisional. It consists in one definitive "Word," spoken in an act of unreserved, and hence perfect and final, divine self-disclosure. God appears in many places— indeed, in every detail of the universe he has created—but nowhere does he appear fully except in Christ. No other reality, therefore, illuminates being and human life as does Christ. On this, all orthodox Christians agree.

Christianity, then, embodies a definite sense of superiority to other religions and other doctrines of life. Does not such an attitude naturally and logically rule out tolerance? What grounds does it provide for anything but a policy of trying to force everyone to acknowledge the single and exclusive truth embodied in Christ?

Christian tradition does not have ready answers to such questions; Christianity has not in fact been a very tolerant religion. What concerns us here, however, is not how Christians have in fact behaved but how they should have behaved in view of the real meaning of their faith. Approaching the matter from this angle, we can see good reason for saying that Christianity truly understood is a tolerant faith. These reasons are not altogether plain and simple; otherwise they would not have been missed by so many Christians. But we can begin with some relatively plain and simple considerations that point in the direction of tolerance. These mainly concern human nature.

That human beings are essentially free—capable of choice—has swayed Christians toward tolerance from the beginning. Choice enters as inevitably into knowing as into acting. To know the truth, one must choose among alternative doctrines, just as one must choose among alternative courses of action in order to do what is right. Choosing among alternative doctrines is not arbitrary, to be sure. One must be persuaded; arguments must be heard, evidence and logic taken into account. But the process of persuasion can take place only among those who can freely reason and freely grant or withhold assent. To profess the truth without having been at liberty to think and disagree is a mechanical or cynical act, not a sign that the truth is genuinely known.

This applies to religious truth with particular force. Scientific truth rarely engages the deep personal concerns of scientists. And in any case, the evidence leaves relatively little room for personal choice; liberty is needed in order that relevant evidence can be freely gathered and fairly assessed, but the coercive character of the evidence is such that science is often successfully pursued even in dictatorships. Religious doctrines, however, bear on the destinies and the fundamental anxieties of all who consider them; and never do they have empirical backing of the kind that enforces assent regardless of all personal propensities. Choosing among them is not arbitrary, but neither is it purely rational. It is an act of the full integral self. It depends heavily, therefore, on liberty. In other words, faith in its very nature is free.

It follows that tolerance is unavoidable. To wish that others would adhere to a particular faith is to wish that they would use their liberty in a particular way. Liberty cannot be separated from the end desired. Some Christians may yearn for the human race to be a single vast company of believers (that would not be illogical or necessarily inhumane), and they may, accordingly, be willing to spread Christian faith with violence. *Agape* would not necessarily stop them, for what greater gift could love bestow than faith? What would stand in their way would not be *agape* but the capacity of human beings to choose—or, more precisely, their incapacity for choosing authentically without choosing freely.

Even God, it can be argued, had to reckon with our essential freedom. Hence the "exceptional, vague, and enigmatic" revelation that provoked the complaints of the Grand Inquisitor. God was compelled—by conditions divinely established in the creation of human nature—to seek free assent in order to obtain authentic faith. The scandal of the Crucifixion responded to this necessity. Making it easy for people to disbelieve, it made it possible for them freely, and thus in their full humanity, to believe. Is it going too far to suggest that Christ reveals not only God's love but also his tolerance?

Our fallibility, as well as our freedom, has important implications for tolerance. We are fallible not only because we are finite, and thus inherently limited in our understanding, but also because we are sinful; instead of cautiously keeping our limits in mind we proudly ignore them. The implications of our fallibility can be simply expressed. We are, so to speak, incapacitated for intolerance. To be intolerant is to ignore our own limited and erring understanding.

But here an objection may be raised. In view of our fallibility, every route to the truth is fraught with danger. Intolerance may express undue self-assurance and thus enthrone one great error, but it may enthrone the truth. Tolerance, however, will never enthrone the truth. It will give rise to a confusing and ultimately destructive variety of beliefs, with the truth at best one among many obscure contestants. Intolerance may therefore be safer.

The answer to this objection is that the dangers of tolerance and intolerance are not equivalent. Tolerance implicitly recognizes our fallibility, whereas intolerance implicitly denies it. Tolerance not only makes it possible for people in their fallibility to be humbled and corrected but encourages them to submit to this unpleasant discipline. Intolerance, however, encourages those who define the truth for everyone to forget their fallibility; in doing this, it raises to the highest degree the danger that error will be unchecked and consequently will flourish.

There is another possible objection, however, which is harder to answer. If all human beings in all circumstances are fallible, then every belief they profess is doubtful. But if every belief is doubtful, then Christianity is doubtful. A truly tolerant Christian would be so doubtful of Christianity itself as scarcely to be a Christian at all. How can the recognition of fallibility be combined with faith? This objection forces us onto a difficult terrain of thought and cannot be quickly disposed of.

The Christian answer to the objection is, in substance, this: the truth has been given us by God; at least, the truth of Christianity has. Hence, we can know the truth in spite of our fallibility. The difficulty with this answer, of course, is that it apparently nullifies the practical consequences of fallibility and thus overturns the argument for tolerance. If God provides the truth, are we not for all practical purposes—such as defining the truth and imposing it on others—rendered infallible? That depends on the kind of truth that God provides.

The crucial fact, arguing on Christian principles (but not along lines all Christians would willingly follow), is that God does not provide truth that can be adequately translated into words and doctrines. Christian faith rests on a particular human being and his life—on Jesus. This man and his life are interpreted in doctrines, but it is not in the doctrines themselves that Christians believe but in the personality and events the doctrines interpret. The truth God has given us is concrete and historical; when we step into the realm of the abstract and theoretical, we are no longer in immediate contact with Christian truth.

Christian truth cannot even be adequately put into the words that make up a story. Christians do not have faith in the Gospels but in the person pictured in the Gospels. And that person, Christians believe, is not dead; although he died, he arose from death into eternity. He lives in all Christians and all destinies.

Christianity, then, contains two kinds of truth—the original truth of Jesus' personality and life, beyond words, and the derivative truth embodied in stories and doctrines. One is divine, the other human; one is sure, and the other doubtful. The Word of God can be relied on unconditionally, but the human words that purport to explain the Word of God must be doubted. Christians believe that we humans are in touch with the truth, for we are recipients of revelation; but we do not possess the truth, for we are fallible. Clearly, it is not wrong for us to translate revelation into words, for we must. The stories are absolutely indispensable; without them, there would be no Christianity. And even the doctrines, although more questionable than the stories, are needed. Human beings cannot respond fully to revelation without bringing their intellectual powers into play, and the Gospels would not be as luminous as they are were it not for the doctrines that bring out their meaning. Words, then, are essential. They are a human response to divine revelation. But they are a *human* response, and in one very significant way they are incongruous with revelation: they can be erroneous.

The principle that Christianity consists in two kinds of truth, one absolutely reliable and one not, was recognized by Paul. Pointing to revelation, to the truth given by God, he wrote that "it is the God who said, 'Let light shine out of darkness,' who has shone in our hearts to give the light of the knowledge of the glory of God in the face of Christ." Then he added, alluding (one may surmise) to the human truth that interprets divine truth, that "we have this treasure in earthen vessels."[14] Human beings are consequently able (although Paul himself did not say this) to be both firm in their faith and tolerant. When God "shines in our hearts," we know a truth we cannot doubt. When we try to put that truth in a form we might force others to accept, however, our fallibility surges forward. We create "earthen vessels."

In sum, the only truths we possess are truths we possess through words, and words are vulnerable to the fallibility that necessitates tolerance. On the other hand, the one truth that is invulnerable to our fallibility is a truth we do not possess (it possesses us) and cannot force others to profess.

It can be argued that our words not only *may* be in error but in some sense *necessarily* are. They put in objective and propositional form things essentially nonobjective and nonpropositional. Unavoidable error of this kind may show up in verbal contradictions—for example, that God is both three and one—or in false objectification—exemplified by the proposition that God exists, as though he exists in the same sense that a rock or a house exists. If this argument is well founded, tolerance is not merely useful in allowing for the correction of occasional errors. It is an acknowledgment of the inherent error in verbal formulas and helps us to remember the mystery that our words are supposed to represent but often conceal. Thus, an orthodox Christian may be glad that there are vocal unitarians to keep us from forgetting that God is one as well as three. Even atheists may help Christians to remain aware of the truth that is not contained in their words; by attacking the elemental proposition that God exists, they can help deliver Christians from their captivity to propositional forms. On this argument, tolerance is a way of being mindful of the truth that is pure only as the Word of God and that human beings, even in their most cautious and indispensable statements, in some measure betray.

We have been speaking all the while not only of the character of man but also of the character of God. If God in his final revelatory act was respectful of human freedom, he also was heedful of his own mystery and majesty. He made himself available to humanity in a way that did not compromise his transcendence and glory. In sending forth a revelation that was "exceptional, vague, and enigmatic"—that is, incomprehensible in human words and statements—he impelled human beings toward a consciousness of their finitude and their fallibility; and in witholding himself from our intellectual grasp, he demonstrated his mystery and transcendence. The frequent intolerance of Christians, on one side pride, on the other side is a denial of God.

It may be objected that intolerance is not always an expression of pride—not, at any rate, of pride alone. It may express a sincere sense of responsibility for the truth. When this is the case, no disrespect for God is implied but rather a desire to be of service to God. It must be admitted that intolerance, or at least religious intolerance, may reflect a genuine concern with safeguarding the truth; in fact, it probably does so almost always. Is it true, however, that this implies no disrespect for God? Not, it seems, on Christian terms.

Christians who are very anxious about the fate of God's truth must have forgotten the doctrine of the Holy Spirit, which implies that God does not send his truth into history like a ship that is launched and then forgotten. He is the source at once of the truth human beings face and of the inspiration that enables them to recognize it as the truth and, in a measure, to understand it. If God were not the Holy Spirit, who provides understanding, his Word would be inaudible and the life of Christ without significance. It was not his intent that revelation should be inconsequential. His Word, he assures us, "shall not return to me empty, but it shall accomplish that which I purpose."[15] Need Christians, then, fear that God's voice will be drowned out by human error? When they succumb to the temptations of intolerance, do they not betray an assumption that God is incapable of caring for his own concerns?

Tolerance in the fullest sense is the same as the prophetic stance. It is communality maintained amid relationships that are not communal but social. It supports liberty as an opportunity for communication. Where communication fails to occur, tolerance becomes a state of communal readiness—a readiness for listening to others when they speak and for speaking when others are disposed to listen. This readiness in itself, maintained in silence, constitutes a kind of community—one consisting more in hope than realization, yet a condition far from alienation or indifference.

Tolerance of this kind is a way of waiting for God. Christianity implies that God is the truth we search for when we speak to one another in the consciousness of our ultimate concerns and the truth we long for when we watch for possibilities of serious speech. In all serious communication, we have God in mind, even if not consciously and not in a framework of orthodox concepts. Tolerance is thus an aspect of the outer form not only of love for human beings but of love for God—of faith.

Accordingly, tolerance is expectant and, if lucid and Christian, eschatological. It is readiness for the community that, in Christian minds, is God's intent in Christ and man's destiny. Through Christian tolerance, I establish relationships that, in the world, exist more in hope and imagination than in reality; yet these relationships are not barren, and they contain premonitions of a community that finally will engulf all alienation and separation.

As a form of communality in anticommunal circumstances, tolerance sets one apart—as does prophetic hope. A tolerant person stands as far as possible from the noise of advertising and propaganda and tries to be independent of the pleasures and distractions offered by a commercial society. Tolerance is thus a posture of detachment; it is not the kind of detachment that expresses indifference or contempt, however, but the kind that is necessitated by attentiveness. When tolerance is Christian, it is a sign of an effort to hear the voices of truth that are nearly drowned out in the world.

Of course, the tolerance I am speaking of is not the tolerance commonly encountered in the Western democracies. The latter arises from the assumption that truth is either unattainable or else unimportant and not worth the trouble involved in employing violence. It signifies an individualism in accordance with which others are regarded with neither respect nor aversion but rather with indifference. And ordinarily, it is thoroughly secular, forgoing the use of force in behalf of God not because God thus is debased but because, supposedly, God does not exist. Tolerance today is largely an expression of unrelatedness.

Christian tolerance is very different from modern tolerance. It is premised on our relatedness. The author of Ephesians says of Christians that they are "no longer strangers and sojourners" but are "fellow citizens with the saints and members of the household of God."[16] Modern tolerance, it might be said, is the tolerance of strangers and sojourners. The tolerance of Christians—and not of Christians alone but of all who sense a destiny in themselves and those they love and all who are conscious of the Logos in the order of creation—provides a foretaste of the liberty of the household of God. Modern tolerance manifests resignation; the tenuous relationships of the present time are assumed to be unchangeable. Christian tolerance is a way of dwelling in an eschatological community.

Yet tolerance cannot be limitless. Some things cannot be tolerated, because they destroy the conditions under which tolerance, as freedom for listening and speaking , is possible. It would, for example, be fatuous for exponents of tolerance to tolerate a movement—one having real prospects of success and not consisting merely of rhetoric that can be safely ignored—to replace a liberal democracy with a totalitarian dictatorship. It would be invalid, moreover, to say that in such circumstances, threatening acts may be suppressed but words of all kinds must be tolerated, for no sharp line can be drawn between acts and words; in politics, we act through words. It follows that we cannot be intelligently and genuinely tolerant by being unqualifiedly tolerant. Tolerance depends on a degree of intolerance. But how, except by a rough common sense that has little philosophical or theological validity, can limits on tolerance be justified?

The question is important because it is equivalent, in substance, to the question on which all political philosophy is centered: How can the state be justified? The state, after all, amounts to a set of highly organized and firmly established limits on tolerance. Anarchism, the denial of all legitimacy to the state, is simply unqualified tolerance. If tolerance is as important a value as I have argued, how can Christians not be anarchists? How can the prophetic stance be anything but a categorical refusal to cooperate with the state and its repressive machinery?

Power

Christianity is not idealistic, in the usual sense of the term, and does not anticipate the development, on earth, of universal and voluntary harmony. Earlier pages on the doctrine of sin have made this clear. Christianity is nearer to Machiavellism than to idealism. Machiavelli maintained that the pride and selfishness of human beings naturally give rise to disorder and that disorder requires the remedy of power; since civilization depends on order, and order on power, there can be no civilization without power. Such views are fully in accord with Christian principles. A statesman particularly illustrative of Christian realism is Abraham Lincoln. He is illustrative partly because he was a Christian and a man of great spiritual depth. But he was also a cunning and sagacious man of power, and the survival of the United States is due largely to this fact. Lincoln can with some justice be characterized as both Christlike and Machiavellian.

If power is pervasive in human affairs, government is a necessary institution. There has been one great Christian anarchist, Leo Tolstoy. But Tolstoy rejected much of orthodox Christian doctrine and is a decidedly atypical figure in the history of Christianity. Orthodox Christians do not deny that governments ordinarily are evil—deceptive, selfish, arrogant—and often are atrocious; but they are indispensable. We should keep them within constitutional limits and subject to popular consent; it would be futile, however, to try to do without them or even to try to substitute for the centralized power of government the voluntary agreement of assembled citizens. The necessity of living under centralized power is one of the most tragic conditions of historical existence. It is inherent, however, in our fallen state.

Christianity accepts even violence, the most shocking form of power. That Christian instincts are antithetical to violence hardly needs saying. Jesus' majestic patience, his mute and unresisting endurance of death, have made an ineffaceable impression on human minds and have shaped Christian attitudes. One cannot believe in *agape*, in the exaltation of the individual and the ideal of community, and in liberty and tolerance without detesting violence. A few Christians, accordingly, have sought ways of eradicating violence from politics.

The doctrine of nonviolence is bound to be regarded with interest and sympathy by any Christian. As framed by Gandhi, it calls not for passivity in the face of evil but for political action shaped altogether—not merely in its ends but in all of its means—by love. It seeks what every Christian must desire, a politics free of vengefulness, resentment, and fury. It contains a mystical vision of world transformation. For Gandhi, the supreme exemplar of nonviolence was Christ.

Yet it is more than doubtful that nonviolence is mandated by Christian principles. Jesus himself apparently accepted violence in principle. This is shown by the well-known incident of his driving the money changers from the temple. It is shown also by his acceptance of government, in essence an agent of violence; one must "render unto Caesar the things that are Caesar's."

It is the realism of Christianity, arising from the doctrine of original sin, that disposes most Christians to view skeptically the doctrine of nonviolence. Christians are apt to notice that nonviolence is a form of power and therefore not equivalent to love. Like violence, it objectifies people, for it contrives ways of influencing their behavior—albeit without using violence. Christians are apt to notice also that nonviolence does not necessarily elicit better moral qualities among its users than does violence. Nonviolence is often linked, in the arguments of its proponents, with qualities like love and humility; violence is linked with hatred and vengefulness. But the American youth movement of the 1960s provides numerous examples of nonviolent actions in which self-righteousness and contempt for opponents were conspicuous. On the other side, history contains numerous instances in which violence has been used by men of moral integrity and even (to name but two, Marcus Aurelius and Abraham Lincoln) of moral grandeur. Evil is rooted in the nature of human beings and not in the means they employ. Human beings are sufficiently ingenious in their perversity to be evil without being violent, just as they are sometimes sufficiently good to be good even while employing violence.

The realism of Christians is apt to be reflected also in the conviction that violence often is unavoidable. The idea that nonviolence can ordinarily take the place of violence manifests less an accurate appraisal of political reality than a prior doctrinal commitment. There are innumerable instances, such as the defeat of Hitler in World War II or of the Persians by the Athenians at the outset of the Periclean era, in which violence, by all empirical evidence, was indispensable.

The dialectical character of Christian political thinking is pronounced in Christian attitudes toward power, however, for if the Christian mind is realistic and unsentimental, in perceiving the necessity of power in the pursuit of common purposes, it is also highly sensitive to the evils of power. Christians look on power from the vantage point of *agape.* Power degrades individuals, however provisionally and benevolently; *agape* exalts them. It is true that *agape* often needs power to attain its purposes, but this implies simply that within history pure *agape* is not possible. *Agape* and power have to be combined, and the greatest political leaders are those who can respond to this tragic necessity, using power as circumstances require but subordinating it to love. The antithesis of power and *agape* is symbolized by the Crucifixion. It is not so much that Rome and Israel, the crucifiers, were terrible but that power is terrible. Even had the Roman

procurator believed in Jesus, he could not, as procurator, have re-
frained from dealing with Jesus and his movement as required by Roman imperial concerns. Pilate was not hostile to Jesus; he was a skeptic and a prudent official.

Power is opposed not only to *agape* in itself but also to its expression in searching and truthful communication. Exercising power is
very different from speaking and listening in a state of unconditional
openness to the truth. Even power that seeks rational persuasion is
very different from *agape,* for using power entails calculating the results of every act, including speech; everything that is said has to be
appraised from the standpoint not only of truth but also of consequences. No form of power is purely communal. The Crucifixion was
an act of power and, in the eyes of Christians, an attack on the Word
of God, an attempt at suppressing the archetype of all communal
initiatives.

Those standing in the "Catholic" tradition (who, let us recall, may
be Calvinists or liberal Protestants) are inclined to interpret power
less negatively than I have here. They are conscious of the benefits
often gained through power; and they are sensitive to the relatively
benign character of certain relationships in which there are elements
of power—those, for example, established by priests and teachers.
They realize, too, that exceedingly few relationships are altogether
free of power. From the perspective of the "Reformation" tradition,
however, it is vital that we bear in mind our essential situation, our
fallenness. That means remembering not only how many human relationships are utterly perverted (which is easy, since such relationships are conspicuous and shocking) but also how very few are un-
tainted by objectification (which is hard, since many relationships
look better than they are). To see clearly how much evil is present in
human relationships depends on defining strictly, and not forgetting,
the nature of power. It is one thing to regard another person as possessing a value beyond calculation and thus as essentially an end; it
is another to view this person in relation to ends that one is pursuing.
There are many power relationships that render this distinction inconspicuous and relatively innocuous. But there are none that nullify
it. It persists even if the other person fully shares the ends that I—as
a power holder—seek, for as long as I seek those ends, I cannot suppress questions incompatible with pure *agape:* Is it true that the

other person fully shares my ends and understands them just as I do? If such is the case at this moment, will it continue to be the case? If some difference of aspiration or undertstanding comes to the surface, what will I do? Should I do anything now in preparation for such an eventuality? It is because of the inevitability of such questions, in a political context, that *agape* is undiluted and fully real only when one gives up everything—all ends, life itself—"for his friends." "Reformation" principles imply that as difficult as it may be to disentangle power and love in practice, we are in danger of flattering ourselves, flirting with pride, if we fail to distinguish them sharply in theory.

The concept of original sin, however, warns us against blaming the evils of power entirely on power itself and thus exculpating the possessors of power. Power relationships are almost always worse than they have to be. Power requires its possessors to do what pride tempts them to do anyway—to look down on others, judging and controlling them. Not many can do that year after year, from duty, without developing a taste for doing it and thus doing more than duty requires, judging and controlling others simply for the enjoyment of dominion. "Power tends to corrupt."

The only weakness in Lord Acton's famous dictum is that the word *corrupt* is so commonplace and vague. It does not tell us specifically what power does to its possessors—that it tempts them to mimic God. Since they are not subject to the limits bearing on most people, they can more or less ignore the fact that they are finite. They are flattered and deferred to continuously and can easily begin to think that they are perfectly wise and good. They are famous and are tempted to mistake being remembered in history for immortality. Such illusions are instinct with cruelty. Men with power may mimic God in his wrath, bringing destruction on those arousing their displeasure. Worse yet, paradoxically, is that they may mimic God in his goodness, attempting to do away with all suffering and injustice. This is so far outside the bounds of human ability that those who attempt it are necessarily blind to their own limits and faults. Ruling with extravagant pride, they create evils worse than those they try to destroy.

It might be supposed that those underneath must either rebel or mutely suffer. The truth is, however, that sometimes they cooperate in pantomiming divine-human relations. Power tends to corrupt not only those who possess it but also those who do not. If power draws its possessors into divine pretensions, it entices those deprived of it into accepting those pretensions. This comes about through a form of idolatry. God as envisioned in Christianity does not immediately quench our thirst for the divine. His glory is often invisible; the redemption he offers must be purchased sometimes with suffering; his sovereignty does not relieve human beings of their freedom or consequent responsibility. It is said that people have a natural yearning for God. But their yearning is ordinarily for a god far more palpable and convenient than the God of Christian revelation. Hence, they readily replace the true God, impalpable and inconvenient, with a human god—a visible being with visible glory, who promises to end their suffering quickly and begins by relieving them of a major source of suffering, their liberty.

Power is a narcotic for both rulers and masses. To be merely human is deeply distressing. It means knowing only a little of reality and being continuously vulnerable to accidents that affect the amplitude and length of one's life. It means being fated sooner or later to die. To be merely human is to have freedom without infallible wisdom or perfect goodness, so that freedom brings anxiety and guilt. Power can enable us for awhile to forget that we are merely human, having no access either to the serenity of gods or the placidity of beasts. It can serve this function for those on both sides, rulers and subjects.

Power is often sanctified in our minds by the assumption that God has power. Is it true, however, that God has power? This is a question we encounter recurrently in discussing the political meaning of Christianity. Of course, human beings can only speak falteringly when they try to characterize God. There is something very questionable, however, about a view that implies that God is basically like a policeman or a soldier, only larger and more irresistible. Such a view is particularly questionable from a Christian standpoint. Christian faith, after all, holds that God is fully revealed in the life of a crucified, and hence wholly powerless, human being. That Christians attribute power to God is perhaps inevitable, for faith would be impossible without the assurance that nothing is capable of obstructing or deflecting his love for the human race. But power is surely one of the most risky of the analogies Christians employ in talking about God.

It is noteworthy that even the limited resources of human language provide a word that is widely preferred to *power* in reference to

God's dealings with human beings on earth. The word is *grace*. Grace is God's kindness in lifting us up. Grace is present when one knows inwardly the exaltation of the individual. Grace does resemble power in one way. It accomplishes what God intends. But if grace is power, it is unlike all human power; it enhances freedom. In a way that surpasses rational understanding, grace and freedom abound together.

The Christian judgment on power is expressed in the ancient conviction that the Church must be distinct from the state. The Church symbolizes the Kingdom of God. As we have seen, it represents, and occasionally and fragmentarily achieves, the ideal of community. Even though the Church is a social group and therefore cannot eradicate power from either its internal or its external relations, power is inappropriate to it. This is expressed in its separation from the state. Leaving to Caesar the things that are Caesar's, the Church testifies to its destiny if not to its worldly reality. At the same time, it allows the state to stand, unsanctified and unapologetically devoted to the organization of power, as a symbol of our fallenness.

It is apparent how divided Christianity is—how near on one side to Machiavellism and on the other side to anarchism—and how pressing, therefore, is the question of how states can be justified. As organized power, the state by its very essence is involved in using individuals as means. It systematically denies the main premise of Christian politics and ethics—the exaltation of the individual. How, then, can anyone striving to maintain the prophetic stance conscientiously accept—much less cooperate and work through—the state? This is to ask, in effect, how the prophetic stance can be political rather than anarchistic.

The State and Its Justification

It would be false to suggest that Christians alone have been sensitive to the moral issue that the state presents. Political philosophy began in ancient Greece with an effort to show how government can avoid being simply an arrangement by which the powerful sacrifice the weak to their own selfish interests. Two basic solutions have been devised, and practically all non-Christian political philosophers accept, in some form, one or the other of these.

The older of them is the theory that the state is justified insofar as it serves the true good of man, which is ordinarily taken to be truth, justice, or some other such universal value. A government serving this good does not sacrifice anyone to the interests of the ruling class. It does not even sacrifice anyone to the good, for anyone who is compelled to serve a good that is truly universal is compelled only to serve his own highest interest. This theory originated with Plato and in modern times, as the theory of the general will, has been influential in the rise of democracy.

The other basic solution to the problem of justifying the state is the theory of consent. An entirely legitimate state would be one that every member, possessing reason and all relevant knowledge, had deliberately and explicitly accepted. Since no such state can exist, proponents of consent theory have ordinarily assumed that consent is inherent in acts that everyone might conceivably perform, such as voluntarily residing in a state. Also, they have sometimes equated the consent of the individual with the consent of the majority. The best-known form of this theory in modern times is that of the social contract.

A Christian can hardly accept either theory. As for the first, a Christian would not deny that a state steadily and reliably serving the good as such, the true ends of the human race, would be legitimate to a degree. Only to a degree, however; for in whatever it does, the state applies power in one way or another, and power is intrinsically evil. When it conduces to the ultimate good of the one subjected to it, it is partially justified; nevertheless, it still destroys liberty. Rousseau's paradox, that one can "be forced to be free," is entirely inadmissible. Respect for individuals forbids us to be cavalier about their choices, even when their choices are mistaken or morally perverse. And this issue aside, a Christian would deny that a state steadily and reliably serving the true and final good of the human race is a practical possibility. Such a state would be not a state but the Kingdom of God.

As for the theory of consent, the problem is in part that it tries to solve the problem of legitimacy without introducing the question of value. Personal preference, regardless of what a person happens to prefer, is made the highest standard of legitimacy. For a Christian, however, political power must be moral. It is justified only if it is instrumental to the highest values—centering, of course, on the dignity of every human being. A second difficulty inherent in consent theory can be very succinctly stated: the individuals coerced do *not* consent. Otherwise, it would not be necessary for them to be coerced. It may, as we have seen, be asserted that they tacitly consent by living within the jurisdiction of the government coercing them. This is not persuasive, however. In ordinary circumstances, what else can they do? To move from nation to nation according to the dictates of one's political conscience is a realistic possibility for scarcely anyone.

From a Christian perspective, then, traditional theories of legitimacy neglect the necessity either that values be freely chosen or that the values chosen be true values. Personal choice in the former instance is left out of account and in the latter instance is made absolute. In addition, we can detect in these theories a tendency to idealize the state, to assume the possibility of a state that either serves universal values or rests on the informed consent of all its members.

By way of such criticisms, Christian principles lead to the conclusion that no state in itself can be fully justified. States may of course be *partially* justified—in terms both of the values they serve and of the consent of their members. Not all states are completely and equally illegitimate. But no state, judged by its own intrinsic qualities, is completely legitimate. If even one individual is sacrificed (made to serve a good not his own) or coerced (even in behalf of his own good), the state is morally compromised. But many are inevitably sacrificed and coerced, even in the best of states. And if this were not so—if true values were served, with all members fully consenting—the state would have no function and would wither away.

Secular theories of the state consistently obscure the evil inherent in the twofold fact that the state always serves ends more or less particular rather than universal and imposes these ends coercively on unconsenting members. These theories thus give rise to a concept that Christianity enables us to recognize as profoundly false—the good state, a concept not only self-contradictory but implying that human beings can organize morally pure spheres of life in the world and in history. Admittedly, Christians have sometimes accepted this concept. In doing so, however, they have allowed themselves to accept a view that is distinctively Hellenic and pagan in its origins, secular and humanistic in its modern development, and contrary to the deepest Christian principles—at least as these principles are understood in the "Reformation" tradition.

If secular theories of the state are unsuccessful, how can the state be justified at all? How can any kind of political activity—serving in public office or supporting specific uses of governmental power—be justified? One must even ask how obedience to a government can be justified, since obedience is a form of support.

As these questions suggest, it is impossible to erase completely the anarchistic elements in Christianity. Love neither sacrifices nor coerces. Jesus forbids all manner of coercion. "Do not resist one who is evil. But if any one strikes you on the right cheek, turn to him the other also; and if any one would sue you and take your coat, let him have your cloak as well; and if any one forces you to go one mile, go with him two miles."[17] The state is organized for the explicit purpose of resisting those who are evil. Love and the state cannot be entirely reconciled.

Yet neither can they be entirely separated, and this fact constitutes a partial—though, as we shall see, insufficient—justification of the state. Only by resisting those who are evil can one defend the weak and helpless. To follow Jesus' injunction literally would mean more than suffering violence and injustice oneself; it would mean abandoning others to violence and injustice. A few may be called by God to strive for the kind of moral perfection that unconditionally refuses to enter into judgment and coercion, leaving the consequences to God. (This, it should be noted, would be to practice not nonviolence, which might better be called nonviolent resistance, but rather non*resistance*.) It is arguable, however, that those not conscious of such a calling should adhere to a humbler and more practical morality, a morality heedful of circumstances and of the commonsense maxim that it is better for unjust aggressors than for their victims to suffer coercion.

The argument that power and violence must be used in defense of the innocent and helpless appeals strongly to common sense. There is a parallel argument that relates more explicitly to the values so far outlined in this essay, however; that is an argument touched on earlier. Without the systematic use of power and violence, by public authorities and according to established procedures and safeguards, there would be no common liberty and hence no community. There would be only the liberty of the strong, which is despotism. In other words, coercion is minimized when it is monopolized under constitutional safeguards. For coercion to be thus minimized is an indispensable condition of community.

To forsake the state in order to safeguard a moral purity that is lost by those implicated in the use of power and violence is to build a wall between moral conduct and human beings on earth. This is disastrous for both. Morality is made irrelevant to the human situation, and humanity is delivered over to evil. And in affirming such a condition, one loses one's moral purity as well. One does not achieve moral goodness by abandoning the earth and the human race, even though the circumstances of earthly existence inevitably involve one in evil.

Scriptural confirmation of this argument may be found in the Incarnation. Christ lived on the earth and in some ways, although not in all, acquiesced in the conditions of earthly existence. He explicitly supported, among these conditions, the state ("Render unto Caesar . . . "), in spite of calling for nonresistance. Christians may conclude that God in this way commands them to enter into history, to accept their finitude by accepting their subjection to historical circumstances, and to find in that way their destinies and God himself. That the state is a lesser evil than anarchy can be seen as a sign of its divine necessity. The state belongs to human destiny; it is called forth by human fallenness and commanded by God.

In summary, I am arguing that moral life—protection of the weak and helpless and the quest for community—is subject to the conditions of historical existence and that the organized use of coercion, the state, is among these conditions. I acknowledge that my argument is inconclusive. This is because Jesus' own position, enjoining nonresistance yet living in the world and sanctioning the state, is inconclusive. It seems reasonable to assume, however, that Jesus did not intend to bring about the immediate collapse of civilized order and that his call for nonresistance is thus to be understood as an eschatological utterance and symbol but, here in history, as incumbent only on those conscious of being called to a distinctive moral practice.

The possibility that some may be called to such a practice is of considerable significance. Its significance must be carefully stated, however, for it can readily be misconstrued. In the first place, the practice of nonresistance is not morally pure. Uncompromising *agape* cannot mean abandoning the weak and the helpless and withholding all support from the realm of common liberty. The truth is simply that love and worldly circumstances are not entirely congruous. To bend before worldly circumstances is to transgress against love in one way; to refuse to bend is to transgress against love in another way. Christians look on Jesus' life of nonresistance (to which, as we have noted, various statements and acts, like driving the money changers from the temple, lend a marked ambiguity) with deep respect; but this is because it was Jesus' life and the life God commanded Jesus to live and not because it exemplifies a universal moral rule.

In the second place, that the practice of nonresistance may lie within the destiny of some people does not invalidate or in any way weaken the concept of the prophetic stance. Maintaining a posture of nonresistance can be genuinely Christian only if it is a way of waiting for God in history. It must embody moments of inaction and solitude as well as attentiveness and availability. In short, only *prophetic* nonresistance can be valid. Jesus' life was formed altogether by eschatological expectancy, by faith in the imminence of the Kingdom of God. I have argued that the prophetic stance normally involves participation in politics and tacit support for the state. But it is not in such terms that I have defined the prophetic stance. Its essence lies in historical hope, sustained in a fallen world.

There is a sense, indeed, in which nonresistance exemplifies a kind of politics. To be sure, it is risky to say this, for our understanding of what politics is—normally, an affair of power and action—is thus put in jeopardy. But we may justify the risk, this once, in order to bring out the fact that nonresistance can embody not simply the kind of hope that is implicit in Christian eschatology—hope directed toward eternity—but also the kind of hope that animates normal politics—hope directed toward particular and proximate historical ends, such as greater economic justice. It is not abjuring such ends that renders nonresisting "politics" distinctive but rather leaving their accomplishment altogether in the hands of God. As impossible as it is to understand Jesus as a political figure, it is not quite satisfactory to say flatly that he was nonpolitical.

Although the practice of nonresistance does not exemplify moral purity and does not invalidate or weaken the concept of the prophetic stance, however, it does—and this is its true significance—relativize the politics through which prophetic hope is normally expressed. Jesus' life of nonresistance is a sign and reminder, reproduced in the life of anyone who in this particular matter follows Jesus, that the state cannot be unambiguously justified and that normal politics, which presupposes the state, is necessarily carried on under a moral cloud. From a Christian standpoint, although nonresistance is no nearer to moral purity than is political action and does not necessarily conform any more closely to the will of God, it bespeaks the subordination of ordinary politics to divine judgment. It rebukes the self-righteousness that threatens continually to subvert the compassion and good judgment of political activists.

Returning to the main theme of this section, traditional theories of legitimacy, such as that of consent, would make us independent of God, justified in a purely human and earthly order of life. For Christians, the inadequacy of these theories throws humans on the mercy and guidance of God; they are justified only transcendentally. The source of justification is the truth in the doctrine of the divine right of kings, a truth that was lost amid modern efforts to replace that doctrine. Not that kings have better claims to sanctity than do presidents or prime ministers. But in the eyes of Christian faith, power can be justified fully only by God, and this is true even of democratic and constitutional power. Politics is a realm of moral darkness, and the darkness cannot be dissipated by human virtue and wisdom.

To stand prophetically, then, is to be skeptical of actual states but supportive of the state in principle. Christian principles provide no basis on which one can claim to know with certainty whether any particular state possesses the legitimacy that comes from God. Some of the most fateful human decisions are made in doubtful cases: in America in 1776, in France in 1789, in Russia in 1917. Sometimes prophetic responsibility imposes the duty of repudiating a particular state. When it does not, however, and a state is nevertheless thrown down, the price may be very high. Casual hostility to the state is indefensible. We can live prophetically only in subjection to the conditions of historical existence—among which, in all of its evil, stands the state.

The same principle that gives or denies legitimacy to a state—that is, the command of God—also justifies or condemns every coercive act carried out by the state. Nothing on earth can do away entirely with the evil intrinsic to taking away someone's liberty or life. When officials of the state do such things, as time after time they must, they become involved in a situation of the kind noted in our discussion of Church intervention in the secular order; they enter a "boundary situation," facing conditions that place them beyond rules that provide unequivocal guidance and full justification. In using power and violence, leaders face the grandeur and the evil, the exaltation and the fallenness, of human beings; they are involved in the conflict of these conditions, which at once condemn and necessitate coercion; and they suffer the fact that nothing we can do, such as subordinating coercion to universal values or to the consent of the governed, can resolve this conflict.

It is characteristic of boundary situations, however, that they not only bring us to the edge of worldly security but leave us, so to speak, with nothing between ourselves and eternity. For using power and violence, there is no full justification on earth. Officials with faith thus face not only the moral dilemmas imposed by their responsibilities but also God, whose commands can guide human beings when rules fail and whose forgiveness can justify them when they themselves fail.

The evil essential to an act of coercion can be conscientiously accepted, and the guilt borne, only by leaders who are at once prudent and prayerful. Prudence is the virtue by which we responsibly occupy a set of historical and personal circumstances. In prayerfulness, human beings acknowledge that they are never justified by anything within those circumstances and must look beyond them.

The question prudence asks is simply whether true values, such as justice, will be better served by coercion than by any other means. Are there alternatives to coercion, such as public discourse, that might serve the same values without bringing the evil inherent in coercion? The principle of consent necessarily enters into prudential calculations; if the values to be served are on all hands repudiated, coercion is likely to be abortive. Prudence is the virtue that enables leaders to take into account the earthly circumstances in which goodness must be realized. The court decisions and legislative enactments that have furthered racial integration in the United States in recent decades exemplify political prudence. The values served were of compelling importance; there was widespread public willingness that they be forcibly promoted; and coercion was employed with painstaking caution.

Statesmen are prayerful when they are conscious that their acts of power and violence can be commanded and justified not by the earthly circumstances that condition them but only by God. When contemplating coercion, they ask—perhaps in words very different from those traditionally used by Christians—"What does God require of us in our present situation?" And even without clear answers to this question, they proceed with confidence in God's mercy. The way Lincoln led the American people into the Civil War exemplifies the prayerful (as well as the highly prudent) use of power. In deep personal anguish, Lincoln pondered the injustice of slavery, the historical significance of American democracy, the mood of the American people, and the probable scale and ferocity of a civil conflict. Nothing provided a clear and binding justification for the catastrophe of the Civil War, and Lincoln's awareness of this entered into his tragic consciousness of his times. Nevertheless, Lincoln was not, in the depths of his being, in doubt. He moved in all of the light he could gain from his own intelligence and from prayer. And even in confessing that both the North and the South believed they fought on the side of God and that in this faith both were probably in some measure mistaken, he was sustained by an assurance of God's forgiveness. Such forgiveness Lincoln did not claim for himself alone but also for his opponents. All was bound together in Lincoln's mind by a prophetic sense of American destiny. In the mystery of divine providence, even the unprecedented violence and horror of his times would finally be redeemed, and those on both sides would be justified.

Implicit in the Christian view of the state, as interpreted in the preceding pages, is the proposition discussed early in this chapter—that the prophetic stance is difficult and equivocal. It means defending liberty and bearing the evils that liberty inevitably brings; it also means denying liberty—not bearing all of the evils liberty brings—so that liberty and the community that depends on liberty may exist. Only within the state can there be an area of common liberty where community can be brought into being. In spite of its necessity, however, the state is essentially evil, because it means the rule of a few over many; and in view of man's tendencies toward self-exaltation and self-abandonment, every state in actuality is worse than its essential nature requires it to be. To maintain the prophetic stance is to face these tensions and live within them.

The Christian justification of the state and its coercive acts must in the final analysis be eschatological. The things we do in history are justified only in the context of eternity. Here in the world, our politics cannot be unequivocally good, nor can our acts of power and violence be fully vindicated. Secular theories, in projecting the ideal of the good state and the image of state acts fully purified by the nobility of their ends or the consent of those they affect, obscure the tragic character of human politics. Those who deny God are under strong pressure to do this, lest they despair of history and our common life. But Christians are under no such pressure. They can acknowledge the tragic significance of the state and of the power and violence we unavoidably use, for these reflect an impermanent situation. They do not disclose our nature and destiny.

If the Christian view of the state is eschatological, so is the Christian view of liberty. No longer is liberty seen, as in the ancient *polis* or in modern versions of ancient political ideals (Rousseau, Hegel, and the English idealists), as being based on the initiative of the state or as being essentially an opportunity for participation in the state. Rather, liberty is a way of recognizing that the individual is grounded in a source of life beyond the state and is perfected by participating in a destiny that, although taking into account the state (as the order human beings create in assuming responsibility for history), may defy it. Liberty sanctions opposition and rebellion. Through liberty, the state acknowledges the singleness and transcendence of individuals; and in doing this, it acknowledges its own relativity.

Envisioning the state eschatologically may help to bring into sharper focus the nature of the prophetic stance. Christians insist on the relativity of the state because of a hope that does not admit that the conditions underlying the existence of the state—estrangement and the consequent dependence of order on force—are permanent. Prophetic hope encompasses eternity, or, it might better be said, is the spirit of one who is encompassed by eternity; the life it imagines necessarily breaks out of the state. This does not mean withdrawal from state activity. As I have already argued, for human beings in history, eternity is destiny, and destiny is not found in a condition of abstraction but in life on earth, within history and hence within the state. It is concrete, and thus political, life. But if truly destined, this life is carried on toward an end beyond the state. Hence the enduring sense among protagonists of the state, such as Machiavelli, that in political matters Christians are never fully committed or entirely reliable. To face political concerns and obligations with prophetic hope is to be mindful that the state defines the circumstances in which our historical responsibilities are fulfilled but does not define those responsibilities themselves. That must be done by every individual. The kinship of prophetic hope and liberty is easily seen. To maintain the prophetic stance is only to live the liberty that marks the limits of the state in authority and significance.

Four

Social Transformation

Prophetic Hope and Social Reform

When we turn from liberty to social transformation, we are not taking up a new subject but rather are entering a new stage in our inquiry into the old one—liberty. The aim of social transformation, for Christians, is community. But we cannot create community. All we can do is remove—or attack—obstacles to community, such as poverty, illiteracy, sharp class distinctions, and secretive and unaccountable governments. That is, we can only set people free for community. Social reform seeks liberation.

The difference between this stage and the earlier stage of the inquiry may be clarified in terms of the familiar distinction between negative and positive liberty. The distinction is not absolute, nor is it everywhere understood in precisely the same way. Roughly speaking, however, negative liberty means simply the absence of governmental restrictions. Liberty is often understood in this sense alone, for government is the most crushing and sinister opponent of liberty. Positive liberty is often defined as the power of choosing and acting; more precisely, however, it means the absence of social conditions that inhibit liberty. (In the final analysis, then, it is also negative.) For example, people enjoy negative liberty where the government does not censor the press; they enjoy positive liberty as well only if good newspapers are available and they are able to read. Negative liberty depends mainly on constitutional safeguards, such as independent courts; positive liberty depends on numerous economic, social, and personal conditions.

As theory, this distinction is somewhat weak, for both kinds of liberty are ultimately negative and the dividing line between them is more or less arbitrary. It is useful, however, because it brings into view an important aspect of liberty, namely, that liberty is not a specific quantum, which is either present or not; it can be indefinitely enlarged. It is not something to be achieved and then simply protected but is rather an endless task. Bringing this aspect of liberty into view has been important historically. There have been strenuous efforts from the beginnings of the Industrial Revolution to the present time to equate negative liberty with liberty itself. The first great victories for liberty were won, prior to the Industrial Revolution, against governments; they established constitutionalism, or negative liberty. The middle-class groups raised to power and wealth by the Industrial Revolution wanted to stop there; but early industrialism created conditions that rendered negative liberty of little significance for large sections of the population. The idea of positive liberty has thus been more than a theory; it has been a cause.

It would be preferable, perhaps, to speak in terms of initial and enlarged liberty. As the most formidable opponent of liberty, government must be conquered first. But to stop with that conquest, with constitutionalism, is arbitrary. The logic of liberty works irresistibly in the direction of the enlargement of liberty—in the direction of social reform. To be protected against governmental thought control, for example, may be of slight benefit for someone illiterate, destitute, or confined to a despised caste. Initial liberty is full liberty only for a few, for those wealthy and privileged enough to enlarge it for themselves. Enlarged liberty is liberty that has been spread from the few to the many; it is common liberty. For the multitudes, initial liberty has significance mainly in the opportunities it offers of working for enlarged liberty.

The liberty sought through social transformation is thus larger in two senses than the liberty that results from constitutionalism alone. It is larger because it is protected against various forces and conditions—employers, poverty, ignorance—and not against government alone. It is positive liberty. It is larger also in the sense that it belongs to more people. It is liberty that does not depend on wealth or social status, on private advantages or special privileges, in order to be real. Hence, it is real for many.

In this way, where liberty is taken seriously, equality must be taken seriously, too. Liberty and equality can unquestionably come into conflict, as we shall see further along in this chapter. Nevertheless, they cannot be separated. Both arise from respect for individual human beings. Liberty has a certain priority over equality, for liberty—protection of the individual against society and government—is the value sought, whereas equality concerns only the distribution of that value. But when a few have gained liberty, there is no secure moral ground on which the claim that all should have it can be resisted. The logic of liberty works toward equal liberty. It can be argued that many will misuse any positive liberty bestowed on them; if protected against poverty, for example, they will not work. Such arguments have merit in many cases, and the enlargement of liberty is a process attended not only by self-interested opposition but also by practical failures and conscientious doubts. But the image of the exalted individual, which evokes the cry for equality simultaneously with the cry for liberty, has great moral authority and keeps defenders of unequal liberty continually on the defensive. From the standpoint of Christian principles, this is appropriate. Where it is a question of removing indignities suffered by individuals, the burden of proof falls on the opposition.

The Christian record in the annals of reform, it must be granted, is not impressive. Christians have accepted, and sometimes actively supported, slavery, poverty, and almost every other common social evil. They have often condemned such evils in principle but failed to oppose them in practice. Faith does not necessarily conquer selfishness, obviously, and is particularly unlikely to do so when connected with an established religion and thus with privileged groups. That Christianity has in many times and places and in various ways been an established religion is perhaps the major reason why it has been so implicated in social evils such as slavery, serfdom, and the oppressive wage labor of early capitalism.

Nevertheless, Christianity in essence is not conservative. The notion that it is probably stems mainly (the historical record aside) from the fact that Christians share with conservatives a keen consciousness of the fallibility of human beings. Christians and conservatives stand on some common anthropological ground. But the consciousness of human fallibility is much keener in Christians than in conservatives, for they are skeptical of human works and arrangements that typically command deep respect among conservatives. Thus, Christians do not assume that the antiquity of institutions provides any assurance of their justice or efficacy. They realize, if they consult Christian principles, that long-standing customs and traditions embody not only the wisdom of generations but also the iniquity—in particular, the determination of dominant groups to preserve their power and privileges.

Christians are also mistrustful of aristocracies and elites. Conservatives typically commend the rule of long-ascendant minorities, those certified by the established order as the wise and noble. But Paul, addressing early Christians in Corinth, notes that "not many of you were wise according to worldly standards, not many were powerful, not many were of noble birth."[1] New Testament passages indicate that Christ had a particular concern for the despised and disinherited, the ignorant and unsophisticated. "God chose what is foolish in the world to shame the wise."[2] The attitude expressed in such passages is remote from the typical conservative reverence for minorities of inherited rank and traditional learning.

Conservatives (like radicals) commonly assume that sin can be circumvented. In the conservative view, allowing only those institutional changes that are slow and protracted and according authority to traditional elites would accomplish this. For Christians, sin is circumvented only by grace. It is certainly not circumvented by society, the form sinful men and women give to the fallen world.

But if Christians are even more pessimistic about human beings than are conservatives, how can they favor reform? How can they do anything but cling rigidly to all institutions, however unjust, that counteract the chaotic potentialities of human beings and achieve a degree of order? There are three interconnected answers to these questions.

First of all, Christian principles place one in a radical—that is, critical and adverse—relationship to established institutions. The Kingdom of God is a judgment on the existing society; the imminence of the Kingdom of God symbolizes its impermanence. Jesus was crucified because his presence and preaching were unsettling to reigning religious and political groups. Jesus did not seek the violent overthrow of these groups, but neither did he show much concern for their stability. His love revealed the chasm between community and the established order. I do not maintain that Christianity is properly revolutionary; on the contrary, I believe it is essentially antirevolutionary, and further along in this chapter, I will try to show why. But it is not, in its basic attitudes, conservative; it is more nearly radical.

The second answer to the foregoing questions is that these basic attitudes have to be acted on. This is a matter of spiritual integrity. To be opposed to the established order in principle, but in favor of keeping it exactly as it is, is an incongruity necessarily destructive of prophetic faith. Beliefs are not genuine unless they affect one's conduct as well as one's mind. To anticipate the coming of the Kingdom of God is merely sentimental, a private frivolity, unless one seeks ways of reshaping society according to the form of the imminent community. The Christian universe is not, as we have seen, an eternal and changeless order; it is a universe moving, under the impetus of the Word of God, toward radical re-creation. This does not mean that all is progress; passages in the Gospels point toward a tragic finale, a time when "nation will rise against nation, and kingdom against kingdom," when "the sun will be darkened and the moon will not give its light."[3] But God's creation is not allowed to rest, and human beings are not immobilized by the historical tragedies they may be destined to undergo. Even if the sinfulness of human beings renders every change in society dangerous and even if attempted reforms are likely to be abortive, we cannot maintain the prophetic stance while taking care that established institutions are preserved in their present form. If we fail to change in response to the coming of the Kingdom of God, our prophetic expectancy will become a mere affectation.

Finally, however, it must be said that Christianity forbids us to assume the inevitability of failure. It requires hope, and hope pertains to the immediate, as well as the eschatological, future. To take it for granted that all attempted reforms will fail would be as presumptuous as to assume that they will succeed. It is not only sinful human beings who are at work in history, Christians believe, but God as well. Need it be said that God may occasionally favor human de-

signs? Or need it be said that God's own designs may sometimes succeed through the failure of human designs? It is reasonable to be
skeptical concerning the possibilities of social transformation. But
human beings have no warrant for holding fixed opinions in this
matter, for they cannot know the kind or degree of change God intends to effect in history. And those who accept Christian principles
do know, through Christ, that all things move toward the Kingdom of
God, however humanly incomprehensible the movement may be.
Agape is not a mere idea, separate from events and powerless. In exalting individuals, it not only sets a standard of personal and political
conduct but discloses the inner meaning of all reality and the goal of
history. Hence, to practice love is to be allied with destiny and to participate in God's history. An anxious immobility would be highly
inappropriate.

As I shall try to show in the pages immediately following, the radicalism inherent in Christianity is unique. Indeed, it contains qualities that secular radicals might call conservative. Because of the hope
called forth and commanded by the imminence of the Kingdom of
God, however, Christianity cannot be conservative. To maintain the
prophetic stance is to be consciously and actively a part of the destiny that is making for the communal reunion of creation.

The uniqueness of Christian radicalism has its roots in the Christian
consciousness of sin. The conviction that we are fallen creatures dis-
tinguishes Christian politics not only from conservatism but from
secular radicalism as well. This conviction precludes trust either in
traditional institutions or in those who set out to reform them. This
does not leave Christians simply standing midway in between; faith
in the coming of the Kingdom of God sets in motion a historical advance that is not dependent on views of human nature. But even
though the doctrine of original sin does not undermine hope, it gives
a highly distinctive cast to the Christian conception of political action and social progress.

Secular conceptions of reform are typically characterized by optimistic oversimplifications and distortions. American reformers, for
example, frequently assume that human beings are both reasonable
and just and that beneficent social change is consequently easy. The
main thing necessary, after identifying a problem, is to devise and

propagate a rational solution. Poverty, crime, class conflict, war, and all other great social evils can gradually and surely be eliminated.

Such optimism was eloquently criticized a generation ago by a great Christian political thinker, Reinhold Niebuhr, but there is little evidence that we have learned from Niebuhr. If we have not, the principal reason may be that liberal falsifications of human nature and the human condition are not just accidental, easily corrected once they have been identified. They are grounded in the difficulty of recognizing simultaneously the exaltation and fallenness of man on the basis of a secular outlook. Liberal reformers are apt to be morally serious people with a genuine sense of the dignity of individuals. But within the framework of their secular views, it is difficult for them to reconcile their respect for individuals with a recognition of the pride and selfishness of individuals. They are thus led persistently to exaggerate human goodness. Trying to match their view of human nature to their belief in human dignity, they fail to see how human beings actually behave or to understand the difficulties and complexities of reform.

They do not notice, for example, that the cause of social reform summons and often strengthens certain highly dubious motives. Many reformers burn with resentment against privileged groups and against society at large, and many are sustained by an unfaltering confidence in their own discernment and righteousness. Righteous work—such as social reform—allows unrighteous motives to be disguised and to grow unchecked. For this reason, it is possible to wonder whether reformers do not on the whole display human sinfulness more fully than conservatives do. Conservatives may be more candidly selfish and cynical but are, perhaps, less pretentious, less naively and immoderately proud, and less contemptuous of those opposing them.

Nor do reformers often fully face the likelihood that their plans will in some measure fail. This is partly because they overestimate the purity of their own intentions and the wisdom of their designs and also because they are unprepared for the ingenious selfishness of those on whose cooperation and goodwill the success of their plans depends. They do not take into account the fact that every human arrangement without exception can be misused and will be, because of the selfish interests that can thus be served. They are insufficiently aware that the difficulties that invariably emerge in the pursuit of any course of action are not matters of chance but are consequences of perdurable human characteristics. Therefore, such difficulties cannot be removed by refinement of original plans or more attentive supervision of their execution.

Christians look at things from a more revealing perspective. Even God encountered major complications in carrying out his redemptive work. The Savior was crucified. This sheds light on the nature of human beings and of historical development. Creatures who can kill Christ certainly can complicate and obstruct the plans of reformers.

In summary, Christianity is not conservative; yet it embodies a realization of human wickedness that is found more often among conservatives than among reformers. How, then, can one characterize the Christian attitude toward reform? Best, perhaps, in terms of the enduring, yet arduous and inescapably equivocal, affirmation of liberty that defines the prophetic stance. At this point in the essay, however, liberty is understood as positive—as liberty that demands continually to be enlarged. Hence the goal of liberation. These terms, I believe, provide access to a more realistic and balanced conception of social transformation than is found in typical writings on reform.

As we have already seen, Christianity alerts us to the certainty that liberty will be abused. In this way, it makes us realize that liberty must be limited; it is inevitably accompanied by coercion. Hence the emphasis, in the chapter on liberty, on the onerous and equivocal character of prophetic liberality. Such qualifications become sharper when we turn to positive liberty. For liberty to be richer and more real than mere legal liberty, and for it to belong to all members of society, is for it to be more dangerous. True, there is room for all individuals to work out, in their own lives, the meaning of human existence; but there is also room for the debasement of an entire society, as is demonstrated by much of popular culture in the Western democracies. Moreover, positive liberty solidifies the connection between liberty and coercion, for positive liberty does not merely lead to coercion as a corrective when liberty is abused; it is attained by coercion (the government frees workers from unsafe working conditions, for example, by coercing employers). Often, the liberty gained is clearly worth the price paid in coercion. Still, as positive liberty grows, so must the coercive activities of the government. This is why, where the aim is total liberation, the result is often despotism.

The difficulty of the prophetic stance, particularly in its liberality, can now be fully seen. Although leaving people free is an essential aspect of waiting for God in history, it is not a simple undertaking; those left free are fallen beings. When we seek not merely to leave them free but to make them freer, and to assure that all are equally free, we take up a task infested with complexities and dilemmas.

The qualified ideal of social transformation that emerges from Christianity is particularly congruent with the concept of justice developed earlier in this essay. *Un*qualified ideals of social transformation have often been inspired by visions of perfect justice. As I have argued, however, such visions are oblivious of our fallen nature and condition; our proper aim is the elimination of particular injustices, not the creation of perfect justice. Our aim, in other words, should be to increase the number of liberties we possess and the number of people who possess them. Such an aim does not encourage complacency, for there can be no end to the ways in which liberty can be enlarged, no end to the injustices that call for action. It is a relatively modest aim, however, for it contains no image of an earthly paradise. This is what recommends it.

Tocqueville commended Christianity for tending to make the imagination of a people "circumspect and undecided" and "its impulses . . . checked and its works unfinished."[4] This expresses well the spirit of reform inherent in Christian principles. Christianity is in a true sense radical, but it is also hesitant. Partly, of course, this is simply because it checks our self-assurance. There are complexities, difficulties, limits, and occasional tragedies involved in efforts at social transformation. Caution and repeated consideration of actions being taken are in order. But Christian hesitancy has deeper grounds than prudence and more compelling motives than wariness of possible blunders. Hesitation is expressive of the posture of waiting for God in history, which is the essence of the prophetic stance. Waiting, as we have seen, is not the contrary of action but a preface and approach to action; hence, it belongs to the work of social transformation. Recent decades have seen heroic political commitments, but hesitation has been evident mainly in the service of self-interest (for example, when vested interests have imposed checks on governmental action). The idea of prophetic hope, however, indicates that hesitation should have a part in our most conscientious deeds. It is a recognition not only of our finitude and fallibility but also of others who are present with us in history. Christianity calls upon us to hesitate before human beings and before God.

Communal Liberation and the Will of God

Hesitation before human beings is for the purpose of listening and, perhaps, speaking. It is communality. The aim of reform is community, and Christian hesitancy is an effort to lessen the difference between action and communication, thus forestalling the conflict between means and ends that has been so fatal to modern revolutions. Pausing in the midst of action to listen and speak means remembering that human beings have a worth that is not measured by their utility and that the end we seek in action is the end we seek also in communication—sharing the truth with all men and women.

Communication is of the greatest urgency in changing society. Justice is not a prerequisite of community, as Marxism implies. The reverse is the case. How can we know what needs to be done unless those who suffer from injustice can speak and be heard? There have, of course, been many reformers, typified by Lenin, who have thought that they themselves comprehended quite clearly the nature of existing injustices and the actions needed to correct them; communication was unnecessary. But such an attitude betrays an arrogance that, as experience amply demonstrates, in action becomes despotic. Thus, community is not merely an ultimate ideal but also an immediate necessity.

This pertains particularly to the outcast and oppressed. Of all the injustices they suffer, the most degrading and destructive is that they are not seriously listened to. There is no more radical denial of the humanity of any group than the refusal of attention. Nor is there a more effective way of rendering social wrongs irremediable than by denying those subjected to them the opportunity and ability to speak.

The imperative of communication, however, applies not only to the oppressed but also to the oppressors, who ordinarily inspire so destructive a self-righteousness among reformers that the reformers are unwilling to extend them the courtesies of common discourse.

The imperative of communication applies, indeed, to all of the interests engaged by any measure of reform. Briefly, to recommend communal hesitancy is to recommend persuasion. Insofar as possible, political action should be carried on through persuasion rather than manipulation, legislation (a form of coercion), or violence. This is not because persuasion, even of the most rational kind, is not a form of power. It is, as we have already seen; it is a way of pursuing preconceived ends and inducing others to support those ends. But persuasion is power mixed with communality, action restrained by the conditions inherent in dialogue. Persuasive power is far more deserving of commendation than is nonviolent power. To refrain from violence and employ demonstrations and other political tactics common among practitioners of nonviolence does not necessarily express respect for one's opponents; to listen and speak with them, however, does, for it means treating them as reasoning beings and as persons.

To engage in persuasion, of course, is often impossible. Even where there is little violence and the air is filled with words, as in many industrialized societies today, it may be that no one is speaking reasonably and no one is willing to listen. Hence, manipulation, legal coercion, and violence (let us call these "force") sometimes seem unavoidable. When is force justified? As we have already seen, there are no unequivocal answers to this question. Contemplating the use of force places one in a boundary situation—before the freedom that demands respect and the evil that demands the curbing of freedom. No clear rules can apply. One must await the sense of necessity that for a Christian is the sense of destiny, or the will of God. One must "appeal to heaven." But this does not signify that the standard of communality, or persuasion, has been abandoned. The aim of force is not to achieve justice, or community, or any such final end. It is rather to make persuasion possible. Force can never be justified unless the ultimate intention is to create a situation in which dialogue can occur. And those engaged in the manipulative, legislative, and violent activities connected with social change can never know whether such a situation has been created except by pausing frequently to listen—by hesitating.

Persuasion minimizes the evils of action—unthinking assurance of one's own wisdom and virtue and unwillingness to consider others except as means to one's own ends. To listen to others and to speak to them in circumstances that permit them to respond freely—hence, perhaps, in ways violating one's own preconceptions—require a degree of humility. They also make it necessary to remember that others are beings like oneself.

One reason Marxism is almost always disastrous in practice, in spite of the truth it contains, is that it logically precludes persuasion. The views of opponents of social change, it is held, result from economic and social conditions and cannot in any significant measure be changed unless those conditions are changed. Hence, efforts at persuasion are in most circumstances quixotic. Only *after* the transformation of society can there be an appeal to reason. But once society has been transformed, reason will have lost its greatest function, that of helping human beings find their way together through history. One of the chief failures of liberation theology lies in its neglect of this issue. Liberation theologians ordinarily claim to use Marxism only as a technique of social analysis and not as an overall interpretation of human life. But in forbearing to challenge the Marxist emphasis on the conditioned character of human intelligence and communication, they leave standing a highly destructive political doctrine. Moreover, they are inattentive to what is surely one of the major presuppositions of Christian faith, that human minds and conduct are determined, beyond all else, by God, the Holy Spirit, who can be present within and work through human dialogue. This points to the other dimension of Christian hesitancy.

To hesitate before human beings is only a way of hesitating before God. At least, this is true where hesitancy is based on Christian principles and is lucid and entirely serious. When human beings listen and speak, they search for God's truth; and they do this in the company of creatures made worthy in Christ for finding and knowing God's truth. Community is inquiry, and the object of inquiry is our destiny. Inquiry that is worthy of being called dialogue is an effort to clarify in common the meaning of our lives and the requirements God and our destiny place on us. It is obvious that political speech is not often so serious. But the standard is not wholly unrealistic. To read some of the greatest speeches of Lincoln, for example, is to become aware of a leader standing at once in the presence of human beings and of God.

Hesitating before God, however, has for Christians a particular purpose: to discover God's will, which defines our common destiny and is the highest standard of political action. Moreover, political and moral rules are of less value than many conscientious people suppose, failing perfectly to fit even ordinary situtations, to say nothing of the boundary situations in which politics is often carried on. Moral rules derive their authority from God. Those who deny this, I think, always accord the supreme rules themselves a tacitly religious weight and authority. So at last we—or Christians, at any rate—must always ask ourselves what God commands, and since God does not speak to us in audible words, we can rarely be sure. Hence the need for frequently reexamining our minds and our circumstances—for hesitating.

If it were not for the will of God, if God were not engaged in human history, then—from the Christian perspective—our fallenness would make our lives hopeless. The two great poles of the Christian universe are human beings in their sin and God in his mercy. These are not unrelated. We can act, and must, because God is not indifferent to human affairs, nor is he unable to counteract our misdeeds and failures. Destiny, therefore, is not subject to disruption by human foolishness and malice, and hesitation is not merely a matter of worldly prudence. Christians—and all others who act with a sense that history is informed with the Logos Christians see in Jesus—hesitate because they are acting before the sovereign of all being and under the command of destiny. They repeatedly ask whether they are doing the things destiny requires that they do. Knowing they are finite, they are ready to encounter limits. When they do, they ask what their limits tell them not only about the worldly conditions they are dealing with but also about the ultimate meaning of creation and the moral necessities facing them.

The Christian doctrine of human sinfulness does not enable us to know in advance just where our limits will be found to lie. No definable boundaries of social transformation can be inferred from the principle that we are fallen beings. Socialism, for example, cannot be ruled to be forever incompatible with what we know of human nature. We are not acquainted with God's historical intentions. We cannot know what God intends to accomplish in spite of human failures; nor can we know how far God intends, within and through history, to change human nature. Prophetic hope must be absolutely open because it is based on the faith that God is absolutely powerful and good. Such, at any rate, are the implications of Christian faith.

The doctrine of the fall disallows political presumption rather than any particular historical hopes. It is presumption when people deny or ignore the evil in human nature and assume that everything we assiduously strive for in history can unquestionably be gained. Christians may properly play the role of political skeptics. When the hearts of human beings are lifted up by confidence in their plans and calculable prospects, it is proper for Christians to call attention to human failings and to the historical limitations they may entail. Christians should be a sobering presence in the political world. Reinhold Niebuhr sets an admirable example. The symbol of original sin was used by Niebuhr to temper the potentially murderous naïveté and pride of political man.

If Christians are the salt of the earth, however, their political role cannot be that of spreading discouragement and rendering life unsavory. Hopelessness is as sinful—and, indeed, as presumptuous—as pride, and Christianity does not recommend historical dejection or political lassitude. It does, however, call for something extremely difficult; so far as our uncertain insights and unsteady moods allow, we must follow the leadership of God in history. This means forsaking the posture of command and replacing it by one of receptivity. It entails the harsh discipline of waiting—of conquering impatience and remembering that political plans always in some measure fail and that they often, in proportion to their scope and the assurance with which they are undertaken, flatly contradict the ends intended. We can act righteously only if we are capable of waiting, and in that sense waiting has priority over action. The prophetic stance is an ideal of taking full cognizance of our common worldly circumstances, being mindful of both our limitations and our responsibilities, and in that frame of mind waiting for God.

We recognize the priority of waiting when we hesitate before acting. We thus take time to remember our finitude and sinfulness and to remind ourselves that the initiative does not belong to human beings. Hesitation is a formality required of us when we cross the frontier between waiting and action; it is also a formality that in the midst of action we occasionally pause and repeat. Like all significant formalities, it is a mark of respect—for God and the creatures with whom we share the earth. And it expresses humility: there are values and realities beyond our understanding and control.

The greatest failure of liberation theologians is their inattention to the two poles of the Christian universe. They pay little heed to human sin or the political role of divine grace. Their call for action is compelling, based as it is on the Christian ethic of love and the Christian faith in the coming of the Kingdom of God. But they habitually speak of action as though it were carried out by beings who, on the whole, are humane and wise. They are victims of the same illusion that fatally handicaps secular revolutionaries. As a result, they neglect the only reality that can overcome the consequences of human sin—the will of God, working through the will of men and women who are attentive, and working in spite of the indifference and opposition of all others.

When sin and grace are neglected, social reform is misunderstood. Sin is equated with personal and social derangements of the kind human beings can comprehend and correct. Liberation and redemption become the same. It is not seen that social and political changes in themselves are insignificant—that only spiritual changes are significant and that spiritual changes come only with the eradication of sin and therefore are beyond human powers. It is not seen, in short, that being unable to bestow redemption, we cannot do anything for others that is of ultimate importance. Although liberation is commanded by *agape* and pursuing it is essential to our spiritual integrity, it would be of no benefit to others were it not the human work that accompanies divine work. Liberation is the task human beings are allowed and commanded to undertake in connection with the divine task of redemption. Thus, political action is significant only through grace. If this is ignored, either social reform is confused with redemption, giving rise to revolutionary arrogance, or it is dismissed as meaningless.

It hardly needs saying that the radicalism of Christianity is very different from the radicalism of twentieth-century revolutionaries. To see more fully why and in what ways this is so, however, can shed further light on the Christian view of social change and on the nature of prophetic hope.

Revolution

However divergent from the attitudes of secular revolutionaries, Christianity has a revolutionary flavor. This is owing primarily to the idea of the exalted individual. The faith that God has given every individual a worth beyond human measurement is socially explosive. It does not merely condemn manifest injustices. It questions all inequalities of wealth, rank, and power. These, perhaps, can be defended as necessary to the efficient functioning of society and as just if they are proportional to merit. But Christianity is not concerned primarily with social necessity, and *agape* casts doubt on the significance of merit. The image of the individual in the setting of eternity renders the defects of the social order painfully conspicuous and makes even the perfections of the social order unimpressive.

There can be little doubt that the Christian evaluation of the individual is at the origins of the modern revolutionary temper, in spite of the typical hostility of revolutionaries toward Christianity. When Christianity first began, scarcely anyone was revolutionary in the modern sense of the term; and the orientation of Christians was eschatological rather than historical. But a worried awareness of the insurrectionary forces latent in Christianity can be seen in Paul's insistence on unqualified obedience to governments; and when the idea of revolution began to develop in modern times, it happened first among Christian thinkers. True, by the time the modern revolutionary creed had reached its full Promethean proportions, Christian faith had grown dim in many minds, and Christians were often on the side of the established order. But the ancient idea of the exalted individual lingered, an antique memory, in a self-confident and irreligious world. The memory has been powerfully influential. Nothing is more important in explaining the modern revolutionary ethos than the conviction, lacking almost altogether in antiquity, that ordinary men and women without exception are as important as noblemen and kings.

The revolutionary flavor of Christianity is enhanced by the communal and eschatological dimensions of the idea of the exalted individual. The Christian imagination is paradisiacal. There is a habit of mind, particularly entrenched in modern bourgeois society, that is oblivious of paradise as a possibility or even a fantasy. Practicality and convenience are the supreme standards. That is not a habit of mind much encouraged in the Bible. Both the Old and New Testaments envision "new heavens and a new earth," and in a famous passage in the Revelation to John, God says to a group of professed Christians, "Because you are lukewarm, and neither cold nor hot, I will spew you out of my mouth."[5] The concept of *agape* lends the paradisiacal imagination a peculiar precision and power. It defines perfection in human relationships without compromising in the slightest degree with worldly possibilities, and it implicitly prescribes the extension of such relationships over the whole earth. This radical communality is central in Christian faith. Not only Jesus' message but his life might be summarized in terms of *agape* and the destined reign of *agape* in the Kingdom of God.

To the moral judgment on society, moreover, Christianity adds something surprisingly unsettling: all societies are impermanent. They are condemned not only by the paradisiacal standards inherent in *agape* but also by the passage of time, in which is hidden our destiny. Societies are awesome because they seem immortal; but they are shaken if the impression that they will last forever is destroyed. One of the main reasons for Marx's immense historical impact is that he so forcefully depicted bourgeois societies, apparently so prosperous and flourishing, as passing phenomena. In this way, he deprived them, so to speak, of ontological authority. Christianity does the same thing, although in a different way. History is a drama of divine wrath and mercy, in the Christian vision. Not only are all societies eroded continually by time; finally, all history will end in an annihilating manifestation of God's sovereignty and goodness. Jesus' proclamation of the Kingdom of God struck no less decisively than Marx's communism at the stability of established societies. This is reflected in the charge against Jesus at his trial—that he had forecast the destruction of the Jewish temple in Jerusalem.

The basic distinction between Christian radicalism and the radicalism of twentieth-century revolutionaries is not, as so often supposed, that Christianity provides "pie in the sky"—an eternal happiness rendering earthly happiness, and the social changes calculated to procure it, unimportant. Christianity does point toward eternal happiness and, no doubt, thus makes earthly unhappiness bearable. But it does not make the imposition of earthly unhappiness on others, or even unprotesting acquiescence in the earthly unhappiness of others, morally acceptable, for such acts imply the absence of faith and love. A Christian feels bound to obey the commands of *agape*, and accordingly to seek the well-being of others and the social changes such well-being requires, because those are the commands of God, and not because failing to obey them would inflict irremediable suffering. Since nothing is irremediable for God, one person cannot do another person any ultimate harm, and the political attitudes of some cannot affect the ultimate well-being of others. But that does not make it a matter of moral indifference how others are treated. The respect owed every human being is grounded in divine *agape* and calls for opposition to every institution that treats human beings neglectfully and oppressively. In this sense, "pie in the sky" does not nullify but rather underlies and supports Christian radicalism.

Christian prophetic hope is set apart from modern revolutionary hope simply by the unwillingness of Christians to accept the revolutionary view of human nature. The vitality of twentieth-century revolutionaries arises from their confidence in human power and goodness. Our limitations and faults, they assume, are due to social influences and can therefore be erased by social changes—by revolution. The vicious circle suggested by such reasoning—that the qualities needed for a successful revolution will be produced by a successful revolution—is broken by the concept of a revolutionary vanguard, a working class or intellectual elite. The vanguard is the natural product of historical evolution. Members of the vanguard are distinguished from the masses and from earlier elites not so much by their goodness, in the traditional sense of the term, as by their possession of a science of history. They know objectively and surely what history allows and requires. It is assumed, in Hellenic fashion, that their knowledge will determine their conduct. Hence, through their leadership, society will be recast as community, and pride and selfishness and the injustices these create will disappear. In the writings of Marx, this is said more often indirectly than explicitly, and much of what is said explicitly is presented in the guise of science. In this way, the magnitude of the trust placed in man is concealed. There is little exaggeration, however, in saying that human beings are raised implicitly to the status of gods. Now, instead of the individual exalted by God, we have the human race, or a representative portion of it, exalted by human understanding and power. The self-conception of modern revolutionaries is an uncompromising affirmation of the man-god.

It is easy enough for people of common sense to see the qualities in human nature that revolutionaries neglect—the finitude, or historical immanence, that makes sweeping programs of social reconstruc-

tion impracticable and also the selfishness that affects both the build-
ers and the inhabitants of any new society. How can the theorists and
makers of revolution have been so blind?

Of course, there is scarcely any flattering illusion about ourselves
that our pride will not entertain, and pride has probably become less
restrained with the decline of religious faith. Under pressure from
the need Dostoevsky noted, that of worshiping something, we have
become increasingly inclined to worship ourselves. Nevertheless,
reasons play a role; and among the reasons inducing men and women
to exalt themselves to positions of historical sovereignty, perhaps
none are more important than those embodied in the idea of a science of society.

The full reality and the implications of our finitude are concealed
from us by what has become with many people today an unques-
tioned assumption—that we can understand society objectively and
comprehensively. Society is supposedly an organized totality, a "system," accessible in its entirety to observation, objective description,
and—in principle, at least—scientific understanding. Through such
commonplaces, elaborated in countless different ways, we entertain
the fantasy that we can sooner or later overcome the consequences of
our finitude and thus of our historical immanence; we can control
the future. The Marxist conception of social science admittedly is
distinctive. It has played a crucial role, nonetheless, in arousing the
aggressive self-confidence characterstic of contemporary revolutionaries, practically all of them Marxists.

Our consciousness of sin likewise has been enfeebled by the faith
in objective knowledge. Sin can supposedly, like all other human
phenomena, be scientifically understood; and since it can be understood, it can also, through psychotherapy or social reform, be controlled and eradicated. I have already shown that in thinking this
way, we are no longer thinking of sin. This is not realized, however,
in an age so powerfully influenced by social science. It is taken for
granted that all disruptive qualities in human character can be brought
under rational control. Again, although Marxists have expressed this
faith in distinctive ways, without it they could hardly have had the
self-assurance that has made them such formidable revolutionaries.

It is not only a consciousness of finitude and sin, however, that separates the prophetic attitude from modern revolutionary attitudes.
Missing from the latter is the exalted individual. This may seem para-

doxical, since modern revolutionaries not only exalt man as a social and historical engineer but also, as I have noted earlier, are moved by a real concern for ordinary individuals. The ghost of the exalted individual lingers in their minds. That it is only a ghost that lingers, however, is quite understandable, since the individual is and can be exalted—Christians believe—only by God, by an eternal destiny that revolutionary leaders do not have it in their power to bestow. Hence, in denying God and assuming divine prerogatives themselves, they necessarily, however compassionate and noble in character they may be, rob individuals of their grandeur.

Here, we approach the irony of modern revolutions—that they simultaneously affirm and grossly violate human dignity. Devoted ostensibly to liberation, they produce enslavement. The self-exaltation of revolutionaries is morally destructive. It blinds them not only to their own limitations and defects but to the destiny that originates in a being who overshadows us all. Revolutionary leaders have illustrated on a vast historical canvas the truth of Jesus' declaration that "every one who exalts himself will be humbled."[6] They have been humbled by their flagrant failures. Indeed, whole societies and perhaps all modern peoples—all of us alike, represented in our worldliness and self-confidence by the revolutionary leaders—have been humbled by the degradation that revolution has almost everywhere brought.

One of the starkest signs of this degradation is despotism. Revolution time after time crushes liberty. Nothing shows more clearly the absence of the idea of the exalted individual. Lacking a principled consciousness of the dignity of persons, revolutionary leaders necessarily also lack an understanding of community and of the dependence of community on liberty. Efforts to create community therefore bring into being, instead of community, monolithic societies. Presiding over these societies are revolutionary despots.

Willful and domineering rather than expectant, these despots maintain a stance that is the polar opposite of the prophetic stance. The mystery of personal destiny disappears in plans of action. And even the future—which, as a genuine future, is not embodied in present plans but is truly new—is excluded from their vision.

A major boundary marker between revolutionary will and prophetic hope is the ideal of negative liberty, or constitutionalism. Twentieth-century revolutionary leaders and their many admirers in Western societies take it for granted that such liberty must often, must perhaps normally, be sacrificed for the sake of social change. Christians will rarely, if ever, be willing for that to happen.

The concept of liberty provides another way of defining the hesitancy that characterizes Christian radicalism. The great truth underlying prophetic politics is the exalted individual. Before this truth, originating in transcendence, human beings in their fallenness are bound to pause. How can we understand and do justice to the mysterious glory of a human being? Politics that is free of revolutionary arrogance must be carried on in fear and trembling. It is quite true, as I have taken care to bring out, that negative liberty is not the whole of liberty. But without it, the rest of liberty, positive liberty, is probably impossible. The arbitrary and totalitarian revolutionary regimes of our time are evidence that negative (or initial) liberty is indispensable for positive liberty to come into existence. Where constitutionalism is discarded or not established, liberation turns into a process of governmental enslavement; liberation does not occur.

Dostoevsky issued a prophetic warning when he said that revolutionaries in times to come would write on their banner, "Feed men, and then ask of them virtue!"[7] For Dostoevsky, "feeding men" meant carrying out the basic, often brutal, reorganizational work of revolution. "Virtue" meant, among other things, liberty; and liberty, for Dostoevsky, was unquestionably liberty against government (although he was concerned with other kinds of liberty, too)—the liberty of which the totalitarian Grand Inquisitor had relieved his human-animal subjects. The maxim against which Dostoevsky warned was thus the one proclaimed in various ways by innumerable revolutionaries since his day: Let the bloody tasks of revolution be done without moral compunction or political restraint—without hesitancy. Only when those tasks have been completed can men live in liberty. Dostoevsky voices the prophetic attitude. Respect for individuals is not something we can set aside and take up again as historical expediency dictates. It is a matter of our humanity before God. And one of its elemental requirements is the protection of liberty against its most formidable enemy, government.

Many will argue that if negative liberty is made so nearly absolute, liberation will never occur. Efforts at significant change always encounter resistance from powerful groups. How can such efforts succeed if the liberty of all—even those highly organized in opposition to social transformation—must be resolutely respected? There is no simple and conclusive answer to this question. We must recognize that the ideal of social transformation presents dilemmas that no one, of any party or persuasion, has resolved. The character of most present-day revolutionary regimes, however, shows that throwing liberty aside for the sake of revolutionary reconstruction can be ruinous. It opens the doors to the political monsters foreseen by Dostoevsky. On the other hand, it cannot be said that constitutional restraints altogether block social transformation. In the course of this century, the Western constitutional democracies have accomplished changes that are deep and significant even though not as sweeping as many reformers rightly desire. It can be argued, indeed, that they have accomplished changes no less fundamental than those carried out in the revolutionary nations. Are the differences between present-day and Edwardian Britain slight in comparison with those between the Soviet and czarist regimes?

Having reflected on the prophetic attitude toward social change, we must examine some of the conditions that—to many, at least—cry out for change.

Inequality and Minority Rule

The human race is going through what we might call "an ordeal of equalization." It began, if exact dates can be assigned to events so large, with the eruption of the French Revolution in 1789. The idea of equality had, of course, been implanted in the Western mind much earlier. The seeds were sown not only by Christianity but also by Stoicism, in which, even before the time of Christ, it was maintained that all human beings possess a rational capacity for discerning the moral law and in that decisive respect are equal. Only in modern times, however, has equality come to seem a practical possibility. Vivified by the sense that no longer are there insuperable material obstacles in the way of equality, the idea has become an imperious demand. Since 1789, multitudes that have been silent and acquiescent for thousands of years have in every civilization become conscious, vocal, and inclined toward violence.

Equalization has been an ordeal because of the great—so far, insurmountable—difficulties it has involved. It has brought violence, since the privileged and powerful are rarely willing to accept equality peacefully. It has presented intractable moral dilemmas, a familiar example being the extent to which, when people are chosen for public office, places in selective universities, and so forth, ability can legitimately be ignored in behalf of equality. Further, where equalization has occurred, it has had extremely injurious side effects, such as uniformity of manners and vulgarity of taste. And finally, equalization has not occurred to the degree that appearances suggest. In America and Western Europe, although the general population has attained a standard of living once enjoyed by only a few, that is due more to expanding production than to equalization, and wealthy and powerful minorities remain securely in place.

Does Christianity, with its principled but so far imperfectly practiced egalitarianism, provide any help in understanding our plight? I think that it does. For one thing, it can make us more realistic and thus help us to understand why equalization is so difficult.

For example, the doctrine of original sin indicates that inequality is a structural necessity of the social order. It is one of the evils reflecting our fallenness and the consequent necessity of creating and inhabiting societies. Primarily because of the disorderly character of human impulses and aims, order is not spontaneous but artificial—dependent on artifice. Some must have power and authority; there must be government. And to reinforce government, probably some must have greater wealth and higher standing in society than others. These are rather obvious points but surprisingly often are ignored. It is forgotten that efforts at equalization are apt to fall afoul of social necessity.

Moreover, people are actually unequal. They are unequal in emotional balance, intelligence, beauty, health, and every other measurable characteristic. Conventional and natural inequalities, of course, never correspond perfectly and often do not correspond even roughly. Natural inequalities nevertheless place serious obstacles in the way of equalization. Christianity helps us to see this, not by taking visible inequalities very seriously but by insisting that the source of equality is something invisible and immeasurable—the creative and redemptive power of God. In this way, without denying that many personal inequalities are social in source, it deflects the sentimental tendency of secular liberals to obscure or ignore the persistent and perhaps inalterable inequalities that are so embarrassing to their social aims. It frees us to see people, in their empirical nature, as they are.

Finally, the Christian consciousness of sin can bring home to us a crucial but little-noted fact about the ideal of equality: that few are fully committed to it. Creatures who are often passionately proud yet are liable, when defeated in their pride, to fall into despairing efforts to forget themselves through unthinking busyness, sensuous enjoyment, or some other form of voluntary enslavement cannot be wholehearted supporters of equality. They wish to be masters; and strangely enough, if they cannot be masters, they would often rather be slaves than comrades. A stable state of equality is hard, and perhaps impossible to attain.

Since equalization collides not only with the inequalities inherent in society and human nature but also with an aversion to equality that arises from the depths of sin, progress toward equality depends on the determination and often ruthlessness of its proponents. The consequence is that those fighting for equality themselves become a new ruling class, destroying equality in the very act of establishing it. It is not only where Communists have come to power that this has happened. It has happened, although more subtly and humanely, in bourgeois societies as well. The middle-class groups that were disadvantaged and revolutionary in 1789 became dominant and conservative. The lower classes have not strenuously resisted; this is illustrated by the spontaneous development everywhere of the "trade-union consciousness"—the contentment with wage increases and shorter hours—that Lenin deplored. The populace has shown more interest in the pleasures and distractions of industrial abundance than in governing.

Egalitarianism that is not a product of envy and pride is an acknowledgement of the dignity of persons. It is an expression of love and is thus a kind of goodness. It is naturally rare.

Christianity does not merely help identify the difficulties underlying the ordeal of equalization but also helps meet them. Christian egalitarianism is less vulnerable to discouragement than the egalitarianism of more worldly and pragmatic creeds.

This in part is because equality for Christians is not a counsel of prudence, at the mercy of worldly conditions, but a command of God. It originates in *agape,* and *agape* calls for a certain neglect of worldly conditions. Our obligations are not decided by the structural necessities of society or the varying abilities and virtues that people display—although these cannot be ignored. One standard in all circum-.. stances is supreme, and that is the love with which God in Christ has dignified every human being. A Christian might conclude that a considerable measure of equality must be sought regardless of its practicality by worldly standards. Contrast this attitude with the attitude of Marx, as impassioned an advocate of equality as one can readily find on the secular side. For Marx, the inequalities of the capitalist system were evil because, in the natural progress of history, they were increasingly inefficient and disruptive. As keen and genuine as was the moral indignation that these inequalities provoked in Marx, his condemnation of them was not moral but pragmatic. Where does this leave Marxists if it transpires—as many intelligent observers, of course, hold that it already has—that inequality (such as that inherent in a free market) is far more efficient economically than equality? Of course, Christians, too, must face such questions, but not without rich resources for responding to them.

The standards of Christian politics are prophetic, not merely moral. Equality lies in our destiny. The standard of equality may be at odds with present conditions, but it conforms with the innermost order of human life and history. God's commands are not in the nature of exhortations that may turn out to be ineffectual; they reveal the intentions of one whose power is not limited. It must be granted, and indeed emphasized, that these considerations do not justify a dogmatic egalitarianism, blind to circumstances and deaf to objections. Because we are finite and fallen creatures, it would be inappropriate for us to act as though we did not live within the world; and it would be wrong for us to act as though destiny commanded that all social relations immediately be equalized. The rule of hesitation applies to equalization, as to all other social changes. But the link between *agape* and equality cannot be severed, and as long as we keep ourselves free of self-righteousness and resentment, we can in good heart press toward realizing the egalitarian implications of *agape,* knowing that such action is not only required of us morally but is sustained by the destiny that defines God's history.

Christian egalitarianism has deep foundations in the doctrine of God. This must be emphasized because, just as the power of God has seemed to sanction the power of human rulers (a matter discussed in the preceding chapter), so the supremacy of God has seemed to sanction human inequality in general. God is exalted, and rich, and powerful; human beings are lowly, and poor, and weak. Should not people who view things in this fashion organize society along analogous lines, distinguishing sharply between aristocrats and commoners, employers and workers, rich and poor? This parallel has sometimes seemed plausible to Christians themselves; it is nevertheless misleading.

For one thing, the logic is defective. As noted in our discussion of liberty, from the principle that God rules absolutely over men it does not follow that men rightfully rule absolutely over one another. Likewise, it cannot be inferred from the incomparable honor, splendor, and riches of the household of God that some human households should be set off from others by such distinctions. It is true that human rank and hierarchy are taken for granted in the New Testament; there is no call for rebellion. As we have seen, however, the rich and honorable are accorded scant respect, and this is precisely because of the ascendancy of God, who infinitely transcends all human beings alike and is not respectful of human rank or riches. Luke writes that God "has scattered the proud in the imagination of their hearts" and "has put down the mighty from their thrones, and exalted those of low degree."[8] The inequality prevailing between God and human beings seems to condemn, not sanction, inequalities among human beings.

And not only is the logic defective in a justification for social inequality that is derived from divine-human inequality; so is the premise. The picture of God as high and ascendant conforms very imperfectly with the Christian concept of God. As defined in the doctrine of reconciliation, God as Father is exalted, rich, and powerful but as Son became lowly, poor, and weak. God not only became incarnate in a human being but in a man who was homeless and impoverished, friendly with marginal and dispossessed people, and finally humiliated and executed as a criminal. Rather than being a ruler, he was subject to rulers—specifically and fatally to the emperor Tiberius and his procurator in Judea, Pontius Pilate. God is not dethroned, but his royalty is decidedly ambiguous. Without abandoning his divine glory, he became fully human; and without loss to his human nobility, he became poor and powerless. The ideal of equality could hardly have deeper roots, for Christians, than it has in the doctrine of reconciliation.

The conclusion seems inescapable. Prophetic hope is egalitarian. Maintaining the prophetic stance entails an obligation, not to pretend that obstacles to equality are slight, but to strive against those obstacles, looking constantly for ways of overcoming them. Racial inequalities are illustrative.

Anyone with a sense of our fallenness must admit that racial discrimination may be partially irremediable. Racial differences provide terribly convenient leverage for pride; the very irrelevance of those differences contributes to their convenience. Since racial discrimination is rationally indefensible, those who support it are not encumbered by any need for rational defenses. They free themselves from reason right at the outset. Thus, racism offers ascendency to those with little reasonable claim to it and will probably always appeal to many people. Christianity helps us to see unpleasant realities of this kind. Moreover, it helps us to see them without self-righteousness, asking us, in the words of Paul, "You then who teach others, will you not teach yourself?" It reminds us that the impulses we are contending against are probably not confined altogether to our political opponents. But it does not allow us to stop contending against them. Resignation and inaction are absolutely condemned, for nothing could be a grimmer contradiction of God's *agape* than the notion that it exalted not all of us together but a particular race.

Inequalities of power are like inequalities of wealth and social standing. Some can be erased, but not all. Christian realism tells us that some are so implicated in the structural necessities of society that they will presumably persist throughout history. And it tells us that power appeals so irresistibly to pride that rulers will, as long as the need for rulers endures, strive for more power than their duties require. Christian realism also offers uncomfortable insights into the normal results of taking power from minorities and giving it to majorities. Where majorities reign, powerful and dominating minorities do not disappear. Rather, they become servile and irresponsible; this is recognized in the pejorative use of the word *politician*. And they learn secret ways of gaining privilege and wielding influence, thus undermining authenticity and morale in public life.

Christianity nevertheless implies democracy. It would be easy to object that Christianity seems always to take its political colors from its times, being monarchical in monarchical ages, capitalistic in the era of capitalism, and now, when democracy is the prevailing standard, being democratic. History seems to show not only an embarrassing adaptability on the part of Christians; it also suggests that Christianity is basically neutral—that it implies no particular standard of government. This objection, however, leaves out of account *agape* and the exalted individual.

These standards make it impossible to regard democracy as merely one among several equally legitimate political forms. It is the only political form based on the idea of equality. It prescribes equality of power. Needless to say, there cannot be equality of power; if there were, there would be no government. But the ideal can be approached, and Christians must always be considering and testing possibilities of transferring power from the few to the many. A skeptic might ask why it took so long to discover the connection between Christianity and democracy. The answer, I think, is simply that we do not bring to light the meaning of Christ for human life merely by drawing logical inferences from revelation but also by living in history. Christians must learn from their times and often must learn from people who are not Christians. The present democratic age, for all of its turmoil and degradation, has much to tell Christians about the meaning of their faith.

It is difficult to argue the egalitarian implications of Christianity without touching on the doctrine of predestination, which appears to be ferociously inegalitarian. Does not the notion that by an eternal decree of God some are destined for heaven and some for hell imply that there are two great ranks of human beings, separated by a distance more vast and untraversable than any gap between ranks within human society? Such a question can hardly be answered in a page or two. But a few brief comments may clarify the issue involved.

I have already noted the terrible dignity implied in the idea of someone's being eternally damned. God does not damn animals, we assume, because God does not take them seriously enough (which does not mean he is indifferent to them). He takes human beings seriously, however, and not merely as a species but in every particular representative of the species. A human being is not a replaceable embodiment of a type but a destiny. Hence his dignity—a dignity not denied by the particular concept of destiny embodied in the doctrine of predestination. This doctrine differentiates radically among destinies; it does not, however, assert that any human beings are beyond the scope of God's concern—bereft of destinies. To have been appointed by God to eternal suffering is a far more real, if more appalling, dignity than any possessed by even the most highly developed animal.

There is a question, however, whether the doctrine of predestination, at least in its starkest forms, really belongs in Christian theology. Some of its force lies in the fact that it explains, or at least helps make acceptable, an incongruity that for some is a serious obstacle to faith: the coexistence of God and evil. How can God be omnipotent and good and allow some not only to suffer but, assuming hell, to suffer eternally? The answer given in the doctrine of predestination—if it be an answer—is simply that God in his incomprehensible majesty (far transcending ordinary human conceptions of good) has decreed that this should be so. God's power is limitless and his goodness beyond our understanding. The economy of salvation is thus rendered logical, and God is enfolded in a terrifying glory.

The great drawback of the doctrine is that the love of God for humanity is tacitly denied. Thus is lost the central tenet, many would say, of Christian faith. One may bow before the appalling mystery of a Creator who dooms many or most of his creatures to an eternity of unavailing torment. One cannot, however, any longer say with John that God is love.

The latter tenet of faith, many Christians feel, must be retained at all costs, and can be retained. Thus, Berdyaev asserts that hell indeed exists but is not everlasting. Barth—a Calvinist—argues that God elects some and rejects others but does not in this way establish eternally changeless categories. We must be open to the possibility, Barth suggests, that all in the end will be saved. And many Christians would be inclined to say that since God's love is sure, the economy of salvation is not a matter we can or need to explain; reason must halt in trust before the mystery of divine power and love.

These comments simplify drastically. Perhaps they serve to show,

nevertheless, that Christian equality does not melt away in the fur-
nace of the doctrine of predestination. Let us, then, pursue somewhat
further the question of what this equality—and the prophetic hope
that embraces it—means.

Private Property and Capitalism

The essential facts are well known. Christianity has usually been on
the side of private property and allied with the owners of private
property (assuming that we count feudal land holdings as private
property). Many Christians in the early Church, of course, were poor.
However, during the Middle Ages, the Church not only supported the
feudal property system but was itself a feudal landholder on an extensive scale. And in the modern world, the Christian clergy has more
often than not, except when trying to save feudalism, supported
capitalism.

Not all Christians, however, have shared in this consensus. Monasteries have represented an ideal of life spiritually unencumbered by
personal wealth or private holdings, and various Protestant sects
have expressed and practiced such an ideal. Furthermore, in modern
times, a number of Christian theologians and thinkers have been
socialists.

Thus, we again encounter ambiguity. A sense of human fallenness
favors any arrangements making for a workable society; this means,
ordinarily, private property. On the other hand, faith in a paradisiacal
destiny gives rise to social criticism and social change in accordance
with the ideal of community; that implies limitations on private
property, if not common ownership. And again we can specify a clear
order of priority. Prudence must be subordinate to prophetic hope.
On Christian principles, the Kingdom of God must impinge on the
present order of things. If it does not, in what sense is it, as Jesus held,
near at hand?

The prudential element in the Christian attitude toward property can
be brought sharply into focus if we note the profound difference between the prophetic hope of Christians and the radical assurance of
Marxists. Although Christians view private property and capitalism
from a radical perspective, they do not grant these things the axial
historical significance they have for Marxists.

In the view of Marxists, once industry has been developed and nature is potentially under human control, private property remains as the primary source of remediable evils; it is the basis of class conflict and of man's subjection to nature. Some evils, such as old age, are presumably inherent in the human condition. But others, such as poverty, estrangement, and stultifying work, can be erased. This will happen (assuming the extensive development of man's technological powers and cooperative capacities through capitalism) when private property is abolished. With the human race no longer divided between those with property—and social standing and political power—and those without, society will be transformed into community.

For Christians, this is a fantasy of pride. The primary source of evil is not any particular property system (which is not to say that all property systems are morally equivalent) but the character of human beings. By tracing all remediable evil back to private property, Marxists exculpate human beings. They ignore, or rather explain away, the persistent and ingenious selfishness of individuals and groups. They close their eyes to the enduring capacity of men and women to pervert and misuse even the best institutions.

Seen from a Christian vantage point, the Marxist conception of private property partakes of what might be called "negative idolatry." Private property is a negative idol in the sense that its abolition is expected largely to end human suffering. Negative idolatry in this case is accompanied by positive idolatry. The primary agents in the conquest of suffering will be human beings without property—the proletariat, a messianic class. When it began to appear that the proletariat could not fulfill a messianic role (that it manifested mere "trade-union consciousness" if allowed to develop spontaneously) it was replaced by the party, and from that idolatrous transposition comes the despotism that prevails wherever Marxism has won power.

Christians, of course, cannot idealize private property any more than they can think that abolishing it will open the gates to community. But they can hardly help recognizing some of the manifest advantages of private property, given the fallenness of humanity: the protection it provides—both against powerful minorities and against the pressures of mass society—for personal and private life; the care it calls forth from owners; the division of power that prevails where economic and political power are in different hands. Although these are mere considerations of common sense, and familiar since the time of Aristotle, bearing them in mind can be important for preserving elementary decencies and is far easier for Christians, with their realistic view of human nature, than for Marxists.

Christians may go even further and recognize the practicality of capitalism. Although in recent years many Christian theologians have been socialists, Christian principles militate against accepting any property system as ideal. If evil is rooted in human nature, we must be wary of expecting too much from institutional arrangements, and socialists ordinarily expect a great deal from common— or governmental—ownership of the means of production. Christians are apt to be less surprised than secular-minded socialists by the personal sloth and bureaucratic arrogance usually afflicting socialist systems. And they are apt to be readier than most reformers to admit that even though capitalism has moral weaknesses, it is attended by practical benefits, such as productive efficiency and freedom from arbitrary governmental interference. Without being enthusiastic supporters of capitalism, Christians will be open to the possibility that among economic systems, all of them highly imperfect, capitalism may be the most workable.

Christian realism is such that even poverty is not unqualifiedly condemned. Jesus apparently held, contrary to practically everyone today, that poverty may entail moral advantages. Inhabiting an uncomfortable world, the poor are less likely than the rich to be worldly; hence Jesus' advice to the rich man who asked what to do to inherit eternal life—he must give away all of his wealth.[9] And aside from possible moral benefits, poverty is ineradicable. "You always have the poor with you."[10] To such statements many people today react with exasperation and hostility, sensing in them support for unjust privilege and power. We should remember, however, that Jesus was a poor man and neither shared nor showed much sympathy with the complacency of the wealthy. ("It is easier for a camel to go through the eye of a needle, than for a rich man to enter the Kingdom of God."[11]) Moreover, modern economic conditions provide some support for Jesus' attitudes. For the majority in the industrial nations, poverty has been replaced by affluence, and few would argue that this has brought moral improvement. Nor has poverty disappeared. Despite the strenuous efforts of reformers, we still have the poor with us (a matter, of course, for repentance rather than complacency).

Here, we begin to see the paradox of prophetic hope from a new vantage point. One must recognize the inescapability of private property, of capitalism, at least in limits, and perhaps even of poverty. But to allow such worldly necessities to define the eternal human state and the scope of political imagination would be to abandon the prophetic stance. Prophetic hope requires not only paying sober attention to worldly realities but also looking beyond them.

Concerning property, there is deep prophetic wisdom in Jesus' parable of the rich man who gathered in a plentiful harvest, resolved to build bigger barns to hold all his wealth, and contemplated with pleasure the prospect of saying to himself, "Soul, you have ample goods laid up for many years; take your ease, eat, drink, be merry." At that moment, God spoke to him. "Fool!" he said, "This night your soul is required of you; and the things you have prepared, whose will they be?"[12] It is plain in this parable why private property is not sacred. It encourages its possessors to concentrate exclusively on their own well-being, to interpret well-being in terms of physical pleasure and economic security, and to set themselves apart from all others. Property owners are disposed to settle down comfortably in the world, shut off from the human situation in an illusory fortress of material treasures, rich in ephemeral blessings but, as Jesus noted in concluding his parable, "not rich toward God."

Private property subverts the true meaning of physical reality. Christians pray for "bread," and it may be said that physical reality—at least the portion of it we must use and consume—is ideally bread. It is a gift from God (this is implied in praying for it); it is given only as needed (hence Christians pray merely for "daily" bread); its purpose is the fulfillment of a destiny, not mere physical satisfaction (the petition for daily bread immediately follows petitions for the healing of relations of human beings with God and one another); and it is freely shared (Christians pray for *our* daily bread). Each one of these standards is apt to grow dim or disappear when the prevailing ethos strongly favors private property. The very concept of human ownership is in tension, if not outright conflict, with the idea that the things we need are given to us by God; people are likely to wish not merely for things that meet present needs but for barns full enough to provide independence from the daily gift of bread; property laws can say nothing of destiny and thus tend to sanction any use that personal preference dictates; and unlike bread, private property is essentially mine and not ours.

The subversion of physical reality reaches its logical climax when wealth is money. The amount that a person owns (his worth!) can be precisely calculated, thus giving to the independence and security wealth supposedly provides an appearance of unassailable objectivity. Holdings in money can be indefinitely increased; one's barns become infinitely capacious. And since money is readily convertible into a variety of physical possessions and personal services, it adds to the charm of ownership the allure of power. It is not surprising that "the love of money" is characterized in the New Testament as "the root of all evils."[13]

If a prophetic outlook entails deep misgivings about private property, how much deeper must those misgivings be about capitalism. All that is dubious in private ownership seems, at least for the owners, to be emphasized by the capitalist system. People are forced into acquisitive rivalry; to await a daily gift of bread would be the mark of a fool. Acquisitive success is candidly equated with virtue and personal worth naively measured in terms of monetary possessions. Charity is often bestowed on the needy, but it is a matter of personal generosity or opulent display, not of justice or community; and it is unsanctioned in capitalist theory. No principles could be more thoroughly anticommunal than those of capitalism. Indeed, capitalism is probably more anticommunal in theory than in practice, for human beings cannot be as consistently selfish and calculating as capitalist doctrine calls on them to be. Capitalism has one bond with Christianity—the premise that human beings are ordinarily selfish. A system that enables an industrial society to achieve order and efficiency without depending on either human goodness or governmental coercion cannot be entirely despised. But any support Christians give to capitalism must be regretful and qualified; after all, Christian faith embraces the doctrine not only of original sin but of *agape*. Even if capitalism worked as perfectly as its supporters claim, it would by Christian standards fail morally and spiritually. And Christians will doubt that capitalism does work as perfectly as its supporters claim. They will be deeply suspicious of the maxim that the invisible hand of the market is always to be trusted in preference to the visible hand of government. Such a maxim has a look of idolatry. The principle that only God, and never a human institution, should be relied on absolutely suggests a far more flexible and pragmatic approach to the issue.

Regarding poverty, to say that prophetic attitudes involve grave misgivings, as with private property and capitalism, would be insufficiently emphatic. The only poverty a Christian can acquiesce in unprotestingly is his own. When Jesus told the rich man to give away his wealth for the sake of eternity, he told him to give it to the poor.

These attitudes reflect the hesitant radicalism described earlier in this chapter—hesitant in recognizing that ultimate and immediate possibilities do not coincide and that the destiny ordained by God cannot be enacted at human pleasure; radical in insisting that ultimate possibilities shape the immediate moment.

A secular radical is apt to find such an attitude fatally divided. People are too eager as it is to find excuses for inaction, since inaction is usually safer and easier than radical action. If hesitation is encouraged, inaction is inevitable. Christians can hardly disagree, maintaining as they do (and as secular radicals ordinarily do not) that people are disinclined, by a primal perversity of their nature, to take risks or make sacrifices for the common good. Christians must claim for their divided attitude not that it is free of danger but that it reflects the truth—that human beings are divided in their nature and condition, at once fallen and exalted, inhabitants of time and destined for eternity. Ambiguous in their character and situation, they must be ambiguous in their politics.

The hesitant radicalism embodied in the prophetic stance is confirmed not only by basic principles of faith, however, but also by recent experience. The simple affirmations and denials of ideologies have been refuted empirically, so far as empirical refutation outside of laboratories is possible. Contrary to the slogans of recent generations, it is now manifest that neither private nor public ownership provides a key to the just and effective organization of economic life. Likewise, experience has shown that capitalism cannot, without unacceptable costs, be allowed either to operate unchecked or to be wholly eliminated. And poverty, as already noted, has been found to be far too complex and mysterious to be theoretically comprehended or practically mastered by social scientists and governmental administrators. Many in modern times have been contemptuous of revelation and have called on societies to rely wholly on experience. What is striking, however, is the degree to which the political implications of revelation and the apparent lessons of experience coincide.

Various conditions encountered in efforts at reform have prompted hesitation—bureaucratic inefficiency, dishonesty among beneficiaries of governmental aid, and so forth. No other cause of hesitation, however, has been as compelling as a great social disorder, apparently caused by equalization and, for many, calling into question the very idea of social transformation. The examination of this disorder brings us to a major turning point in these reflections.

Mass Society

The most serious failure of modern social reform has been idolatry of the people. Reformers have let themselves assume, and often assert, that when true equality is achieved, society will have been perfected. They have been blind to the disadvantages and perils connected with equality and popular rule. Marx exemplifies this failure. There is little exaggeration in the observation, now commonplace, that for Marx the proletariat had the historical role that Jehovah had in the faith of his ancient Jewish ancestors—that of avenging the injustices of the past and establishing justice. True, Marx showed an awareness in his early writings of the dangers of equality. But he attributed these dangers to false forms of equality, and he held throughout his life that when working people had been organized and equipped in the ways mature capitalism made possible and tended to effect, the dawn of community would be at hand. The workers were not, for Marx, merely one class among others; they represented the people, universal humanity. Owing above all to the influence of Marx, tacit deification of the working class became widespread and has lasted into our own day, even though many social critics (Marxists of a sort among them) have pointed out its divergence from reality.

The truth obscured by such idolatry is that equality brings with it some surprising, and potentially disastrous, consequences. Equalization is a dangerous undertaking. Many thinkers have brought this out. But one of the earliest of these, and perhaps the greatest, was a

Christian, Alexis de Tocqueville, whose critique of equality was set forth in his youthful masterpiece, *Democracy in America*. Tocqueville was by no means an embittered enemy of equality, even though he was a landed aristocrat and experienced the aftermath of the French Revolution. He saw equality as inevitable and in many ways benign. He entertained no desire to return to the *ancien régime*. Nevertheless, he argued in his study of American democracy that equality tended to attenuate social relations, undermine moral standards, and vulgarize language and literature. Although such results were not inevitable, since a people alert to the dangers could do much to obviate them, equality set up currents that could carry a people into an unprecedented and peculiarly desolate form of existence. Individuals would be isolated and insecure, moved mainly by monetary and hedonistic impulses and bereft of many of the disciplines and satisfactions of traditional civilization.

Tocqueville described what has since come to be called "mass society"—society debased by the reign not of tyrants or incompetent kings but of an atomized and degraded people. In a mass society, the people are both oppressors and victims—oppressors because they are sovereign, victims because they are not inherently base but become so in the circumstances created by modern equalization.

Mass society is a threat to liberty and community alike. Impending over liberty, Tocqueville saw the possibility of a "tyranny of the majority." Individuals within a democracy, deprived of traditional authorities by the process of equalization, are inclined to seek guidance from the one authority in existence, an authority always near at hand: everyone. An uncertain and unsupported individual is likely to think and do what all other individuals think and do. Moreover, "everyone" is strongly inclined to exercise authority and is able to do so with an efficacy no other ruler can match, for "everyone" is everywhere and can wield power merely through a disapproving glance.

This was a political, as well as a social, condition in Tocqueville's mind. The tyranny of the majority is maintained not only through social censure but also through popular dominance of every governmental institution. Tocqueville asserted—prophetically—that democratic governments tend to become large and centralized, while remaining democratic. He sensed, however, that formal democracy might be abandoned and that mass society might become dictatorial and totalitarian. The most terrible of the surprises that equality might bring was that of a complete reversal, the rule of the people becoming the rule of a despot.

The threat to community that is inherent in mass society has been clarified through the concept of alienation. This term, of course, denotes a state of separation not just from particular people, such as a former friend, an unfair employer, or a tyrannical ruler, or from a particular group, such as a town, neighborhood, or class; it is separation from the entire society to which one belongs. And since it is separation from one's own society, by which one's values, opinions, and character have been shaped, it is separation from oneself. Alienation is the most complete imaginable defeat of community, for all ties are attenuated or severed. Although such a condition might be experienced in more than one kind of society, it is associated in most analyses with mass society. The masses render social relationships intrusive and uniform and leave little room for the diversities, hesitations, and inner explorations that underlie serious communication. Conformity, rather than communication, is the principal bond. Tocqueville succinctly described the way in which the masses destroy liberty and, in destroying liberty, suppress community when he wrote that in democracies "to live at variance with the multitude is, as it were, not to live. The multitude require no laws to coerce those who do not think like themselves: public disapprobation is enough; a sense of their loneliness and impotence overtakes them and drives them to despair."[14]

Equalization unifies and magnifies society. At least it does so where it gives rise to mass dominance. Individual and group diversities are obscured or destroyed; society *en bloc* is empowered. Individuals are isolated and weakened, and communal relationships become more ephemeral and fragmentary than ever. And the weight of society becomes even greater when democracy becomes not only social and political but economic, assuming the form of consumer's capitalism and the welfare state. Then society is supported by something Tocqueville thought was encouraged by democracy, the "passion for physical gratification."

One conclusion to be drawn is that social transformation—as liberation—does not come automatically with equalization. Such a proposition may seem elementary, yet it is not as widely accepted as one might suppose it would be. Those pursuing social transformation have been committed so strongly to equalization that they have not faced, or even been very conscious of, the dangers of mass society. On the other side, those most acutely aware of mass society and the perils of equalization have in many cases been conservatives, with little interest in social transformation. Reformers prepared to resist not only powerful minorities but also dominant masses are rare. When the realities of mass society are faced, however, it becomes obvious that reformers must be prepared to oppose equality, in some of its manifestations, as well as to further it. The sword of reform must be two-edged.

Christians are well placed for wielding such a sword because their faith can help them stay free of the idolatry of the masses. But if one edge of the sword is traditional reform, what is the other edge?

Part of the answer was given by Tocqueville. He did not put it succinctly anywhere, but it can perhaps be summarized in a word: prudence. Much of the damage done by democracy consists in destroying things that are important to civilized life and cannot easily be restored once they have been lost. Therefore, equalization should be pursued with care. Tocqueville was not conservative in any precise sense of the term. He believed that historical movement was inevitable and potentially beneficial and did not attach great importance to stability; and ancient institutions as such did not have value in his eyes. But some things grow rather than being deliberately constructed; some of them are essential to our humanity and are imperiled by equality; hence, as we move toward democracy, they should be treated with particular care. The following are examples of these things; in each case, I am concerned more with the spirit than with the details of Tocqueville's suggestions.

Authority. One way of stemming the tide of the masses is to safeguard the power and status of small and respected groups that are governed by objective standards and not by the pleasure of the people. Lawyers and judges were perhaps the most important of these groups for Tocqueville, but the general principle applies not only to law but also to literature and the arts, science and learning, and government. Tocqueville's attitude is not "elitist." No particular group holds the key to civilization and justice, nor does some particular balance between the few and the many define good order. It is prudent, nevertheless, to leave room in a democracy for minorities with the discernment and influence to defend true values when they come into conflict with popular taste and fashion.

Established groups. Democracy will be more benign, and liberty and community more secure, if the people are not entirely homogeneous and society not entirely undivided. Relationships with the depth and solidity that come only from time—those found in families, neighborhoods, towns—are worthy of care. And in democracies, they are in particular need of care, for equality tends to erode them— today, for example, by weakening parental authority and dividing generations. There should be no implicit reliance on society or any of its groups (no idolatry). But established relationships can become channels of community and should not be casually abandoned to public opinion, administrative decree, or any of the other alienating forces that flourish in modern democracies.

Morality. One of the most ominous consequences of equalization is erosion of the standards of morality. Tocqueville discussed at length the acquisitiveness and the "passion for physical gratification" that he thought democracy encouraged. In the twentieth century, we see the spread of pornography, sexual promiscuity, and casual abortions. That American reformers have nothing to say on such matters is one of their gravest failures. They are afraid, apparently, of offending voters. One of the consequences of their failure is that the defense of morality is left largely to reactionary moralists for whom a simple and rigorously enforced set of traditional moral rules and a cessation of social reform suffice to define a good society.

Culture. Although cultivated taste is far from the same as religious faith, and is often proudly antithetical to it, it is difficult to think that the diversions and melodramas that constitute popular culture in the Western democracies are favorable to Christian insight and faith. Culture is closely allied with religion, and great art often communicates religious intuitions. Hence, Christians and cultured nonbelievers might logically unite to defend beauty and meaning against the owners and managers of the mass media, who with keen singleness of mind consult one standard alone, popularity.

Constitutionalism. One of the principal themes of *Democracy in America* is that government under stable and enforceable limits has not become less important with the rise of the people to power. Rather, it has become more important, for the majority is apt to capture every governmental institution; then, the informal social power of the masses is reinforced by legal and political power. Constitutionalism bars the worst political evil, tyranny; the danger of tyranny is not eliminated by democracy but only presented in novel forms—as the tyranny of a majority or of a popular despot. Constitutionalism is one of the elemental values of the political universe and needs to be guarded against the idolatrous notion that if the people govern, no limits on government are required.

These are not, as I have noted, counsels of conservatism. But neither are they counsels of social transformation. To be careful of authority, of natural groups, of moral standards, of culture, and of constitutionalism is not so much a goal of collective action as a limit upon such action. They are cautionary notes—counsels of hesitation. They would help to prevent the rise of mass society and to check its dangers. Is nothing further necessary, then, for the process of social transformation to continue?

That is doubtful. In one respect, mass society has a significance comparable to that of Marxist totalitarianism. It emerged from actions intended to create or encourage community, and it brought into being something very unlike community. Mass society and Marxist totalitarianism alike compel us to pause and think again about political action. Why has such action brought results so at variance with original intentions? Although mass society is a less terrible spectacle than Marxist totalitarianism, it is in one way more disturbing. The latter demonstrates the dangers of proud and sweeping action. The former shows that even cautious and piecemeal action, action as guarded and gradual as the long series of measures that led to the emergence of the egalitarian republic that Tocqueville observed in the Jacksonian era, can have results that are both unanticipated and highly undesirable.

Are we forced into political skepticism, into quietism? As I have argued throughout this essay, Christian premises decisively rule out any such conclusion. Despair of action cannot be justified on the basis of a faith that tells us we are morally bound not only to take responsibility for our fellow human beings but also to carry on our lives with hope. But mass society does point toward the necessity of attaching important qualifications to ideals of action common among modern reformers. Two such qualifications deserve to be mentioned here.

The first is that the kind of political action on which the Western democracies have concentrated during the past half-century or more is of limited value and, blindly pursued, may be destructive. I am referring to action that aims immediately at equalization—at eliminating poverty, providing security for everyone, and reducing the privileges and powers of the wealthy. Not that wealth has been even nearly equalized in any nation, and not that the inequalities remaining are just or in any way morally acceptable. Nevertheless, the vast majority of people in the Western industrial nations now have access to roughly similar economic goods. The poor are a small minority, and the rich do not live in ways dramatically different from the ways in which most people live. In that sense, equalization has occurred. And the result has been a reinforcement of mass society; this is evident in gigantic public and private bureaucracies, degraded popular culture, growing uniformity, and pervasive alienation. Hence, the very meaning of social transformation needs rethinking. Admittedly, justice requires far greater equality than now exists; but for reformers stubbornly to concentrate on that one goal, ignoring the ambiguities it entails—ambiguities well known since the time of Tocqueville and conspicuous in present-day democracies—is to invite futility, or worse. Political action needs to be more broadly and diversely conceived. Presumably, there are measures awaiting discovery that would open the way to community and thus bring us nearer to the ultimate purpose sought in equalization, even though they do not immediately enhance equality. For example, there are probably ways of organizing the mass media of communication that would facilitate their serving their natural and proper, but now almost wholly forgotten, end—community. In the absence of such measures, equalization loses much of its point. Effected in the setting of a mass society, it may only give its beneficiaries access to a degraded life and may only widen the empire of stultification and estrangement.

The second conclusion toward which mass society points is that no form of political action whatever can reach the ultimate end that action seeks. The end is community. Through political action we create conditions of community but never community itself. Spontaneous, uncontrivable acts are needed—acts of communication. If these fail to occur, the best institutional forms will be empty. Political action requires a communal response and otherwise is fruitless. Mass society brings home this truth. Communal forms, such as social equality and democratic rule, flawed as they are, have come into existence. But there has been little communal response. Instead of entering into common efforts to uncover the truth of the meaning of our lives, which for the first time in history is now a practical possibility for entire populations, we devote our time and abundant resources to every pleasure and diversion to which people can be profitably attracted.

Briefly, fruitful political action brings liberty, but that is all. When liberty is not used for communal ends, action is thwarted; and when liberty is not even created for communal ends, it is misconceived. Mass society is indicative of extensive misuses and misconceptions of liberty.

To gain a better understanding of the relationship of action to liberty, we must recognize one basic principle; this, at any rate, is suggested by Christian doctrine. The principle is that spirit is prior to order. Christianity began with Paul's critique of the law, of the order that Paul's Jewish forefathers believed incumbent on followers of God. Paul affirmed the priority of a certain spirit, faith. Here, we cannot explore the rich political implications of Paul's critique. We can, however, take note of its bearing on modern attitudes toward order.

Order, a set of external arrangements, is a product of action. Thus, the modern belief in action has carried with it belief in the efficacy of good order. The solution to any practical problem, it is assumed, lies in rightly arranging social and political forms. Hence the faith in equalization; a more equal society would be a better society and nearer to true community. Ordinarily neglected or forgotten is the fact that a good order is doubly dependent on a certain spirit—the spirit needed to create and sustain such an order and the spirit needed to use its liberties in a way that brings it to fruition. On the whole, reformers have been blind to the perverse uses that could be made of the enlarged liberties they sought. How many of them imagined, for example, that when most men and women had the legal rights and educational opportunities needed to participate in intellectual and political life, the air would be filled, as it is now, with advertising, simplistic political slogans, and the obscenities and frivolities concocted by an "entertainment industry"? Showing us such things as these, mass society shows us the need for "a new and right spirit" if social transformation is to occur and be fruitful. Mass society makes plain for us what the law made plain for Paul: that good order is stultifying and destructive without the appropriate spirit.

To focus on the primacy of spirit is to see again the insufficiency of justice, which is what we usually call the best order. A just society can suffer moral and cultural degradation—conditions destructive of community. Although community presumably cannot exist without justice, mass society shows that justice can exist without community. Someone may object that the justice attained in Western societies is marred by a multitude of imperfections, and, as I have acknowledged, this is certainly true. Mass society, however, seems to arise from the *perfections* of the outward order—from the various forms of equality characterizing modern society; that is certainly Tocqueville's view. Consequently, there is little reason to think that further equalization, unaccompanied by a communal spirit or by measures designed to create communal openings in the midst of mass society, would do anything to alleviate the alienation and superficiality of modern life.

Nothing I have said is intended to suggest that "old-fashioned" reform—equalizing reform—is no longer needed. Even though the first days of the New Deal lie over half a century in the past and were succeeded by decades of attempted reform (often interrupted, to be sure), there remain inequalities in the distribution of wealth and power that are entirely indefensible. Although less dire poverty is found now, in America, than in 1933, the political agenda of past decades still cries out for fulfillment. My argument is only that we need to remember the point of equality—community, an end to the estrangement of classes—and to reflect on the fact with which mass society presents us: that equality can in some circumstances be destructive of community. It is this fact that shows us the need for a new and right spirit and for a reformist imagination that is alive not only to the penultimate end, equality, but also to the ultimate end, community.

If now we ask the question posed in the New Testament and echoed so often in later times—What, then, must we do?—the answer is that we must seek the spirit needed for continuing the work of social transformation and for rendering good order, or equal justice, fruitful. How can we seek this spirit? The Christian answer lies in the main argument of this essay. We must train ourselves to wait, in history, for God. To say that spirit is prior to order is to say that human beings depend on something they cannot at will acquire but can only be ready to receive. The spirit they need must be given to them. Mass society confirms the principle of waiting, along with its corollaries— solitude and inaction, attentiveness and availability. Now, however, it becomes clearer than earlier in the essay what waiting means. To begin with, it requires an acknowledgment of spiritual poverty, which, as an incapacity for action, is also political poverty; we do not have and cannot deliberately supply ourselves with the spirit we need in order to fulfill our political purposes. Such an acknowledgment consists essentially in facing our ignorance and weakness and our moral inadequacy; it therefore implies effort. It is not mere passivity.

In addition, waiting requires anticipation, or hope. It is not merely living in the consciousness of one's own limitations but is also watching for the spirit ("You do not know whence it comes or whither it goes."[15]) that will enable us to act fruitfully. A confession of spiritual poverty is insignificant unless accompanied by a watchfulness expressive of hope. This, too, implies effort.

Here we begin to discern a dimension of the prophetic stance that so far we have scarcely acknowledged. It involves concentration and discipline. Maintaining the prophetic stance is a form of spirituality. This we must examine before concluding the essay.

Five

Prophetic Spirituality

Politics and Spirituality

Spirituality is, for Christians, the concentrated effort to open one's soul to God, to be fully available to Christ. It has a narrower and a broader meaning. According to the narrower meaning, spirituality consists only in those activities that have no other purpose than entering into relationship with God. Prayer is the preeminent spiritual activity. In addition to prayer, studies in spirituality are concerned with disciplines such as meditation, ascetic self-denial, and confession, which are intended to open the way between God and man. Spirituality in this narrower sense is highly organized in monasteries, with the monks committed not only to obedience, chastity, and poverty but also to a rigorous regimen of prayer and worship.

In the broader sense of the term, spirituality comprises any activity whatever that is carried on with the faith that it will open pathways between man and God. Thus, physical labor and work of other kinds have often been regarded as spiritual activities. Serving the poor and disabled, although today often carried on merely by bureaucrats pursuing careers, readily takes on a spiritual character. And suffering can become a form of spirituality under the power of faith. In suffering, one gives up the worldly self, shaped in response to the opportunities, pleasures, and standards of the world—one dies, but in dying one can be reborn as the self shaped by God.

The suspicions with which many Christians, typically Protestants, regard spirituality are not groundless. It can become an effort to ascend to God, and then spirituality becomes pride. We think we are ascending to God when in fact we are descending to a deity of our own imagining. Standing on the Christian doctrine of God, one may well ask: What are our prayers and spiritual disciplines measured against the majesty of the Lord of heaven and earth? On Christian grounds, it is easy to answer that they are nothing, or worse than nothing—human presumption. Nevertheless, a serious Christian can hardly refrain from striving to turn toward God and can hardly think that God does not wish this to occur. God said, according to one of the Psalms, "Seek ye my face," and the Psalmist prayed, "Hide not thy face from me"; and Jesus declared "Seek and you will find."[1] Granted, our ways of seeking God are bound to be incommensurate with their goal, as are all of the religious activities we undertake. But Christian principles allow one to believe that God can bring these efforts to their goal and allow us to pursue them in hope and good conscience.

Since any aspect of life can be incorporated in spirituality, politics and spirituality can be joined. Obedience to a political sovereign can be carried on in a way that gives it spiritual significance; so can disobedience, as is suggested by movements of nonviolent resistance to racial segregation, movements often led by Christians. Political action can be a spiritual activity, as can the suffering that many governments bring so abundantly to the people under them. Moreover, it is not only spirituality in its broader meaning that can be joined with politics. Christians regularly pray for "the peace of the world," for their governmental leaders, and for "the poor and the oppressed, for the unemployed and the destitute, for prisoners and captives, and for all who remember and care for them."[2] These are political prayers. One might carry on meditation partly to understand one's historical situation and obligations, and then it would be political meditation. When Simone Weil deprived herself of food (which, in England, she could have had) in order to share the sufferings of her countrymen under German occupation, she practiced a political asceticism.[3]

We are so used to thinking of spirituality as withdrawal from the world and human affairs that it is hard to think of it as political. Spirituality is personal and private, we assume, whereas politics is public. But such a dichotomy drastically diminishes spirituality, construing it as a relationship to God without implications for one's relationship to the surrounding world. The God of Christian faith entered into the world and disclosed the coming transformation of the world in Christ. The notion that we can be related to God and not to the world—that we can practice a spirituality that is not political—is in conflict with the Christian understanding of God. Moreover, true spirituality will be not merely political but radical, since it will be a method of waiting with ever-increasing discernment and strength (provided God brings spirituality to its goal), for relationships radically different from any of those existing in the world. It will be prophetic.

And if spirituality is properly political, the converse also is true (however distant from prevailing assumptions): politics is properly spiritual. The spirituality of politics was affirmed by Plato at the very beginnings of Western political philosophy and was a commonplace of medieval political thought. Only in modern times has it come to be taken for granted that politics is entirely secular. The inevitable result is the demoralization of politics. The idea of the exalted individual grows dim. Politics loses its moral structure and purpose and turns into an affair of group interest and personal ambitions. Government comes to the aid only of the well organized and influential, and it is limited only where it is checked by countervailing forces. Politics ceases to be understood as a preeminently human activity and is left to those who find it enjoyable, profitable, or in some other way useful to themselves. Political action thus comes to be carried out for the sake of pleasure, power, and privilege.

I have suggested as examples of the prophetic stance two figures, one fictional and one actual—Pietro Spina, in Silone's *Bread and Wine*, and Dietrich Bonhoeffer. In connection with spirituality, a third example comes readily to mind—a man mentioned in the preceding pages, Thomas Merton. As a Trappist monk, Merton spent many hours every day in prayer and meditation. Confined almost entirely to the monastery, he was necessarily more or less inactive politically; inside the monastery, he and the other monks, even though constantly in one another's company, were solitary in that they were not normally permitted to converse. Yet Merton was thoroughly political. He saw monastic life as a way of inhabiting the world rather than withdrawing from the world. He was intensely conscious of current political issues, such as the war in Vietnam, and was strongly committed to certain political positions. He was able frequently to make his positions publicly known, although he could not engage in demonstrations or other such forms of political action. It is noteworthy, too, that he emphatically opposed racial segregation, in that way supporting social transformation. For Merton, solitude was the obverse side of a universal attentiveness, or communality; and contemplative spirituality was the fountainhead of political responsibility.[4]

That politics and spirituality can in such ways be fused has an important bearing on the political situation of our time. Reformist political action, as I have argued, has been brought to an impasse by mass society. Faced with a social order in which there is considerable equality but little community, we do not know what to do. Only one clear requirement arises from this situation, construed in the light of Christian principles, and that is a requirement bearing on each individual singly: to stand, open to God and to human beings. Communality must be maintained as a personal orientation even though we are not sure what communality now requires of us in the sphere of political action. This is a paradoxical posture, for it is solitary even though communal; although reforming society demands solidarity among reformers, being open is something one must do alone. Solitary communality cannot strike readers of this essay as strange or impossible, however, for it is simply the prophetic stance.

But now, from the perspective of spirituality, we see the prophetic stance as a way of siding with social transformation even at a time when the actions required for social transformation have come into doubt. In the midst of the alienation of mass society—alienation apparently furthered by past reformist (equalizing) action—one waits for the community that God, as understood in Christian faith, is bringing into being in Christ. This is not passivity, however. To wait prophetically is only to hesitate until the commands of God are heard, perhaps in human words or perhaps in historical conditions and events.

Through spirituality, the radical posture inherent in solitary communality becomes serious and disciplined. In meditation and prayer, one seeks God and strives for the clarity of spirit in which other human beings can be heard and answered. In prayerful reflection, one tries to attain an understanding of history and the Kingdom of God and to speak and act appropriately in response. Spirituality is cultivation of the receptivity essential to prophetic hope and to the task of maintaining a radical relationship to the established order. The receptivity gained in solitude can be carried into everything one does in the world, into obedience and disobedience, action and suffering. Through spirituality, the prophetic stance becomes something more than an occasional attitude. It becomes an activity, perseveringly practiced, continually deepening the roots of communality and hope.

Can such spirituality have any meaning for, or in any way be practiced by, one who is not a Christian? I believe that it can. There is an openness toward transcendence, an agnosticism that is not tacit atheism but genuine religious uncertainty; it is not hostile to the idea of God nor indifferent to the question of God's reality. It is a readiness to hear of God and a willingness (although not, as in James, a will) to believe. An openness of this sort may be expressed in philosophical reflection, and it is possible to understand Socrates (depending on how one interprets his professed "ignorance") as representing such an attitude. Some Christians would dismiss this openness as religiously insignificant, for it is clearly quite different from faith. But can they rightfully do this? Is it valid, given the faith that God is love, to maintain that God condemns and leaves in utter darkness—a darkness unilluminated even by hints of human destiny and historical meaning—human beings who are sincerely open to the light? Indeed, can Christians rightfully deny that a genuinely open-minded agnosticism may be a sign of grace?

At any rate, communality sustained and deepened in solitude—whether in the solitude of Christian spirituality or in the solitude of an agnostic openness toward transcendence—must finally become manifest in political action and have historical repercussions; this is implied by the faith that personal depths and historical events are united ultimately in destiny. And such action must aim at reform. Communality is radical because it is interpersonal openness maintained in opposition to social impersonality. It must sooner or later reanimate the work of social transformation. There is no knowing how or when. But let us dwell for a moment on one example of how a deepened communality, and the spirituality in which it has its source, might enliven political imagination. This example is closely connected with preceding discussions; it concerns the mystery of poverty.

A certain spiritual—rather than narrowly political—challenge is inherent simply in trying to think about poverty in a true and balanced way. The challenge is indicated when we speak of the *mystery* of poverty. As brought out in preceding chapters, poverty is neither the essentially soluble problem that traditional reformers have often thought it to be nor a manifestation of the just distributive workings of a free economy, in accordance with typical assumptions among conservatives. We do not have the knowledge or command of social reality to eliminate poverty, but neither have we the right to acquiesce in it or to ignore it. This ambiguity is accompanied by another. Christians must admit that poverty may make for spiritual depths that wealth tends to close off; yet at the same time, they must see it as a shame and an outrage. They must oppose it in every way they can but, recognizing the mysteries of grace, in a certain way accept and respect it. Admittedly, all evidence suggests that Christians view poverty much as does everyone else—either as a mere problem awaiting solution or as a changeless condition, like our mortality. They evince no unique wisdom. It is not unreasonable to think, nevertheless, that Christian spirituality—or the disciplined openness toward transcendence that corresponds to spirituality among agnostics—may offer a way to the wisdom for which the persistence of poverty amid industrial wealth calls. It warns us away from ideological oversimplifications; it leads us to reflect on the fallenness, evident in different ways among the rich and the poor, to which poverty testifies; and it might enable the powerful to consider the poor with an *agape* free of both sentimentality and political ambition.

The spiritual challenge of poverty, however, is one not merely of understanding but also of action. The challenge arises from the fact that those who have the wealth and power to act effectively are not compelled by circumstances to act at all. We inhabit a new situation in the history of the industrial world. In recent decades, governments have tried in various ways to help the poor primarily because the poor constituted a large, enfranchised, and visible majority—a group with the power to compel attention. But the situation has changed fundamentally. Governmental help (along with rising productivity) has been effectual. The poor now constitute a relatively small minority, armed with few votes and afflicted by conditions, such as illiteracy and despair, that make it difficult for them to organize for political action. Sequestered in urban ghettoes, moreover, they are little seen by the prosperous majority. Weak, disorganized, and inconspicuous, they are easy to ignore. The consequence for the rest of society is simply that poverty now demands a far freer—a more gratuitous—concern than it ever did before. In the absence of outer necessity, there is needed a strong inner prompting; spiritual qualities of a kind rarely considered by reformers have become politically essential. In this way, spirituality, the disciplined cultivation of spiritual qualities, has been brought into close proximity to action.

A like conclusion emerges when we consider the situation of the impoverished multitudes outside of the wealthy nations. Here, too, poverty calls for attentiveness on the part of those from whom attentiveness is not exacted by immediate political urgencies; and it calls for respect for strange and distant peoples on the part of those inevitably tempted by their privileges and possessions to lead lives of self-centered enjoyment. Admittedly, there is an enormous question of practical possibilities—of what wealthy nations can do to help nations that are not only destitute but also illiterate and often despotically and inefficiently governed and at war among themselves. Admittedly, too, some nations may be destined to endure a poverty that will in the long run be more spiritually fruitful than the prosperity—so far spiritually stultifying—of the industrial nations; the Cross seems to belong in a Latin American slum or a South African homeland as it does not on Madison Avenue or Wall Street. But for us to forget that every person who lives is exalted by a destiny that is universally human, and that such matters as geographical proximity, voting power, and cultural matrix have no bearing whatever on the respect and consideration that destiny commands, would be to lose our spiritual moorings. The sea of misery that covers the earth requires that we examine those moorings, and this is not merely an intellectual task. It is a task of prophetic spirituality.

In sum, as a condition we can neither remove nor accept, poverty drives us toward reflection and prayer; it hints of the practical relevance of spirituality. In the mystery of its persistence, it fuses inwardness and action.

The political significance of prophetic spirituality, however, should not be measured only by actions and changes of the kind historians can observe. If God, as Christians maintain, is the ultimate sovereign of history, and if God's purposes and his ways of reaching his purposes are not entirely comprehensible to us, we must think that prayer and meditation, and other forms of spirituality, may have historical consequences that we cannot explain or even clearly perceive. "Thoughts that come on doves' feet guide the world," according to Nietzsche.[5] Christians believe that the axis of history lies in the shameful death of an obscure person, an event that altogether escaped the notice of ancient historians. History does not consist entirely in the events everyone watches and discusses. Secular radicals will regard with scorn the idea of seeking social transformation through meditation and prayer. Christians, who pray, "thy Kingdom come," will not.

If spirituality can have political significance, it is natural to look for a spiritual ethic—for a comprehensive and coherent set of rules showing how political spirituality should be carried on. These would help one know what prophetic spirituality means in practice. But no such ethic can be provided, and it is important to understand why.

A major premise of this essay is that we have no abiding city—no full and enduring community—in this world. Preceding chapters have brought out this theme in various ways. We must inhabit two fundamentally different orders, society and community, and we must meet the conflicting requirements of liberty and social transformation. We must attend at once to our fallenness and our exaltation. Our lives are divided and will be healed by Christ but not by human devices.

An objective and reliable set of rules governing spiritual life would constitute a kind of earthly city, an adequate and satisfying order of life in this world. The relative optimism of the ancient Greeks is shown by the fact that they not only devoted immense philosophical energy to the imaginary construction of ideal cities but even, when facing the impossibility of actually building those cities, called on men to inhabit cities built in their minds. The Greeks were sometimes cognizant of the tragic character of the political world but did not, like Christians, recognize the tragic character of all spiritual effort that originates in human will and reason rather than in grace. For Christians, there are no human capacities that enable us to construct and inhabit a good order here on earth, not even an inward and spiritual order.

This implies not that spiritual effort is futile but that spirituality depends on grace. Unable to withdraw into an inner, spiritual city, we must—Christianity tells us—rely entirely on God. The coherence of our lives does not come from rules we can prescribe for ourselves but from the destinies God gives us. And the form of our spirituality must come from God. Prophetic spirituality is of many different kinds, ranging from private meditation, perhaps politically signifying nothing more than quiet watchfulness, to self-sacrificial lives like those of Dorothy Day and Mother Teresa, who have given up all wealth and comfort for the sake of the impoverished and forsaken.

Particularly noteworthy from the standpoint of the discussion that follows is that reflecting on prophetic spirituality presents us with theoretically irresolvable conflicts. Should I obey or disobey? Act decisively or, in humility and faith, simply endure the sufferings imposed by political circumstances? Try to frame politically efficacious ideals or dissolve all ideals in a meditative consciousness of the mystery of being? Such questions cannot be answered in terms of unequivocal rules. Obedience and disobedience are both—occasionally even at the same time and in the same place—called for by prophetic expectancy. The same is true of action and suffering, meditation and ideological construction. In each instance, both extremes belong to prophetic spirituality. Tension and uncertainty—and reliance on grace—are unavoidable.

It follows that prophetic spirituality is best discussed by reflection on dilemmas. And these dilemmas are merely exemplary. One can easily think of dilemmas other than those dealt with in the following pages. Furthermore, the pairs of principles I examine are not exclusive; action, for example, is in conflict not only with suffering but also with communication. But the incomplete and unsystematic nature of the discussion is a reminder that spiritual achievements are not merely human. Spirituality—not only the spirituality of Christians but that of their non-Christian comrades in history as well—is simply a concentrated and disciplined way of waiting for the meaning of history to unfold.

Obedience and Disobedience

When we consult traditional Christian teaching concerning obedience and disobedience, we find assertions incongruous with the

Christian emphasis on the individual. To some people, these assertions are offensive. They are emphatically on the side of obedience—
assumed by many to be the side of conformity and apathy. "Let every
person be subject to the governing authorities," Paul wrote in a famous passage. "For there is no authority except from God, and those
that exist have been instituted by God. Therefore he who resists the
authorities resists what God has appointed." Paul draws the logical
and crushing conclusion that "those who resist will incur judgment."[6] Such is the authority of Paul that even if nothing else in this
vein could be found among Christian writers, it would still have a
powerful influence on Christian attitudes. Counsel conforming with
Paul's, however, abounds in Christian literature.

The duty of obedience is strongly stressed both in the Catholic tradition, by St. Augustine, and in the Protestant tradition, by Luther
and Calvin. It is possible to discover or infer qualifications. For example, one must disobey a governmental command that clearly con-
travenes a command of God. Moreover, Christian history contains
a revolutionary line of thought, beginning at least as early as the
twelfth century with John of Salisbury's defense of tyrannicide and
culminating in the twentieth century with liberation theology. Hence,
Christianity speaks on both sides of the issue. It seems fair to say,
however, that it speaks more frequently and forcefully on the side of
obedience.

Such counsel, of course, is not absolutely binding on Christians,
and many will be tempted to challenge it immediately, for it seems to
breathe a spirit of subservience and to clash with the Christian ideal
of personal responsibility. Still, in dealing with the Bible and with the
greatest Christian writers, Christians are bound to use their critical
freedom with care and therefore to ask: Is there truth of some kind in
the demand for obedience? I think that there is.

It is a rather simple truth, although an important one, if I understand it correctly. Obedience is our normal duty. It is a duty inherent
in the twofold fact that order is a fundamental human need but disorder a powerful human inclination. Disobedience can only be an ab-
normal obligation; if it were more than that, civilization would be
impossible.

Government is an ineffaceable sign of our fallenness, and obedience is an acknowledgment of that sign. In obeying, we recognize

our moral state and accept the conditions it imposes on us. In disobeying, however, except under an imperious moral necessity, human beings manifest a heedlessness of the human situation. They tend, moreover, to create conditions that disturb their relations with God—relations conditioned by civilization and order. To think that one must almost always obey may seem injurious to human dignity, but it expresses a humility befitting fallen creatures.

Here, Christian and secular radicalism are sharply divergent. Although Christianity is suspicious of the established order, it is fearful of disorderly human inclinations; and it attributes the evils in society to human qualities that are not confined to ruling groups. Secular radicals typically depict the oppressed as entirely innocent. Such is an expression, however, of the idolatry of the many, which we have already discussed. Christianity does not deny that some are more wronged than others, but it does deny that any are guiltless or properly free of the normal obligation to obey the governing authorities. Social and political criticism is therefore an invitation not only to anger and rebellion but also to repentance and submission, for none of us are innocent.

Obedience would be idolatrous, however, if it were unconditional. This is clearly implied by the principle that God alone must be obeyed in all circumstances whatever. Obedience rendered to governments or any other human agencies must be critical and deliberate. Christianity cannot avoid this principle, however marked its emphasis on obedience.

I have already mentioned a Christian of our time who was mindful of the conditionality of political obedience—Dietrich Bonhoeffer. Bonhoeffer is a noteworthy illustration of the qualifications Christianity is bound to attach to the duty of obedience. This is not only because of his stature as a Christian thinker and a man but also because he was a Lutheran. The duty of obedience is stressed more strongly in Lutheranism than in any of the other major traditions; Bonhoeffer himself had strongly reiterated that theme in his book *The Cost of Discipleship.* Yet Bonhoeffer found himself, while still in his youth, in a situation that made it impossible, he felt, to obey the government over him and God as well. This situation was created by the anti-Semitic and anti-Christian policies of the Hitler regime, and in response to these policies, Bonhoeffer embarked on the course of resistance that culminated in his execution.

Some may think that they hear in the doctrine that God alone must be obeyed continuing overtones of subservience and conformity. If this impression were accurate, the whole idea of Christian liberty, brought out in earlier chapters, would fall under a shadow. Accordingly, it must be noted that obeying God is not, in Christian faith, an act of self-suppression, as is always more or less the case in obeying a man. "The commandment of God," Bonhoeffer wrote, "differs from all human laws in that it commands freedom."[7] Bonhoeffer did not mean that God commands you to do anything you feel like doing but rather to do what your authentic being, or destiny, requires. He commands you to be truly yourself.

Even if disobedience never in fact occurred, the principle that in some circumstances it is morally unavoidable transforms the obedience normally rendered. Every act of obedience becomes a responsible choice. I may obey the government invariably, but I do not thereby avoid responsibility or the necessity of thought. I become morally involved in history.

The possible duty of disobedience has sometimes been obscured in Christian thought by those who have unduly stressed the importance of order. Augustine, for example, did this. One suspects, however, that Augustine did what many supporters of order do: that he silently read into the concept a moral content it does not logically contain. Order is assumed to be *good* order. But of course it is not, necessarily, and as soon as this is recognized, the concept of order loses some of the authority it is often accorded in political discussions. Order can be so evil as to justify disobedience. This reminds us of the importance of incorporating in every order methods of peaceful change. Then one can obey and still seek change.

The possible duty of disobedience also is sometimes obscured by suggestions that eschatology entails passive obedience. It is said, for example, that anarchistic impulses in Christianity were quieted among the early Christians by expectations of the imminent coming of the Kingdom of God. There was no reason to rise up against a world so soon to end. The truth, however, is that eschatological expectancy has a flavor of rebellion, for it implies that established societies are morally condemned and historically doomed. None resemble the Kingdom of God, and none will survive its coming. In this way, eschatological expectancy separates individuals from society and provides a vantage point for social criticism. Granted, worldliness may lend urgency to rebellion, as the example of Ivan Karamazov shows. But eschatology places demands on history even while affirming that destiny is not finally determined by history; it does not still rebellion.

Both obedience and disobedience are elements of prophetic spirituality. Obedience can be an act of humility and penitence, an admission that we human beings are of such a nature that order depends on the artful contrivances of rulers and on the habitual obedience of all others. Measured by the standard of love, obedience is unquestionably a degraded relationship, far different from the dialogical search for truth that defines community; intrinsic to it is an inequality that, as we have seen, cannot be rendered entirely unobjectionable either by the values ultimately served or by the consent of those who obey. That our fallenness compels us to enter into this relationship can be apprehended, and our understanding of this necessity deepened, in meditation; and in prayer, we can make obedience an act not only of humility and penitence but also of faith. The course of history is entrusted to God.

Throughout this essay, I have tried to link the concept of the prophetic stance with attitudes such as critical detachment, attentiveness, and hesitation. Obedience can express all of these attitudes. Summarily, in Christian terms, it can be said that obedience is a form of waiting for the Kingdom of God. An ethic of obedience contrasts with the ethic of mastery and accomplishment that prevails in the secular civilization of the twentieth century. In obeying, one endures a degraded relationship, recognizing—so far as one obeys on grounds of faith—that mastery and accomplishment belong more to God than to human beings. But doing this with trust in God means that there is no despair and no apathy. There is, rather, watchfulness—attentiveness to events and the people taking part in them, a readiness for truth and for liberation.

Disobedience, too, can be an element of spirituality. It is not this, of course, when it is proud defiance. But it can, like obedience, be an acknowledgment of aspects of the human situation—of the incongruity of society and the individual and of the solitary responsibility thus bearing on the individual. From the fact that society and government manifest our fallenness, it follows not only that we must ordinarily, in humility and penitence, obey but also that our obedience often makes us accomplices in evil, as when the taxes we pay finance an unjust war. Disobedience can be a refusal of such complicity. And it need not be reflective of pride. Making the dissonance of society and the individual resound, disobedience can be carried out in an eschatological spirit, in the expectation not of immediate harmony in history but of God's community.

Obedience and disobedience condition one another morally. The normality of obedience brands disobedience as an exceptional and perilous act. The principle that one who disobeys must freely accept the punishment involved is immensely important; accepting punishment, one acknowledges in the very act of disobedience that a norm inherent in our fallenness has been violated. On the other hand, the possibility of disobedience, as morally unavoidable, reveals the personal responsibility that is not erased by the normal duty of obedience, and it reminds us of the complicity in evil that normal obedience inevitably brings.

Christianity provides no rule telling one when to obey and when to disobey. It suggests, on the contrary, that to seek such a rule is to flee from the mystery into which we enter when we make moral decisions in response to grace rather than in conformity with a rule. In a situation that renders obedience questionable, one can only observe, reflect, and pray, hoping to see the moral necessity given by destiny—the moral necessity that enables one to say, as Jesus said to Pilate, "For this I was born."[8] Many will feel this to be inadequate guidance. But in Christian faith, to look for guidance except in grace is, in the final analysis, idolatrous.

The results have always infuriated politically serious people. Christians are traditionally, in their relations with governments, obedient yet disrespectful. Thus, they violate the ethos both of secular radicals (disobedience grounded in disrespect) and of conservatives (obedience grounded in respect). Eschewing absolute principles, they are unreliable allies of either left or right.

Their attitude, however, is anything but frivolous. It goes down to the first principles of Christian faith. Estranged from God, from human beings, and even from ourselves, and in our perversity continually reaffirming our estrangement, we would be overwhelmed by chaos if we did not ordinarily submit to the order contrived by political rulers. On the other hand, we are, in the Christian vision, recipients of the mercy of God, and if we obeyed unconditionally, we would replace the exalted individual with exalted governments. The resolution of this conflict is effected in the mystery of destiny and divine grace.

Although the Christian attitude arises from the first principles of faith, it contains common sense and is confirmed by twentieth-century political experience. Recent decades have shown that revolutions usually bring tyranny, either immediately or as a remedy for chaos, and that chaos is worse than all but the worst forms of order. But these decades have also displayed the universal evil of governments—ineptitude and deception on the part of the best governments, corruption and terror on the part of the worst. It is thus manifest that conduct unsettling to orderly government is not to be entered into lightly but, at the same time, that governments rarely deserve much respect. Thus, experience, apart from faith, urges us toward the regretful and conditional obedience called for by Christian principles.

The dilemma of obedience and disobedience is intrinsic to the prophetic stance, by which one lives within history toward the end of history. Living within history necessitates normal obedience, whereas faith in a destined end of history imposes a responsibility for judging, and perhaps resisting, political rulers. As an eschatological being, man is always critical, normally acquiescent, and potentially rebellious.

Suffering and Action

Action is not simply activity of any kind. For example, neither conversation nor listening to music is action. Action is directed toward the production of preconceived results and is exemplified in the activities of engineers and revolutionaries. Conversation is not action because participants are open to the spontaneous progress of the dialogue and are not contriving a particular outcome. Listening to music is not action because listeners are not aiming at a specific result but are ready for whatever results, in feeling and insight, the music brings. To engage in action is to seek changes envisioned at the outset. It is necessarily to exercise power, sometimes over persons, sometimes over material objects alone.

Today, we are called to action from all sides. A fervent belief in action, as both morally wholesome and practically efficacious, is one of the most distinctive characteristics of our age. Secular radicals, seeking swift and sweeping changes in society, are among the most conspicuous advocates of action. More striking is the fact that bourgeois opponents of these radical activists are activists themselves. They oppose political radicals not from moral or pragmatic doubts about action but from a desire for action carried on by different groups, in different ways, and for different ends; they are business activists, ordinarily, rather than political activists. It is noteworthy, too, that in both of the superpowers today, the human race is envisioned as continually engaged in world-transforming action. Thus, both within and among nations, there is profound conflict over the nature and the ends of action but no disagreement about man's duty and ability to act.

Not always has the human race been so committed to action. Human beings always, of course, have acted, and sometimes with impressive results; witness the Roman Empire. But with some peoples, speech and contemplation or prayer and worship have had prior importance. And probably never—not in ancient times or in the Middle Ages—have human beings been so sure as today that they are potentially masters of reality and that every problem has a practical solution.

Christianity casts doubt on modern activism, and some of the reasons for this will be familiar to the reader. Modern activism is premised on human innocence. Human beings are not assumed to be everywhere and always good, but they are assumed to be (as in the "idealism" discussed in an earlier chapter) capable of making themselves good through psychotherapy, social reform, and other such expedients—in other words, through action. From the Christian standpoint, however, action has no foothold outside of sin. Even if directed against sin, it is affected and distorted by sin. And where action is carried on under an illusion of innocence, sin is apt to be particularly pretentious and unrestrained.

Christianity places modern activism in question also by reminding us of our finitude. The meaning of finitude for action is simply that unforeseen consequences are inevitable. It is commonly assumed that trial and error will enable us finally to avoid the mischances that have always bedeviled our efforts to manage our lives. But only within the artificially stabilized and limited setting of a laboratory can we finally, by experimentation, learn to anticipate every result. In the ever-changing and unbounded context of history, assured action will forever be impossible.

Moreover, Christianity—or at least the "Reformation" tradition of Christianity—passes not only a practical but also a moral judgment on action. However good its purposes may be, action in itself is never good. To engage in action is to objectify; to incorporate persons in a project of action is to treat persons impersonally. Action is power, not love, even when love provides its motives. To aim even at so broad and benign a result as that of enlightening someone's mind introduces into a relationship elements of calculation and appraisal that preclude love in its purity.

And action necessarily diverges not only from love but also from truth. One cannot act in human affairs without reducing truthfulness to a conditional imperative. One must always ask not only what is true but also whether the truth can be prudently revealed. This is something of which all teachers are aware. Teaching is a form of action presumably closer than any other to pure and sustained truthfulness. Yet teachers, even in universities, must oversimplify and circumscribe the truths they are teaching. They are compelled repeatedly, in view of the results they are seeking, to draw back from the candor of pure communication. The tension between communication and action is reflected in modern democracies. The standard of democracy requires truthfulness; effectiveness requires dissimulation.

It is strange that people regard power with suspicion but action with approbation, for the two are inseparable. Effective action is a demonstration of power, and power is exercised only in action. And just as power tends to corrupt, so does action. People engaged in action are inclined to exaggerate their own virtues and powers and to neglect the sufferings their actions inflict. In this way, action is morally destructive. And the point may be broadened. Lord Acton said not only that "power tends to corrupt" but that "absolute power corrupts absolutely," and there is evidence suggesting that this part of the maxim, too, can be applied to action. If there is such a thing as

absolute action, it is presumably that carried on by the despotic re-
deemers of our day, who have promised to eradicate the great evils
afflicting human society. The results are those that Christian principles, and Lord Acton's maxim, might lead us to expect: evil becomes extravagantly manifest among men dedicated to the utter destruction of evil. Even God—the God of Christian faith—moved
toward human redemption along the mysterious road of divine weakness, suffering, and death.

Representatives of the "Catholic" tradition ordinarily view action,
as well as power, less negatively. They are attuned to the many good
things human beings do—studying, teaching, worshiping—and cognizant of the inseparability of action—even in some of its harsher
forms, such as revolution—and historical responsibility. But "Reformation" principles do not imply an ideal of passivity or withdrawal;
the whole of this essay will have made that clear. What they do imply
is the importance of remembering that approaching another person
in pursuance of a goal cannot be a pure expression of love; however
noble the goal, however subtle and considerate the actor, the other
person becomes a means and an object of influence. Narrow and definite limits may be placed on how the other person can be "used"—
limits excluding not only physical coercion and lying but even strenuous persuasion. Within those limits, that person still is a means and
an object. My definitions of *activity* and *action*, though designed primarily to etch sharply the character of action and differentiate it
from the kind of doing that is expressive of love, also embody a recognition that some of the things we do are relatively or entirely free of
means-ends calculations and thus of the moral taint attendant on action. These definitions thus free us from any compulsion toward
quietism; at the same time, they can help us understand and distinguish the various moral situations in which we place ourselves in
facing our historical responsibilities, and they can help alert us to the
temptations and illusions infesting those situations.

The modern love of action, so lacking in reservations, reveals the
modern indifference toward spirituality. The prayer of Christian
spirituality is one that resigns the ascendancy gained in action:
"Teach me to do thy will, for thou art my God!"[9] This is not a prayer
of passivity but reflects a faith in God as the origin of all deeds. The

modern assurance that every problem is humanly soluble suggests a very different spirit; it suggests a confusion between the human and the divine.

Yet inaction, too, is antithetical to spirituality. (I am referring to inaction as a settled and final state, as distinguished from the moment of inaction belonging to the prophetic stance; to mark the distinction, let us call it "perpetual inaction.") Every one of the standards according to which action is condemned demands action. Although the dignity of persons is inevitably violated in action, this dignity would be far less recognized in the world than it is had it not been supported by actions such as the establishment of constitutions and the fighting of wars in defense of human rights. Action must be untruthful, yet religion, science, philosophy, and the arts, the main forms of absolute fidelity to the truth, could not survive were they unsupported by action. Action cannot but be anticommunal in some measure, yet communal relationships would be almost nonexistent without areas of peace and order, which are created by action. We must act hesitantly and regretfully, then, but still we must act.

The antithesis of perpetual inaction and spirituality does not lie just in the abandonment of spiritual values that such inaction implies, however. It lies also in illusions that ordinarily accompany inaction. There is, for example, what might be called the illusion of infinitude. Action always involves taking a position, favoring one policy and opposing another, supporting one candidate among several candidates. To refrain from action enables me to entertain the impression—necessarily without careful thought—that I might occupy all possible positions at once. In fact, of course, I cannot. I cannot even stand off from all positions, for however I live, I live in a way that has consequences, even though I do not calculate those consequences and hence do not act. Thus is my finitude manifest. But I do not feel my finitude. Abstaining from action, I am unaware of having to stand in one place and no other, enter one set of relationships and no other, be one kind of person and no other. Finitude means that when one position is taken, many others are rejected. This is realized in lucid action but obscured by inaction.

Something else is obscured as well: moral responsibility. Perpetual inaction gives rise to an illusion of innocence. To refrain from consciously siding with any of the unsatisfactory alternatives before me allows me to suppose that I am morally uncompromised. Being unaware of occupying any particular position, I do not feel vulnerable to any of the criticisms to which any particular position is always exposed. The guilt most often obscured by such illusions of innocence is probably that of complicity in the evils maintained and perpetuated by one's own society and government. Law-abiding inaction is a position in support of the established order, and that is never an innocent position (although rebellion is never innocent, either).

Here again, the life of Bonhoeffer is illustrative. For Germans of the Hitler era, the only alternatives were (1) complicity—active or tacit—in the evils perpetrated by the Nazi regime and (2) resistance. Both entailed, although in very different ways and for very different ends, involvement in violence and even in murder. It was impossible for finite beings in such circumstances to be simply detached and innocent, although a great many honorable Germans understandably tried to be. Bonhoeffer's greatness lay partly in the simple fact that he took cognizance of the necessities inherent in the situation. With deep moral seriousness, he rejected all illusions of moral purity.

Bonhoeffer's life exhibits at once activism and spirituality and in this way exemplifies the main inference to be drawn from the illusions encouraged by perpetual inaction: action can be an element of spirituality when it is divested of pride. This is because it can dissipate the illusions of infinitude and innocence that inaction encourages. It can bring a consciousness of both the human responsibilities and the human limitations implicit in being one among many. Obviously, it does not do this necessarily. It carries the same dangers as perpetual inaction—one lives with no clear consciousness of one's finitude and moral imperfection, and thus true spirituality is precluded at the outset. But Bonhoeffer proved that action can be humble and can open the doors to spiritual life.

Having noted the evils and dangers of both action and inaction, it is important to guard against the mistaken conclusion that the two are on the same moral and spiritual level. It is true that each has its evils—such as objectification of persons in the case of action and neglect of the weak and innocent in the case of inaction—and that each has its dangers—pride of power on one side, for example, and illusions of innocence on the other. There is nonetheless a crucial difference between them. To engage in action is to recognize that we are fallen beings and therefore cannot obey the commands of love without sometimes transgressing against the dignity of persons and the integrity of truth; we are compelled to use power and deceit. Action is a way of lucidly inhabiting the human situation. This cannot be said of perpetual inaction, save with one great qualification.

The qualification is implied by Jesus' ethic of nonresistance, already discussed in connection with the state and its justification. The ethic of nonresistance is, in effect, an ethic of inaction. The conditions under which such an ethic is valid are suggested by Jesus' life—a unique personal destiny, requiring complete abstention from the use of power and a willingness to enter fully into the human situation in other ways, as did Jesus in his poverty, homelessness, and crucifixion. As I have already suggested, however, it seems appropriate for those not called to the unique moral posture of inaction to subject themselves to the ordinary conditions of human existence, conditions in which common sense tells us that it is better for unjust aggressors than for their victims to suffer coercion and that only through the organized power and violence of the state can there be a realm of common liberty.

Although the possibility that some may be called to a life of inaction does not condemn political action, it does seem fitting here to recall the point made earlier in the discussion of the political significance of nonresistance. I suggested in that discussion that nonresistance, without setting a universal standard, relativizes ordinary politics, serving as a reminder of the incongruity of politics and *agape,* of state and community. Here, a like point can be made. A politics of inaction is, from a Christian standpoint, a sign of God's judgment on the politics of action through which the prophetic stance is normally maintained. Granted, the same strictures that apply to nonresistance apply to perpetual inaction. To eschew action without inner certainty of a unique vocation is a presumptuous effort to stand beyond the circumstances that condition the moral practices of finite and fallen beings; and it violates *agape,* abandoning the weak and helpless and ignoring our responsibility for creating and maintaining a realm of common liberty in which community can be sought. Nonetheless, it remains true that action also violates *agape;* moreover, in some measure, it almost always fails. Only through humility, awareness of these moral and practical limitations, does action have spiritual integrity. Those called to inaction remind us of this and help overcome the temptations to pride that inhere in action.

This qualification aside, perpetual inaction must be condemned. Rather than the intense moral seriousness of nonresistance, it manifests neglect of the truth that whatever we do, or refrain from doing, has consequences for others and that action is only choosing among those consequences and consciously bearing the guilt that such choice brings. Perpetual inaction, therefore, even when divested of all illusions of infinitude and innocence, cannot be a way of spiritual life. Action, as exemplified by Bonhoeffer, can.

We see again, accordingly, that the prophetic stance does not mean waiting without acting; it means waiting in preparation for acting and acting in a spirit of attentiveness and humility. It implies a mode of action resting on two premises—that human action is good only in response to the requirements of destiny and that human action is significant only as a counterpoint to the actions of God. But it is far from perpetual inaction.

Here, however, another mistaken conclusion suggests itself, namely, that if action is imperative, suffering is unconditionally evil. But this is not so, for suffering is not the same as perpetual inaction and does not fall under the same condemnation.

There is perhaps no better way of exploring the subject of suffering, especially its relationship to action, than to reflect on T. S. Eliot's striking dictum that "action is suffering/And suffering is action." [10] Each part of this dictum contains an important insight.

The first part of the dictum is of less importance to us than the second, which bears more directly on our principal concern, the potential value of suffering. The first part deserves brief attention, however, because it helps us to understand that suffering is attendant on action and cannot be identified with inaction. Action that is lucid and free of pride brings an awareness of finitude, of moral fallibility, and of singular personal responsibility. These all are types of painful knowledge and show why "action is suffering." Perpetual inaction is tempting because it is comfortable. Action may be tempting, too, of course; it may minister to our pride and cause "our hearts to be lifted up." But action can only do these things under cover of delusions—for example, of perfect human knowledge or righteousness. When our minds are clear, action humbles us, because it brings us into contact with the limits that define our finitude and the failures that mark our moral fallibility. To be humbled in these ways is far from agreeable.

The second part of Eliot's dictum, that suffering is action, points to the potential value of suffering and expresses a classical tenet of Christian faith, symbolized by the Cross. Suffering, like action, may have consequences that are much to be desired. In what way?

The answer is in part readily understandable to common sense. When Paul wrote that "suffering produces endurance, and endurance produces character," he voiced a truth to which common experience attests (even though Paul no doubt rested his statement more on faith than on common experience.)[11] Suffering can make us stronger and more steadfast. It does not do this necessarily; as everyone knows, suffering in some circumstances is destructive. People who have never gone through serious suffering, however, are apt to be soft and vulnerable. Character needs testing and refining. This implies, however, that suffering, although evil in itself, can have good consequences and can be endured in anticipation of those consequences. This is one sense in which "suffering is action."

As Christians understand it, however, the potential value in suffering is not confined to results of the sort to which common experience attests. Paul added to the foregoing statement that "character produces hope, and hope does not disappoint us, because God's love has been poured into our hearts."[12] Here, he was obviously appealing to faith, referring to the mystery that has its primal form in the suffering of Jesus. Although suffering naturally produces endurance, and endurance character, character does not naturally produce hope, at least not the kind of hope that "does not disappoint us." That depends on grace—on the love that God has "poured into our hearts."

Presumably, Eliot was thinking of grace when he said that suffering is action. It is not *our* action, however, if it is grace. It is God's action. At the center of the Christian vision is the proposition that God's most critical act since the creation of the heavens and the earth came about through the suffering of Jesus. That single instance gives meaning to all of the suffering human beings undergo. We must each one, as Paul declared, suffer with Christ, and when we do—Christians believe—we shall also be raised to life with Christ. How this happens is not within our understanding. We can be confident, nevertheless, that suffering has a part in human destiny and is not sheer waste and humiliation. Even the deepest anguish, even death, may bring nearer the Kingdom of God.

It is noteworthy that suffering can be carried on for others, just as action can. Suffering can be vicarious. Christians believe that Jesus suffered in behalf of us all. This does not mean that he relieved the rest of us of all suffering; but he made it possible for our suffering to be an act of participation in his own suffering and in God's redemptive work and not simply a stark and utterly crushing consequence of bad luck or guilt. In that way, he suffered in the place of all human beings. The principle of vicarious suffering suggests that no suffering is wasted. It suggests that the suffering of even a single solitary and unseen person (and Christians have no grounds for asserting that this person must be a Christian) may be an enactment of universal destiny and may bring humanity nearer the eternal fulfillment foreshadowed in the resurrection of Christ.

The phrase "political action" is heard again and again. Christianity allows us to pair this prominent phrase with another that is almost unknown: political suffering. If suffering works in natural and supernatural ways to bring the Kingdom of God nearer to us, then it has consequences for our lives together. And the consequences may be political; suffering may accomplish things that we try to accomplish also through political action. Not that all suffering is political; to say that would deprive the concept of politics of all reasonable meaning. But perhaps, by grace, suffering is political when it is borne in a mood of prophetic hope, and perhaps even the most singular and intimate suffering can take on such significance.

Christ on the Cross thus has a meaning that is spiritual and political at once. We see a single individual, forsaken by all, reduced to complete helplessness, and finally killed, and we see him, through the suffering thus endured, changing the course of history. For Christian faith, the Cross represents for every person a possible form of historical responsibility, an image of the "politics" of powerlessness and inaction. To die "uselessly"—like many political martyrs, unseen and forever unremembered—may be a crucifixion with historical consequences, even though no historian could relate those consequences to their causes or perhaps even perceive them.

We shall consider one more dilemma involved in prophetic spirituality. This dilemma is of particular interest because it involves at one pole an activity that is at the center of spirituality and that is closely connected with saving personal being from social degradation and at the other pole an activity that our involvement in society renders inescapable.

Meditation and Ideology

The word *meditation* is used here to designate several solitary spiritual activities—scriptural reading, theological reflection, remembrance and thanksgiving, and prayer. These are distinct activities, but they go naturally together and make up a set of spiritual pursuits traditional among Christians. As already suggested, philosophical reflection carried on without faith but in a spirit of genuine openness toward transcendence can be a form of meditation. Meditation is not exclusively Christian.

The solitary character of meditation is particularly to be noted. Meditation calls an individual out of society and into an inner universe. It is true that meditative activities are often carried on collectively, and in view of our communal nature, that is appropriate. But no one who wants to read thoughtfully, reflect deeply, or pray undistractedly will be satisfied with doing these things only with others. Withdrawal will prove essential. Meditation is a form of active inwardness, and it is necessarily carried on in large part away from the world.

As is made evident by its solitary character, meditation is a source of individual independence. It is a deeply personal way of searching into reality, and the truths it uncovers are deeply personal—not necessarily different from the truths of others but so much one's own that to give them up would be a sacrifice of selfhood. It is not only the personal nature of the search that makes meditation a school of personal independence, however, but also the object of the search, that is, God, or transcendence. Meditation is a quest for the creative and saving source of personal being. Totalitarian governments would no doubt oppose meditation were it at all widespread, for it brings a person into contact with one who insists that Caesar receive no more than the things that are Caesar's.

Christian faith inspires and demands meditation. There is, it might be said, a Christ of solitude. More familiar to the world is the Christ of crusades, charities, ceremonies, and other public activities. But Christ has also impelled people to read, think, and pray. The inwardness thus attained has been absolutely indispensable to Christianity; without it, there would have been little Christian doctrine and few Christian saints. It is doubtful that anyone can live and grow as a Christian without occasional meditation. Christianity is joined indissolubly with subjectivity, as Kierkegaard insisted, and subjectivity is cultivated in meditation.

In modern times, a very different concept of truth and of our proper relationship with truth has become widespread. Solitude, subjectivity, and personal independence are excluded; searching is assumed to be unnecessary; God is denied or reduced to an idol. Truth of this sort may be referred to as "ideology."

Broadly, an ideology may be defined as a doctrine propagated in order to mobilize the masses for action. An ideology may be revolutionary or conservative, reactionary or liberal. The crucial characteristic of an ideology is not its doctrinal content but its purpose, which is to serve as an instrument of mass mobilization. This requires that it provide simple prescriptions, such as abolishing (or preserving) private property; that it take in life as a whole, with its prescriptions responding to all of the major problems human beings experience; and that it claim finality, purporting to provide not merely sensible advice but changeless truth. Above all, an ideology must be redemptive, calling for action that will fully and finally resolve the major dilemmas of human life.

Ideologies are highly attractive in times of confusion. They provide inner certainty, and they bind together people who feel desolate and forsaken. They offer an escape at once from doubt and from loneliness. It is not surprising that ideologies have flourished in our own tumultuous and bewildered century.

Christians are bound to resist the ideological tendency of our age and to regard all ideologies, regardless of content, with suspicion. Ideological commitment is fundamentally different from faith. And it is antithetical to the meditative search for truth.

Although an ideology is defined primarily by purpose (mass mobilization) rather than content, purpose has an impact on content. For one thing, ideologies tend to be worldly, or, in philosophical terms, "naturalistic." This means that they deal in palpable, present realities, in things that supposedly can be comprehended and controlled. They are intolerant of mysteries, of realities that surpass every human faculty, are known only by revelation, and are never under human control. Without a naturalistic bias, ideologies could not offer prescriptions that purport to be comprehensive, final, and redemptive. If they acknowledged realities such as destiny and God—mysteries—they would have to be far more circumspect. They would have to be humble, hesitant, and open. Were they in these ways circumspect, however, they would not be ideologies. Essential to their appeal is the claim to assured knowledge and powers of confident action. Ideologies promise dominion over history. This is the way they attract the support of the masses (made up, perhaps, of intelligent individuals but existing as a unified historical force only through ideological simplifications, distortions, and falsehoods). History cannot be brought under human dominion unless it is exhaustively accessible to human understanding. This is the source of ideological naturalism.

Ideologies must be not only naturalistic but also, at least tacitly, atheistic. Within a universe that in all of its depths and distances is nothing more than a vast conflux of comprehensible and controllable realities, there can be no God. If a Christian ideology were to be framed (which happens when faith is reduced to inalterable dogma), God would have to be in some way tacitly denied.

The difference between an ideological commitment and Christian faith, however, is deeper than this comparison may suggest. The belief that the world is all and the belief that beyond the world there is God are not on the same footing; they are not reducible to mere contradictory assertions. Rather, they express dramatically different ways of approaching reality. One expresses an attitude of mastery, the other of openness; one is unapologetically proud, the other aspires to humility; an ideological commitment represents a venture in historical sovereignty, whereas Christian faith is fundamentally responsive. The crux of the matter is that whereas worldly realities can be known and mastered by human beings, God cannot. The God envisioned in Christian faith speaks to us but is never an intellectual possession; we can appeal to God but cannot act upon him to produce calculated consequences.

Christianity does not consist primarily in doctrines, nor is a Christian someone who accepts Christian doctrines. Christian faith is steady attentiveness and availability to God in Christ. Numerous doctrines have been formulated to help us understand all that this means, and some of these doctrines are of incalculable historical and personal importance. Nonetheless, one becomes a Christian not by assenting to doctrines but by entering into daily and hourly relations with the living being whom the doctrines concern.

The difference between Christian faith and political ideologies is manifest in meditation. Christian faith inspires inner journeys that are not arranged or led by social and political authorities. Ideologies are bound to discourage such journeys. They are unnecessary because the truth is already known; and they are undesirable because the point is not to contemplate the truth but to act on it and change the world. It is often supposed that Christians claim knowledge of all truth, and of course some of them do. But Christian faith in essence entails no such claim, as is evident in Augustine's declaration that we believe *in order* to understand. Faith does not mean possessing the truth but rather means confidently searching for it—and that must draw us into meditation.

Attitudes toward ultimate reality determine attitudes toward human beings. The divergence between ideological commitment and Christian faith entails divergent images of man and in consequence divergent social and political philosophies.

Ideologies exalt human beings in an immediate and unequivocal way; they accord humans command over history. They call on them to stand forth in their pride and seize the mastery of events that is proper to the highest living species. In contrast, it may seem that Christians, denying that human beings have either the power or the goodness to dominate history, deny them dignity. As we have seen, however, the Christian abasement of human beings is paradoxical; it prepares for their exaltation. The ideological exaltation of human beings is also paradoxical; it leads to their abasement. The reason is that the ideological image of exalted humanity is false. Hence, it destroys our appreciation of real human beings and our understanding of the requisites for being human. The ideological image is false in at least three different ways.

First, original sin is denied, partly because it is rationally incomprehensible, partly because it would nullify ideological designs and expectations. Unless human beings can be explained and managed and counted on finally to be unselfish and cooperative, and unless some of them even now are wise and good enough to do the explaining and managing, ideologies are nonsense. Their supposed comprehensiveness and finality will prove illusory and their redemptive promises void.

Second, and for similar reasons, death is neglected. It is assumed to be no more than a natural fact among other facts of similar significance (or insignificance). The truth, however, is that death encloses our lives and all natural facts within a mystery. It prevents us from knowing, as we know the things around us, the shape and meaning of our existence. It renders a human being ultimately inexplicable. And it casts doubt on ideological aims, for if death sooner or later extinguishes every person, the value of any earthly paradise is questionable. "Eat and drink, for tomorrow we die." And not least important is that death is humiliating. If the great leaders and inspirers of ideological movements must die as does everyone else, we cannot help wondering whether they really can be sovereigns of history. The ideological neglect of death thus is a falsification of life; it is essential, however, to the plausibility of ideological claims.

Finally, even finitude, in the form above all of unsurpassable limits on our knowledge, is ignored. "O Lord," the Psalmist writes, "thou hast searched me and known me!"[13] He then adds that "such knowledge is too wonderful for me; it is high, I cannot attain it."[14] Ideological leaders and thinkers are less humble. Essential to an ideology is the presupposition that man has been searched and known by man.

Sin, death, and finitude: these are not plain, conclusive facts like the countless everyday facts that fill our lives; they are aspects of the mystery of our humanity. They belong in the sphere of meditation. Cultivating our consciousness of our destiny, unfathomable by our worldly minds but, Christians believe, revealed in Christ, meditation safeguards our humanity. It protects us from delusions of historical sovereignty, delusions of possessing all things at the very moment when we have lost our own being.

Fostering such delusions, ideology threatens our humanity. A human being, as known to us in the world, is a creature of darkness, filled with darkness in the form of sin, moving toward the darkness of death, and hedged about always by the darkness of finitude. The creature exalted in the ideologies is all light, but the light is merely that of everyday factuality, not of revelation. Ideological man is without mystery and hence is not human. To say this is not merely to manipulate abstractions. Ideologies have repeatedly brought to power men whom we characterize as inhuman. And these men, in pursuit of their ideological goals, have reduced entire nations to circumstances we also characterize as inhuman. The logic here is that already noted in the philosophy of the man-god: those who refuse to be human in order to be divine are fated to be neither human nor divine, but monstrous. This logic is often dramatically evident among ideological leaders, whose redemptive pretensions and criminal activities are starkly in contrast.

"Whoever would save his life," Jesus said, "will lose it."[15] The ideologies represent the titanic efforts of human beings in recent times to "save their lives"—to do away with evil through comprehensive programs of political action. In the course of these efforts, they have "lost their lives" in the sense that they have obscured and defaced the human image. Setting out to exalt individuals, they have ended by murdering them.

Ideologies typically promise community (both communism and fascism, for example, stand for a unity more perfect and intense, as they accurately assert, than has ever been realized by a civilized society), and the power of the ideologies is no doubt owing in part to the alienation and uprootedness that make such promises alluring. But they close off the only route to authentic community—free communication. Totalitarian governments systematically subvert the uninhibited speech and spontaneous, roving attentiveness essential to community. This accords with their view of human beings. Creatures whose vision is not distorted by sin or limited by finitude and death need not search for the truth; and their relations with one another need not be burdened with ignorance and disagreement. In short, they are spared the trials of communication. They are ready for the perfect unity of paradise. In fact, of course, they are not. Evading communication, they deprive themselves of the very possibility of community. Just as the ideological leader is a monstrous semblance of the man-god, the totalitarian society is a monstrous simulacrum of paradise. Instead of the open visage of faith, there is the domineering glance of mastery. Instead of liberty and the searching communication liberty makes possible, there is the hysterical unanimity of mass rallies and the despairing silence of concentration camps.

The secularism of the ideologies precludes prophetic hope. Awaiting the Kingdom of God is senseless; men and women must take steps to assure the coming of a kingdom exclusively and defiantly human. This effort, in its proud humanity, will appeal in some measure to almost everyone. Nevertheless, it represents a human effort to perform a divine task.

Meditation, in contrast, sustains prophetic hope. Although carried on in solitude, it is fundamentally communal. It is a search for truths that are universally human and thus belong between and among us. Christian exponents of meditation invariably recognize the imperative of love, and it is hardly going too far to say that meditation is unfulfilled without attainment—even if, paradoxically, in solitude—of the luminous solidarity that is community. Moreover, the community sought in meditation is not merely a personal possibility. It is, for Christians, the Kingdom of God, the purpose and end of history. Meditation thus is a way of standing in history and living our common destiny, and those engaged in meditation may appropriately make themselves familiar with the political and social realities of their time and reflect on those realities in relation to God and the destiny ordained in Christ. Meditation is a way of watching for signs of God's Kingdom and a time for praying for the "clean heart" and the "new and right spirit" that will enable one to see them.[16]

The dialectic of Christian existence is evident here, as everywhere, however. Historical involvement, even that attained through meditation, necessitates ideological thinking. To understand and act upon events is not possible without a set of ideas explaining the historical forces at work and prescribing ends for action. And in spite of all precautions—keeping oneself exposed, for example, to fresh experiences and to challenges from opponents—these ideas will take on ideological characteristics. They will simplify reality, for that is in the very nature of ideas; they will be comprehensive, since it would be arbitrary and careless to ignore anything relevant to the ends we seek; they will carry a quiet claim to finality simply because action requires that at some point inquiry be concluded and minds for the moment closed. These ideas will provisionally leave God out of account because they concern *human* action, and they will provisionally objectify persons because they concern human *action.* And ideologically tinted ideas fulfill not only a personal but also a political need. Those engaged in action need to provide a picture of the realities around them in order to attract the support of other people and of the multitudes.

Even ideal human beings, then, would be forced by the necessities of action to envision their situation ideologically. Actual human beings will always be more ideological than circumstances require. Ideologies appeal to qualities like sloth, which welcomes oversimplification and recoils from thought and observation. And above all, ideologies appeal to pride, to our fierce desire to conceive of all reality as within the scope of our knowledge and command.

Meditation must therefore at times struggle against undue ideological entanglement. Anyone who carries on historically responsible meditation will be—as one who not only meditates but also acts, at least temporarily and tentatively—a liberal, a socialist, a conservative. The act of meditation, however, will aim at keeping such classifications continually in peril. It will be an act of political self-criticism.

The struggle with ideology does not divert meditation from its proper task. Meditation should illuminate one's responsibilities in history, and those responsibilities include the creation and use of ideological concepts. Meditation should render political action wise and compassionate, yet such action cannot be carried on without ideological guidelines. Meditation should envelop historical success and failure (in both of which ideology is bound to have an important part) in a mystical consciousness of the destiny shaping events and time. Ideology reflects our fallenness, and resisting the excesses and corruptions with which it threatens us accords fully with the role of meditation as the center of prophetic spirituality.

"Dying, and Behold we Live"

Prophetic spirituality is a concentrated effort to grasp and embody in one's life the spiritual meaning of the prophetic stance. There are other forms of prophetic spirituality than those discussed above. I said nothing, for example, of dialogue or of the discipline of remembrance, which is so crucial for gaining a sense of one's own destiny. In all of its forms, however, prophetic spirituality is an effort to become deeply conscious, to enter fully into the truth, of our journey through history into eternity. Prophetic spirituality is intensely personal because my consciousness of history is inseparable from my understanding of my own acts of obedience and disobedience, my own suffering and action, my own involvement in meditation and in the use of ideological concepts. It is personal because it is an effort to discern my own destiny. But fully understood, my destiny is universally human. Hence, prophetic spirituality is fundamentally political as well as personal—aimed at discerning, in the necessities and responsibilities that shape my life, the meaning of history.

This meaning could not be more concisely or eloquently expressed than in Paul's words, quoted in the heading of this section. Paul was describing to the Christians in Corinth the experience he and his companions were going through. "We are treated as impostors," he wrote, "and yet are true; as unknown, and yet well known; as *dying, and behold we live*; as punished, and yet not killed; as sorrowful, yet always rejoicing; as poor, yet making many rich; as having nothing, and yet possessing everything."[17] Thus, Paul delineated the dialectic of Christian life, a dialectic based on the destiny set before every person and before all humanity in the crucifixion and resurrection of Christ. Prophetic spirituality is an effort to discern and live this destiny in its full historical—hence, political—sweep.

Accordingly, it might be said that prophetic spirituality is an effort to live and illuminate the crucifixion and resurrection inherent in the prophetic stance. The crucifixion in prophetic existence consists, in the broadest sense, simply in accepting unreservedly the constraints and responsibilities imposed by one's own life situation. In this way one dies. It may seem that a mere situation is not so lethal— that a situation, indeed, may be innocuous. But to inhabit the particular circumstances, some of them always disagreeable and inalterable, that define a situation is something only a finite and mortal being is compelled to do. Hence, to live lucidly within any situation is to know that one's knowledge and powers are limited and that one must die; it is to know also that we are sinful, for every situation is made more constricting and dangerous, festooned with thorns, as it were, by one's own misdeeds and by the past and possible misdeeds of others.

A situation is inherently insecure. One does not create a situation but rather finds oneself within it. And a situation has no knowable boundaries; in the last analysis, it comprises all of the realities that in any way touch on one's own being. In short, to inhabit a situation is to realize the tininess and fragility of the worlds we construct in an effort to dominate reality and live in security. In a situation, one is exposed to dangers continually, although one can identify only a few of the dangers. To enter fully into one's situation is deliberately to become vulnerable, to place oneself in the pathway of suffering. Only in a situation, and never in a world, can there be a crucifixion. This is why people try ceaselessly to evade the consciousness of being in a situation: through alcohol and drugs; through sensual pleasure; through the incessant busyness that keeps us ever from thinking; through the kind of revolutionary commitments in which human beings pretend to be absolute masters of historical circumstances. Wealth is avidly sought because it promises, however falsely, to set one free from all circumstantial constraints. Probably every kind of idolatry is an effort to evade the knowledge that, as human, we are in essence situational beings. But Christians believe that the God who became incarnate as a particular human being, as Jesus Christ, does not allow us to evade circumstances. Rather, he gives circumstances the form of destiny. Faith requires us to enter lucidly and unreservedly into our life situations, like the grains of wheat that fall into the earth and die and only thus "bear much fruit."[18]

Were I to think that my personal situation is peculiarly mine, and mine alone, however, I would be deeply in error. Such an impression would signify either a failure of understanding or an act of abstraction, perhaps unconscious, in which my own circumstances were cut off from those of others. Circumstances important in one person's life, such as wealth or poverty and health or illness, are shared with many others. And they reflect historical conditions. Disease, not only in its impact on lives but in its very character and prevalence, is related to historical times and places; material deprivation suffered by one person reflects national and often global economic circumstances; strains that poison the intimacy of a family can usually be fully understood only against the background of encompassing social trends. In short, every personal situation is also historical.

In prophetic spirituality, one tries to realize that this is so. One tries to submit and respond to one's own circumstances in their universal humanity. And one tries to contemplate the life and suffering even of distant peoples with an awareness that, as John Donne said, "no man is an island."

I have tried in this essay to illuminate diverse aspects of the dying that is inherent in the prophetic stance. I have tried to show that maintaining the prophetic stance is living in the consciousness of being separated from transcendence, alienated from human beings, subject to fate. It is living amidst equivocal demands—that we grant liberty yet coerce people to keep them from harming one another; that we liberate them from oppressive social and economic conditions but safeguard old, and almost invariably unjust, forms of life that hold back the chaos implicit in sin. It is realizing the infinitesimal power and consequent political insignificance of a single individual, while offering one's own weakness in history as a medium for God's strength. ("When I am weak, then I am strong.")[19]

The principle that we are strong only when we are weak, rich only when we are poor, alive only when we are dead, gives Christian hope and the Christian way of living in history the distinctive character that marks off Christian radicalism from secular radicalism. We do not command the future, in the Christian vision, but receive it from the hands of God; and we receive it only by giving up all pretensions of historical sovereignty, in dying. And the future given to us is not confined to the world or describable in terms of worldly realities; the things "God has prepared for those who love him" are things "no eye has seen, nor ear heard, nor the heart of man conceived."[20] Hence, to enter into this future we must abandon the conviction so natural to us, and so essential to our pride, that reality is nothing more than what we can see and hear; and we must resist the nearly irresistible inclination to count on nothing that is not assured by our own power or by some set of human arrangements that we idolatrously trust. In these ways, too, we must die. A radicalism formed by so paradoxical a faith is drastically different from secular radicalism. It is prepared to encounter limitations and suffer defeat; it is impelled by faith rather than self-confidence; in a word—a word that will damn it in the eyes of secular radicals—it is otherworldly. That otherworldliness carries political dangers must be admitted; for Christians, defeat does not bring despair, and the result may be that they are more willing than they should be to suffer defeat. But otherworldliness may have consequences more favorable to a radical posture. It may give rise to a hope, free of arrogance, that cannot be defeated.

It is through hope, through an indefeasible expectancy, that we rise from death into life. Faith tells us that situations, recast by God, become destinies. The resurrection inherent in the prophetic stance comes as we perceive in our circumstances the visible outlines of destiny. Life and expectancy are inseparable. We live in time and thus into the future. The worst situations are not necessarily those that cause the most intense immediate suffering but those that seem to take away the future. Biological death is fearful because it apparently nullifies all expectancy. This is why the awakening of hope, in response to Jesus' proclamation of the coming of the Kingdom of God, is a resurrection.

This rising into life, like the dying inherent in entering fully and lucidly into one's life situation, is at once personal and historical. It is personal, or else it is not real. Christian hope is anticipation of the Kingdom of *God*—the God who, in Christ, exalts individuals and is encountered in the most secret recesses of personal life. But Christian hope is anticipation of the *Kingdom* of God. The God who enters the innermost being of one person is not indifferent to other persons. Christ is the Son of Man—universally human—and we are exalted in company with all human beings. When I discover my own destiny in Christ, I discover a destiny that belongs to everyone and is worked out in history.

In the twentieth century, expectancy is elusive. Severe disappointments have punctuated our times. The dangers of war, of economic dislocation, of contamination and disease are present continuously in our minds and in public discussion. The air is full of alarm, and fearlessness almost seems a token of insensitivity.

But hope is demanded of us, Christians believe, by God. Faith is confidence in the future that God has placed before us in Christ. It is readiness to receive the good implicit in our destinies. Hopelessness is sin, unwillingness to anticipate anything not comprehensible to the human mind and assured through human power. We are drawn into the sin of hopelessness by fear, and fear arises from pride. In our pride, we are fearful unless all things are under our control. But they are not, and the eventual failure of control fans the flames of our fear. Even so, unless broken by grace, we persist in our pride and live without hope; we prefer even despair to humility.

The fearlessness of faith, then, does not come easily. The New Testament shows the apostles witnessing miracles with wonder but forgetting them immediately and confining their expectations to worldly probabilities. In this respect, most people are like them. They gratefully receive gifts of insight and community and for brief moments breathe the air of the destined community that Christians call the Kingdom of God. But soon they fall back into fear. Grace announces itself by dispelling fear; it bestows expectancy. The concept of personal immortality represents the expectancy that faith maintains even in the face of physical death.

Faith in eternal life, however, is not a refuge from an unbearable present time, and the prophetic stance is not merely a way of dwelling in the future. A sense of destiny is a sense of the form and meaning of existing circumstances. To see what is coming is to see what the present time is making for and thus to see anew the situation we inhabit. Looking ahead with prophetic hope thus means realizing that in spite of all confusion and violence "this is the day which the Lord has made."[21] It is a day illuminated by the coming of the Kingdom of God. In the Psalm from which this declaration is drawn, there immediately follows the supplication, "Save us, we beseech thee, O Lord!" Thus, the future is invoked, the present time transcended. But the light of our ordained future falls back on the present time and creates day—an interval of light enabling us to see reality and to live.

Living in the daytime created by God is, in the Christian view, the same thing as living in the presence of Christ. Christ is God in his humanity and in his care for us; he is light and life. As a bodily human being, Christ is no longer among us. As the form and purpose of human life, however, he is present everywhere and gives our existence a meaning that circumstances cannot nullify. We must die— many times, and in many ways—but we can die with Christ, and hence we can live with Christ.

If this is the day that the Lord has made—a day made light by the glory of Christ—we must, as the Psalmist says, "rejoice and be glad in it." The prophetic stance means not sadness and resignation but a paradoxical joy—the joy expressed by Paul when he wrote, "Far be it from me to glory, except in the cross of our Lord Jesus Christ, by which the world has been crucified to me, and I to the world."[22] There is no avoiding the Cross. The politics of the twentieth century, devoted either to maintaining and increasing the pleasures of a consumers' society or else to creating a worldly paradise through revolutionary action, has bent every effort to avoiding the Cross. In this way, sometimes frivolously, sometimes fiercely, we have caricatured our ancient paradisiacal hopes. To the world we have thus created, we must be crucified. The standard of prophetic expectancy forbids us to glory in material prosperity or revolutionary projects. But it does not forbid us to glory. If the Cross means life as well as death, we are not faithful to the Cross unless we live, now, rejoicing in the day the Lord has made.

Postscript:
World Politics

It may seem strange, in an age when sovereign and contentious nations are armed with nuclear weapons, that I have said so little about world politics. Does not the issue of peace have priority over every other political issue? In a sense, of course, it does; if it is not adequately met, we shall all perish. In another sense, however, I believe it is secondary—secondary to the larger problem of discovering, understanding, and abiding by the standards that must guide us in our political lives as a whole. Achieving peace will come about not mainly by our discovering truths peculiar to international relations but rather by our gaining political wisdom. This is why the great classics of political philosophy for the most part neglect international relations and instead are devoted to general political issues, such as the nature of justice. It is not that their authors were indifferent to peace, even in prenuclear times; but they saw political wisdom as the primary issue.

The assumption of the classical writers has governed the writing of this essay. I believe that peace would be near attainment if the political insights and attitudes that inform Christian faith were to become widespread. Thus, I feel that indirectly I have been addressing the issues of world politics throughout the preceding pages. Nevertheless, a few explicit words seem in order; hence this postscript.

Christianity is dramatically universalist and pacific. All peoples are the work of a single Creator; all are addressed by a single Redeemer.

We have seen that *agape* disregards conventional and natural inequalities. In like fashion, it crosses national boundaries and ignores racial differences. "There is no distinction between Jew and Greek," says Paul; "the same Lord is Lord of all and bestows his riches upon all who call upon him."[1]

The prophetic stance means standing apart from the disorder and violence of the world and representing the ideal of a community comprising all nations and peoples. Christians who share wholeheartedly in the self-righteousness of a nation or the conceit of a race have, at least for the moment, suspended their faith. The imperative of social transformation therefore concerns not only relationships within nations, such as those between business and labor and between government and citizens, but also relationships among nations and among civilizations. For a prophetic conscience, the stark absence of peace and justice in the world constitutes a call for global transformation.

Oversimplifications concerning peace and world harmony, however, are perhaps even more abundant than oversimplifications concerning equality and community within nations. The flagrant inhumanity often characterizing international relations seems to inspire particularly vapid intellectual responses. Here, as elsewhere, Christianity can help us to take into account the ambiguities of the human situation and to escape platitudes and illusions of the kind secularism encourages.

Among these is the idea of abolishing nations, all of us becoming citizens of the world. Christians are wary of nationalism but not opposed unconditionally to nations. The prophetic attitude is suggested in the myth of the Tower of Babel. "The whole earth had one language," as the well-known story tells, and men set out to build a great city and a tower "with its top in the heavens."[2] Seeing this as a step in the direction of more ambitious designs, God intervened. He "confused" the language of humans and "scattered them abroad upon the face of the whole earth." This myth does not tell us that the existence of distinct and separate nations is good in itself. It does seem to say, however, that such a condition is a punishment for our pride, and it suggests, in this way, that the abolition of nations is not to be undertaken casually or confidently.

An interesting perspective on the matter is provided by the status of Israel in the history of salvation. Christians believe that God initiated the process of redemption by speaking first not to humanity at large but to Israel, to a particular people. Even Jesus, according to the New Testament, addressed himself primarily to his fellow Israelites. Jesus was not a world citizen. He was far less cosmopolitan than Stoics who had lived centuries earlier. The peculiar role of Israel in the history of salvation does not imply, of course, that national distinctions pertain to eternity or even to all of history. By implication, nevertheless, it does accord them legitimacy of a kind.

How can this legitimacy be described? In less reserved terms, I believe, than many will be prepared to accept. The Christian view of Israel suggests that the nation plays a mediating role in the relationship of an individual to the human race and to God. One participates in human affairs and stands before God—normally, at least—by belonging to a particular society. Such an idea accords fully with the concept of the prophetic stance. Of course, other nations were not hallowed as was Israel, and once Christ had appeared and the Church had been formed, even Israel was no longer God's principal agent. This role was assumed by the Church. But the Church has never claimed to replace the nation altogether, and there are no manifest reasons for rejecting the principle suggested by sacred history—that to live one's destiny in history, one must live in a nation. Thus, Dostoevsky thought that expatriates, people without a nation, were in a sense strangers on the earth—alienated from the human race and usually godless. Dostoevsky is only one of many Christians to hold a view of this kind.

Caution no doubt is in order here, for Christianity does not mandate any very definite view of nations. This at the very least can be said, however: that Christian *agape* does not condemn the unique obligations and affections that link fellow citizens. Although there are dangers in all discriminatory obligations and affections, Christian universalism does not set an all-inclusive love in opposition to moral and emotional bonds with particular peoples and places, for love that is limited still is love.

Christians go further than this, however, in their global realism. When the world is divided among diverse nations and peoples, certain other phenomena are normally present—for example, power politics, war, and nationalism. Some of these Christian morality condemns, but not all of them.

Power politics, for example, is not necessarily contrary to Christian standards. It might seem that it would be, for a world order upheld by the efforts of nations and coalitions of nations to frighten one another into quiescence is surely distant from a world order upheld by *agape*. As we have seen, however, one of the realities inseparable from our fallenness is power. Even within families and among friends, power in various forms has a part. In the relationships of nations, power is bound to have a far larger part. As Reinhold Niebuhr brought out in a book significantly entitled *Moral Man and Immoral Society*,[3] the selfishness and exaggerated self-esteem often found in individuals are much more pronounced and unchecked among nations. Individuals occasionally are moved by love or sympathy to sacrifice their own interests, whereas nations as corporate entities pursue their own interests unswervingly; individuals are sometimes humble, nations almost never. A nation, with its vast size, its indeterminate life span, and its symbolic force as the living presence of a historic past, is a dangerously plausible object of idolatry. Little can check a nation, therefore, but power. In a world of independent nations, power politics is thus inevitable.

And, probably, war—but not necessarily nuclear war—is inevitable, too. Although Christianity is pacific, it does not issue ordinarily in pacifism. By the standard of *agape*, war manifestly is one of the greatest of evils. It is not necessarily, however, a greater evil than any other. It may sometimes be a lesser evil than some other evil preventable by war—a despotism obliterating all freedom and authentic communication, for example. To refuse under any circumstances to fight is to refuse to make such comparisons. Is this tantamount to refusing to face the ambiguities of human existence? Is it implicitly even idolatrous, in a negative way, making one evil, of the many that crowd human life, absolute?

The Christian attitude toward nations, power, and war shows that prophetic hope is not "tender-minded." A hope that is eschatological, neither confined to nor dependent on worldly realities, can accept the harsh conditions of historical existence without being cynical or despairing.

I suggest that the "tough-minded" attitudes of Christianity have not been rendered inappropriate by nuclear weapons. In spite of the terrible risks now involved, world politics goes on as before. There are still sovereign nations; the balance of power governs their relations; and there are frequent, nonnuclear wars. None of this has been altered by the vehement moralizing inspired by the threat of nuclear conflict, and no one has shown how it can be changed in any fundamental way. It certainly will not be changed by a world constitutional convention patterned on the convention that created the United States.

It may seem that Christianity should do something to illuminate circumstances so dangerous as those created by nuclear weapons. I think that it does, but with a light that it has cast on human circumstances from the beginning. Christianity long has held that human life in the world is carried on in close company with death. It has held that men themselves, in their fallenness, are the bringers of death. It has held that sometime, in some sense, death will come upon the entire human enterprise, and history will end. None of this expresses complacency in the face of human trials and suffering, and no one familiar with Christian history and literature can think that it does. Christian composure in the presence of death expresses, rather than callousness, a consciousness that death is not superior to destiny.

The objection may be made that never before has the very continuance of the human species been threatened. But Christianity has always been at grips with something more profoundly unsettling than the possible death of the species, and that is the certain death of every individual. It is the individual that is exalted, after all, not the species, and the death of an individual constitutes a crisis of meaning that is not altered fundamentally by the uncertain future of the species. If we can face without despair the inevitability of the death of each one of us, then our footing is solid; we shall not be overwhelmed by things threatening the human race at large.

It goes without saying, however, that Christians do not take lightly the threat of nuclear war, and one can find in Christian principles, if not a specific answer to the threat, something with an important bearing on it. This is the Christian sense of values and the standpoint it provides for criticizing common secular values. To a greater extent than is generally realized, it may be in our values rather than our political skills that the threat of nuclear war lies. By this, I mean that our vulnerability to nuclear annihilation may be due not as much to the bombs and missiles that make annihilation possible, even though our vulnerability would not exist without them, as to a hidden willingness, or even inclination, to use them. It may be, even while dreading the thought of nuclear war, that we calmly entertain attitudes that make nuclear war a likely eventuality. If so, the nuclear crisis is not fundamentally military or political but moral. It is this possibility that gives Christian values their bearing on our common jeopardy.

Christianity leads us to question the ends pursued in modern global politics. It challenges both the candid selfishness and the ostentatious unselfishness that motivate nations today and keep dangerous company with nuclear arms.

Candid selfishness is found almost universally among officials and is widely affirmed among scholars as well; its usual name is "the national interest." The principle that the national interest is the highest aim to be pursued by a nation in its dealings with other nations is ordinarily defended most strongly by those who also defend the use of power in pursuing national aims. It seems to be assumed that power as a means goes necessarily with national interest as an end. It is difficult, however, to see any logical connection. Power is not necessarily used for selfish purposes. If it ordinarily is, that is due to the selfishness of those who use it, not to the character of power. No doubt, there is a *psychological* connection between power and national selfishness. Those who seek and accumulate power are not likely to be people of the kind who are given to self-sacrifice. But in principle, power can serve ends set by *agape,* and men of power are not inevitably so consumed by selfishness that it is pointless to say that it should. Hence, Christian doctrine, for all of its realism, clearly implies that selfishness among nations is no more justified than is selfishness among individuals. Correspondingly, the notion that nations are obliged to serve only the national interest is no more valid than an ethic of selfishness for individuals.

One may ask why, if Christians accept power as unavoidable, they do not accept national selfishness for the same reason. The answer is that one is a necessary means, the other a freely chosen end. To reject power would be to reject the possibility of reaching any good ends in history. To reject national selfishness, however, is only to reject an evil end, opening the way for power to be better used. Nations will no doubt be selfish as long as nations exist. To acquiesce unprotestingly in the selfishness of one's own nation, however, would be to conform voluntarily to the way of the world, abandoning *agape*.

At the opposite extreme from unapologetic national selfishness is a form of ostentatious unselfishness—ideological universalism. The goals of the nation are completely identified with the supposedly true goals of the human race. The nation claims to serve selflessly the interests of mankind, and these it knows surely and comprehensively. A politics of this kind was practiced by France in the wake of the revolution of 1789 and by the Soviet Union in recent times. It might seem as though a dedicated universalism would be sanctioned by the Christian ethic of love. But Christianity, alert to the deviousness and subtlety of sin, suggests that proud and pretentious unselfishness is no better morally than candid selfishness. The character of saints shows that goodness is unpretentious. And the teaching of Jesus suggests that the goals of love are unpretentious; we are not obliged forthwith to create a good life for the entire human race but merely to help our "neighbors." Modern universalist politics is a sign less of expanding love than of declining faith. It is the politics of the man-god.

Christians must be especially suspicious of ideological universalism that is expressed in war. Pride and pretentiousness are ordinarily exacerbated by war. How far Christians in the past have departed from their own principles is indicated by the fact that the word most commonly used to designate a universalist war, *crusade*, is, as everyone knows, derived from Christian military expeditions. In no period of history are there many examples of Christian resistance to the universalist conceits of war-making governments, and typically Christians have joined enthusiastically and uncritically in the wartime jingoism of their nations. Such behavior, however, exemplifies the weakness and sinfulness of Christians and not the true meaning of Christianity.

The challenge of nuclear war, then, is perhaps simple and primarily moral: for nations to find ways of being neither selfish nor morally proud. The demand on prophetic intelligence is not primarily that of inventing military and political devices to forestall nuclear catastrophe, although such devices might help. It is rather that of discovering—in our national lives—how to affirm and live the ancient idea that the human race is a single community and how to do this unpretentiously. The idea was foreshadowed among the ancient Hebrews, was clearly stated by the Stoics, and was a commonplace of medieval Christian political thought. It is unmistakably implied by *agape*. But in our national lives, we either repudiate it openly or affirm it in pride.

The challenge is probably given its most urgent form by the impoverished and tumultuous multitudes of Asia, the Middle East, Africa, and Latin America. What does love require of us, the prosperous and industrialized nations, in relation to these stricken masses of exalted individuals? The question is exceedingly difficult. We do not know how to lead nations to prosperity, and even less, in our own spiritual squalor, do we know how to teach them true values. But for the wealthy nations, most of them ostensibly Christian, to accept the material poverty and spiritual turmoil of the greater part of the human race, seeking primarily to assure their own safety and material advantages, is, from a Christian standpoint, intolerable.

There is at least one organization in the world that should articulately represent the aspiration toward universal community, and that is the Church. The Church is an implicit condemnation of national pride, and there are no more shameful chapters in Christian history than those that show churchmen uncritically, sometimes fanatically, endorsing the ambitions and moral arrogance of their national governments. To ask nations to forswear national pride—the pride of uninhibited selfishness and of ideological universalism—may be asking too much. But to ask the Church openly to oppose such pride does not seem extreme. Its principles manifestly permit nothing less. A truly universalist Church would defend against both jingoists and ideologues the authority and mystery of the human community envisioned in prophetic hope.

The prophetic stance becomes sharply paradoxical when we look out at the world and try to understand the responsibilities it places on us. The selfishness and pretentiousness of nations and the hatreds and economic disparities dividing them reflect the tragic character of history. And we must acknowledge not only the tragic but also the fateful character of history. Even powerful nations are inept and weak before the tasks of global transformation. Individuals seem altogether helpless. In these circumstances, it is hard for prophetic hope not to be reduced to mere sentimentality, a matter of entertaining vague sympathy for distant peoples, peoples often no more real in one's mind than if they had lived three thousand years in the past. I do not know how atheists can avoid political despair. For Christians, and for all who in any way have faith in human destiny, the ultimate future does not depend on the practical efficacy, or even on the wisdom, of nations and individuals. Our responsibility is only to be attentive to God, or transcendence, to the deepest necessities of history, and to human beings everywhere; and to be available for the future that is given us. We must watch and—if we are Christians—pray. Paul's statement, quoted earlier, "When I am weak, then I am strong,"[4] bears on this situation. In the face of world disorder and suffering, all of us are weak. Prophetic hope rests on the faith that in admitting this, we are paradoxically strong.

Endnotes

Preface

1. Isaiah 1:18 (Revised Standard Version).

Prologue: The Prophetic Stance

1. John 3:16 (Revised Standard Version).
2. I Corinthians 7:29–31 (RSV).
3. Martin Buber, *The Prophetic Faith,* trans. Carlyle Witton-Davies (New York, 1949), 62.
4. Isaiah 5:19 (RSV).
5. David Tracy, *Blessed Rage for Order: The New Pluralism in Theology* (Minneapolis, 1975), 249.

One. The Exaltation of the Individual

1. I Corinthians 1:21 (Revised Standard Version).
2. I John 4:19 (RSV).
3. I John 4:11 (RSV).
4. Romans 9:3 (RSV). ("I could wish that I myself were accursed and cut off from Christ for the sake of my brethren, my kinsman by race.")
5. Luke 22:42 (RSV).
6. Matthew 18:21–22 (RSV).
7. I Corinthians 13:7 (RSV).
8. II Corinthians 4:18 (RSV).
9. Romans 8:28 (King James Version).
10. John 3:8 (RSV).
11. Matthew 13:32 (RSV).
12. Matthew 19:30 (RSV).

13. Galatians 3:28 (RSV).

14. Romans 7:15 (RSV).

15. Fyodor Dostoevsky, *The Adolescent*, trans. Andrew R. MacAndrew (New York, 1971), 389.

Two. Prophetic Hope

1. Thomas Hobbes, *Leviathan, or the Matter, Forme, and Power of a Commonwealth Ecclesiastical and Civil*, ed. Michael Oakeshott (Oxford, n.d.), 57.

2. Isaiah 55:8 (Revised Standard Version).

3. Albert Camus, *The Rebel*, trans. Anthony Bower (New York, 1954).

4. Deuteronomy 8:11–17 (RSV).

5. Deuteronomy 8:19 (RSV).

6. Psalm 27:14 (RSV).

7. Psalm 46:10 (RSV).

8. Psalm 130:5–6 (RSV).

9. Martin Buber, *The Prophetic Faith*, trans. Carlyle Witton-Davies (New York, 1949), 136.

10. Matthew 24:42–44 (RSV).

11. I Corinthians 16:13; I Thessalonians 5:2–6 (RSV).

12. See Eberhard Bethge, *Dietrich Bonhoeffer: Man of Vision, Man of Courage*, trans. Eric Mosbacher *et al.*; ed. Edwin Robertson (New York, 1970).

13. Dietrich Bonhoeffer, *Letters and Papers from Prison*, trans. Reginald Fuller *et al.*; ed. Eberhard Bethge (New York, 1971), 272.

14. *Ibid.*, 276.

15. *Ibid.*, 289.

16. See Reinhold Niebuhr, *Faith and History: A Comparison of Christian and Modern Views of History* (New York, 1951); Nicolas Berdyaev, *The Meaning of History*, trans. George Reavey (Cleveland and New York, 1936).

17. T. S. Eliot, *Murder in the Cathedral* (London, 1935), 61.

18. I Peter 4:12 (RSV).

19. See Andre Dumas, *Dietrich Bonhoeffer: Theologian of Reality*, trans. Robert McAfee Brown (New York, 1971).

20. Luke 17:20 (RSV).

21. Luke 21:27 (RSV).

22. Romans 5:5 (RSV).

23. Karl Barth, *The Humanity of God*, trans. Thomas Wieser and John Newton Thomas (Richmond, Virginia, 1960), 64.

24. Matthew 10:27 (RSV).

25. Karl Barth, *The Epistle to the Romans*, 6th ed., trans. Edwyn C. Hoskyns (London, 1933), 362–90.

26. *Ibid.*, 367.

27. Karl Barth, *Church Dogmatics: The Doctrine of Reconciliation*, trans. G. W. Bromiley (4 vols.; Edinburgh, 1956), IV, Pt. 1, pp. 157–210.

28. Mark 14:50 (RSV).

Three. Liberty

1. Fyodor Dostoevsky, *The Brothers Karamazov*, trans. Constance Garnett (New York, n.d.), 262.
2. John 12:24 (Revised Standard Version).
3. Dostoevsky, *Brothers*, 264.
4. *Ibid.*, 264.
5. Matthew 5:18 (RSV).
6. John 17:21 (RSV).
7. I Corinthians 12:12 (RSV).
8. I Corinthians 12:31 (RSV).
9. John 9:39–41 (RSV).
10. Psalm 27:8 (RSV).
11. Isaiah 1:18 (RSV).
12. Matthew 4:4 (RSV). Jesus here was quoting Deuteronomy 8:3.
13. Romans 8:21 (RSV).
14. II Corinthians 4:6–7 (RSV).
15. Isaiah 55:11 (RSV).
16. Ephesians 2:19 (RSV).
17. Matthew 5:39–41 (RSV).

Four. Social Transformation

1. I Corinthians 1:26 (Revised Standard Version).
2. I Corinthians 1:27 (RSV).
3. Mark 13:8, 13:24 (RSV).
4. Alexis de Tocqueville, *Democracy in America*, trans. Henry Reeve, rev. Francis Bowen and Phillips Bradley (2 vols.; New York, 1948), I, 305.
5. Revelation 3:16 (RSV).
6. Luke 18:14 (RSV).
7. Fyodor Dostoevsky, *The Brothers Karamazov*, trans. Constance Garnett (New York, n.d.), 262.
8. Luke 1:51–52 (RSV).
9. Mark 10:17–22 (RSV).
10. Matthew 26:11 (RSV).
11. Mark 10:25 (RSV).
12. Luke 12:16–21 (RSV).
13. I Timothy 6:10 (RSV).
14. Tocqueville, *Democracy*, II, 261.
15. John 3:8 (RSV).

Five. Prophetic Spirituality

1. Psalm 27:8–9; Matthew 7:7 (Revised Standard Version).
2. *Book of Common Prayer* (New York, 1977), 383–84.

3. See Simone Petrement, *Simone Weil: A Life,* trans. Raymond Rosenthal (New York, 1976).

4. The literature by and about Merton is vast. The most discerning study of his life is Monica Furlong's short book *Merton: A Biography* (San Francisco, 1980).

5. Friedrich Nietzsche, *Thus Spoke Zarathustra: The Portable Nietzsche,* ed. and trans. Walter Kaufman (New York, 1954), 258.

6. Romans 13:1–2. (RSV).

7. Dietrich Bonhoeffer, *Ethics,* trans. Neville Horton Smith; ed. Eberhard Bethge (New York, 1962), 248.

8. John 18:37 (RSV).

9. Psalm 143:10 (RSV).

10. T. S. Eliot, *Murder in the Cathedral* (London, 1935), 22.

11. Romans 5:3–4 (RSV).

12. Romans 5:4–5 (RSV).

13. Psalm 139:1 (RSV).

14. Psalm 139:6 (RSV).

15. Matthew 16:25 (RSV).

16. Psalm 51:10 (RSV).

17. II Corinthians 6:8–10 (RSV); my italics.

18. John 12:24 (RSV).

19. II Corinthians 12:10 (RSV).

20. I Corinthians 2:9 (RSV). Paul is quoting from the Old Testament.

21. Psalm 118:24 (RSV).

22. Galatians 6:14 (RSV).

Postscript: World Politics

1. Romans 10:12 (Revised Standard Version).

2. See Genesis 11:1–9 (RSV).

3. Reinhold Niebuhr, *Moral Man and Immoral Society: A Study in Ethics and Politics* (New York, 1932).

4. II Corinthians 12:10 (RSV).

Index

Abraham, 75, 123

Action: human, 14–16; society as product of, 40–41, 60; secondary to waiting, 69–72, 159, 164; and tolerance, 126; radical, 185; and suffering, 201, 205, 211–21; and finitude, 212–13, 215, 218–19; morally destructive, 212–14; and sin, 212; truth and, 213, 215; differentiated from love, 214; and spirituality, 214–16; and *agape*, 217–18

—political: elements of evil in, 25; justice as aim of, 64; Bonhoeffer and, 73; through words, 133; and nonviolence, 134; original sin and, 156; and reform, 160–65 *passim*; liberation theologians call for, 164–65; order as product of, 193; power and, 211–14; and ideology, 222, 226–28. *See also* Inaction

Acton, Lord, 137, 213–14

Adam, 38

Agape: Christian love, 20–25; and the exalted individual, 26–31, 53–54, 156; and destiny, 31, 156; and universality, 33, 236; and fallenness, 43–44; Nietzsche's attack on, 46, 48; and society, 60; and community, 61, 118–19, 242–43; and mercy, 62; and justice, 66, 119; and hope, 68; and communication, 124; and liberty, 127; and power, 134–37, 240;

and nonresistance, 144; and revolution, 166–68; and equality, 175, 236; and democracy, 177–78; and capitalism, 184–85; and poverty, 202; action, inaction, and, 217–18; view of nations, 237–38, 240–41. *See also* Love

Agnosticism, 201–202

Alienation, 94, 96, 131–32, 188, 194

America (United States): and justice, 12; nationalism in, 35; Constitution of, 67, 107; and materialism, 101, 103; and racial integration, 146; led by Lincoln, 147; reformers in, 151, 156, 190; and equalization, 173; Tocqueville's study of, 187–91

Anarchism, 133, 139, 142–43; elements of, in Christianity, 134, 142, 208

Aquinas, Thomas, 65, 77

Aristotle, 22, 23, 62, 81, 182

Asceticism, 79

Atheists, 130, 243

Athenians, ancient, 56, 58, 60. *See also* Greeks, ancient

Attentiveness, 124, 132, 209; and availability, 69–70, 72–73, 105, 144, 195, 224

Attitude, prophetic, 8–10, 20, 77, 171, 185

Augustine, Saint, 65, 77, 80, 85, 104, 206, 208, 224